T0283525

American Negra

American Negra

A MEMOIR

Natasha S. Alford

HARPER

An Imprint of HarperCollinsPublishers

AMERICAN NEGRA. Copyright © 2024 by Natasha S. Alford. All rights reserved. Printed in the United States of America. No part of this book may be used or reproduced in any manner whatsoever without written permission except in the case of brief quotations embodied in critical articles and reviews. For information, address HarperCollins Publishers, 195 Broadway, New York, NY 10007.

HarperCollins books may be purchased for educational, business, or sales promotional use. For information, please email the Special Markets Department at SPsales@harpercollins.com.

FIRST EDITION

Library of Congress Cataloging-in-Publication Data

Names: Alford, Natasha S., author.
Title: American Negra / Natasha S. Alford.
Description: First edition | New York, NY: Harper, 2024.
Identifiers: LCCN 2023039638 (print) | LCCN 2023039639 (ebook) |
    ISBN 9780063237100 (hardcover) | ISBN 9780063237117 (paperback) |
    ISBN 9780063237131 (ebook)
Subjects: LCSH: Alford, Natasha S. | African American women—
    Biography. | Puerto Rican women—Biography. | Journalists—United States—
    Biography. | Black people—Race identity—United States. | United States—
    Race relations.
Classification: LCC E185.97.A356 A3 2024 (print) | LCC E185.97.A356
    (ebook) | DDC 305.48/896073092 [B]—dc23/eng/20231106
LC record available at https://lccn.loc.gov/2023039638
LC ebook record available at https://lccn.loc.gov/2023039639

ISBN 978-0-06-323710-0

24 25 26 27 28 LBC 5 4 3 2 1

TO MY PARENTS, FOR YOUR UNCONDITIONAL LOVE.

TO THE WANDERERS WHO CANNOT REST UNTIL THEY FIND HOME.

Morenita, morenita men have named you . . .
Not Latina. Morenita.
Negrita chiquita
de Estados Unidos.

—Tracie Morris, "Morenita"

Contents

Pa'l Norte

I am a daughter of northern migrations. A lovechild of American dreaming clashing with conquest and flight, sending two populations who should've been basking in the suns of Southern states and the heat of Caribbean islands, to a new, cold, snowy land they would call home: upstate New York. Most folks don't think of us people way up North, past the Big Apple that gets all the shine, but we are here. The peoples whose families boarded flights, ships, and invisible trains on the tracks of underground railroads just to make it to a land advertised as free. This is the land where I was born.

If you ask Mamí, my birth was a miracle. Not because of complications with the pregnancy or an inability to conceive but because she originally wanted to be a nun. That's right. She had been a woman with a clear goal: the nunnery. Catholicism was in her blood as a Puerto Rican, and she attended mass every Sunday, thanks to the Spanish Empire's legacy of trying to convert the Indigenous and African people on the island they colonized. However complicated the history, *la iglesia* was tattooed on her soul.

As a child, I cherished my Mamí and Daddy's love story like it was the stuff of romance novels. Knowing how different my parents were culturally and personality-wise, and what a miracle of chance their connection was, I was amazed their love could be so strong it transformed a woman who wanted to serve God for a living to cancel her plans and start a family.

"We planned you!" Mamí always insisted, almost defiant, a nod to my being born out of wedlock.

Mamí was from the Bronx and had just finished her college degree at Keuka College in upstate New York before fate introduced her to Daddy. As a Puerto Rican—actually, let me be precise—a Nuyorican, who'd grown up riding graffiti-covered subway cars, dancing to salsa at underground clubs with her twin brothers, taking trips to Coney Island with her little sister, and having picnics on the fire escape of the family apartment building, Mamí thought Syracuse, New York, the cold city she'd moved to after college graduation, was country, but she was only making a pit stop to escape her troubled home, and see what life held for her.

She met my father one night in 1984 when her roommate Olivia, another Nuyorican transplant in Syracuse, invited her out to a nightclub called Grabbers. Grabbers was downtown, and as the club's soul music and latest '80s hits like Prince's "When Doves Cry," played, Mamí was accosted by a guy who saw their whole future before his eyes.

"You and me could get married, and I'll have your bathwater ready every night," he proposed as Mamí scanned the room meekly looking for an escape. Luckily, that's when Daddy saw her in distress and butted right into Mr. Bathwater's convo to introduce himself to her.

Daddy was fresh out of the army, with a short black Afro and six-one military physique, the epitome of cool '70s soul. He had just traded driving around the hills and valleys of the world in his red-and-black Monte Carlo for his hometown of Syracuse to find work and take a break from back-to-back tours in Germany.

Daddy grew up in a large Victorian-style home on Garfield Avenue right next to the I-81—a highway that led to the demolishing of a historically African American neighborhood called the 15th Ward to make way for "urban renewal." His parents were only the second Black family on their block when they moved in, but soon redlining real estate agents encouraged white families to sell their homes by stoking fears about how Negroes would ruin the neighborhood and lower property values.

Daddy was patient with Mamí, an introvert who insisted on only friendship for an entire year, barely speaking as he chatted her up on the phone after her shifts at the care facility where she worked with disabled residents. One conversation at a time he changed her mind about the nunnery. Mamí's father died when she was nine, and she had survived abuse at the hands of both of her drug-addicted stepfathers, each consecutively coming to her home like a wolf in sheep's clothing. Daddy had a troubled relationship with his father, which seemed to overshadow nearly every memory of his youth with a dark gray cloud of angst. My parents bonded over their childhood traumas, each of them with stories of pain that erased whatever cultural contrasts they had and connected them on a human level.

Neither of their families took offense at the intercultural symbolism of my parents' union. My father was a dark-skinned African American man, my mother a racially ambiguous tan-skinned Puerto Rican who was sometimes mistaken for a light-skinned African American woman. It was a romantic pairing common in cities in hoods across America, where African Americans and Puerto Ricans often lived side by side and therefore fell in love, married, and brought children into the world.

"We got Puerto Rican cousins anyways!" was a frequent refrain from my aunt Cyn, referring to our cousins through marriage, who had a Puerto Rican daddy. Aunt Cyn loved Mamí to death and always wanted her to make empanadas to go during Thanksgiving. Meanwhile Mamí loved my grandpa's pig's feet, only endearing her more to her future father-in-law, who had a complicated relationship with his eldest son. There may not have been a ton of Puerto Ricans on the South Side of Syracuse, where Daddy grew up, but according to my aunt Val, she saw right away that my mom was good for her headstrong brother and celebrated their love.

On Mamí's side, the feeling was mutual. Her youngest sister, Titi Nina, had Black American friends. Her twin brothers, Uncle Tito and Uncle Jose, had done their share of ripping and running through New York City, dating and falling in love with women of every color and persuasion. "Your mom bringing home a Black guy? Oh, we didn't care! I dated Black women too," Uncle Jose explained to me many years later, although admittedly he'd caught flak from some fellow Latinos who didn't like the crossing of cultural lines and called him a "nigger-lover." Mamí's family was so far removed from her daily life, with my Abuela being down in Puerto Rico with my Titi Nina, and my uncles down in Florida, that meddling in their independent eldest daughter's romance wouldn't have made sense anyways. So they sent their *bendiciones* through the phone for the two lovebirds.

My parents, who were only in their twenties when they had me in 1986, spent my early years doing the best they could to raise a child on their own, making use of the village they created upstate but doing much of the heavy lifting themselves. My foundation of self comes from my parents: my mother with her big-city upbringing yet shy demeanor, her affinity for *pan, queso*, and *café* for breakfast, her faith, and her compassion for children and the needy; and my dad with his inextinguishable confidence, a walking, talking Black history lesson of endless facts despite having no college degree, with his posters of Malcolm X on our walls and his love of collard greens, yams, and chitlins. Different as they seemed, it turned out my parents had a lot more in common—more history, and culture—than was obvious at first blush.

It all started with each of their families' courage to come up north.

On Mamí's side, Abuela had flown to bustling New York City from Bayamón, a town near Puerto Rico's capital of San Juan. She came from a family of sugarcane plantation workers, carpenters, and working-class laborers. She'd been born in 1936, just two decades after Puerto Ricans had gotten U.S. citizenship through the 1917 Jones Act. The bill was introduced by two U.S. senators who thought extending citizenship to these island natives they'd "inherited" from Spain after the 1898 Spanish-American War would help with "Americanization" and pave a path for English-speaking Americans who wanted to do business on the island. While Puerto Ricans still couldn't vote in presidential elections, they could get on chartered planes to the U.S., come work for little pay in factories and farms, while filling labor gaps for rich contractors.

Abuela found work packing meat in a factory and secured an apartment in the Bronx getting past landlords who discriminated against Puerto Ricans, and mistook her for Jewish due to her ambiguous features and light skin. She had a small frame but a vibrant voice, red dyed hair and a prominent curved nose, her entire face the blueprint for my own.

Abuela met Mamí's father, Abuelo Felix, way back in Puerto Rico. He was a charismatic, dark-haired country church boy also from Bayamón, who also descended from sugarcane plantation workers and had a Black Puerto Rican father and a white Puerto Rican mother. Abuelo Felix and Abuela Sonia married in New York City and had Mamí in 1962, then her twin brothers, one year later, Irish triplets style. Abuelo Felix was drawn to, and eventually eaten up by, the streets of New York, the vices of alcoholism and womanizing taking him away from the family—leaving Abuela and the kids to fend for themselves.

My daddy's people came from the South. His mother, Florence, was from Mims, Florida, the daughter of a successful orange farmer named Fred Cuyler. Orange farming ran in the family, and Fred was the son of Bentley Cuyler Sr., another citrus grower who had actually gotten 40 acres—no mule—conveyed to him by his uncle. Bentley was so passionate about education, he gave land to Brevard County, Florida, to build a school for Black children called the Mims Colored School. Mary McLeod Bethune was his close friend, and right before Great-Great-Grandpa Bentley died, she was there to witness him sign his will.

Although Grandma's family was middle class, they were never fully treated as equals down in Florida. She had memories of the Ku Klux Klan riding through town, and of cowering under her bed until they were gone.

After having a baby in high school ended her educational journey, Grandma wanted work and a new life, so at the invitation of her uncle she headed up north to Syracuse with her daughter, my beloved aunt Cynthia. Grandma found a job at General Electric and met my grandfather.

Grandpa grew up in Pinehurst, North Carolina, by way of South Carolina. A boy with many sisters and brothers, he was rumored to have had a Cherokee grandmama. At a young age he had to drop out of school to work in farming and help his family. He was the descendant of an enslaved Black man named Beachmon Alford, who toiled on the M. B. Gandy Plantation in Darlington, South Carolina.

Beachmon had lived to see Black folks go from slavery to emancipation, and his name was found on the contract for the Freedman's Bureau, where he signed with an "X," promising to continue sharecropping the land of his former masters, to take care of their tools, and of course to keep no weapon or gun on him should he get any grand ideas as a newly freed Black man.

With the blood of survivors running through his veins, Grandpa made his way up to Syracuse from North Carolina, eventually getting a good-paying job at the Crucible Steel Factory and starting his family with Grandma. They had four children together: my daddy, his brother Leonard, my aunt Valerie, and their baby brother Aaron.

Syracuse was Daddy's hometown, and it became mine when I was born. From the time I was a child, I remember the snow. Falling like cold white stars from the sky, blanketing hills, streets, and homes like cozy sleeping bags, and piling high on the street corners into mountains we'd dash up to avoid brown, slushy pools beneath our feet. It was a place of marvelously colored autumns and idyllic summers, welcomed with joy as Syracusans celebrated freedom from their frosty prison.

It was a humble town. The northern rust belt. A city where people knew hard work, clocking into factories like the Chrysler car plant and Carrier air-conditioning plant. Where mom-and-pop shops could thrive. Where families stayed close and for generations. We took pride in *not* being New York City, taking umbrage when confused for being downstaters.

Despite Syracuse's origins as a booming town known for producing salt, once factories started closing en masse, shipping operations overseas, it drove a dagger through the heart of the local economy.

There was poverty, deep, entrenched, and so harsh; there were poor white folks down bad in the struggle. Still there was no question that a quiet line of segregation kept many Black folks and other people of color on the economic and social margins.

My hometown was a tale of two cities, with the famed Syracuse University up on the hill and East Side representing opportunity and some of the best education the area could offer; whereas down on the South and West Sides, the abandoned homes and closed businesses tended to overshadow the beautiful neighborhoods that once thrived in the Salt City.

Even with its challenges, Syracuse was always billed as a great place to raise children, where I frolicked through state fairs, local duck ponds, skating rinks, and pumpkin patches, giving me the kind of quintessential American childhood you see depicted on TV. On weekends with Mamí I tasted some of the best authentic Italian and Irish food at local festivals, ate shortbread cookies at Wegmans, and bought Amish handcrafted souvenirs at the weekend farmer's market.

And yet you could go your whole life not sampling any of these upstate New York delicacies if you grew up in one of Syracuse's poorest and isolated neighborhoods, or didn't have anyone make you feel like it was your city too.

In elementary school I was taught a tidy history of my hometown and the upstate region overall: the "bad" South was addicted to the slave economy, and the "good" North, where we lived, was the heart of freedom. At the top of that holy grail was Syracuse, our wintry liberal abolitionist city, once a stop on the Underground Railroad. Harriet Tubman had lived only forty minutes away in Auburn, New York, a gathering spot and safe space for other abolitionists.

However Syracuse's land belonged to the indigenous Onondaga Nation until in the 1700s it was stolen by the state of New York. While Native Americans fought for decades against land thievery, African Americans were subject to bondage in New York until 1827, less than four decades before federally legalized emancipation in 1863.

And even after slavery was officially ended in the state of New

York, enslaved Black people still had to "earn" their sovereignty with policies like the 1799 Act for the Gradual Abolition of Slavery, which kept existing enslaved Black girls and boys in bondage until they hit twenty-five and twenty-eight years old respectively. Even the good northern folks who wrote the abolition law paternalistically hung freedom out like a carrot in front of Black people.

Truth was, there was no entirely "good" North and "bad" South, but rather an entire country touched by the nation's original sins.

When I was three years old, my parents moved us to Rochester, New York, a sister city to Syracuse an hour and a half west, a carbon copy of upstate charm and cold. We built a new life there, but the hold of Syracuse was so strong that even when my parents got married, they traveled back to Daddy's hometown to seal the deal at Iglesia de Dios on the West Side of the city.

Daddy was never religious. He despised what he saw as hypocrisy in the Christian Church, and memories of his own run-ins with his deacon father during the era of segregation only made the Bible's message more bitter. "When I was growing up, they tried to tell me God was white. You want me to worship a God that looks like YOU and not me? Mannnn, tsk!" Daddy would rant. But out of respect for Mamí's wishes, they married in a church, honoring the God who had gotten her through hell in her childhood. A Santería priestess at a Bronx botánica she was brought to by an aunt, once predicted Mamí would have a hard life, and apparently was not wrong. Nevertheless, it would be nuns and a priest who took her in the day she'd run to the sanctuary during her first stepfather's beatings on Abuela. They fed her an egg sandwich and let her munch quietly, even though she wouldn't confess the reason she'd come for help. This was the God she taught me to believe in.

I was seven years old at that point, and a happy flower girl in my parents' wedding. They had a modest DIY reception at the local YMCA down the street, where I danced the Running Man with my cousin Mark all over the gymnasium, yo-yoing balloons tied to our wrists, as big black speakers pumped hits from MC Hammer and

Luther Vandross. Mamí's family couldn't make it to the wedding, but the Garcias, the Puerto Rican family who had babysat me since I was three weeks old, showed up to support, chattering in Spanish and English with excitement during the reception as the two worlds my parents came from blended into a hybrid that had always been perfectly normal to me.

On Friday nights I sat between my parents on the carpet for "indoor picnics," watching shows like *In Living Color*. For dinner Daddy often ate hot dogs or pork and beans, with collard greens from a local restaurant or from a can, since Mamí didn't know how to cook them. Meanwhile, Mamí ate *platanos*, *bacalao*, and *arroz con gandules*. And I, their picky only child, ate a combination of chicken nuggets and french fries, with a helping of *arroz* and the sticky, crispy treat of burnt rice at the bottom of the pot called *pegao*.

This was not the kind of family you'd see on television, but this was *my* family, sheltered in the safety of our love, though far from the places we all truly originated from.

"You are both of us Natasha. Never let anyone tell you that you can't be *all* of who you are," Mamí would often say to me seriously, almost urgently. "You are African American. You are Puerto Rican. And you are a girl. That's three strikes against you—but you can be anything you dream of being." Looking up at her I would nod dutifully, not understanding the intensity of her message, still wanting to believe, and hoping that whatever I was supposed to be, I was enough.

NEARLY EVERY SATURDAY, MAMÍ AND I TRAVELED THIRTY MINUTES to the home of two married doctors in Rochester, where Mamí worked in the hospital's daycare, to take care of their children. Daddy had picked up a custodian job at the local McDonald's, but Mamí's babysitting allowed her to earn extra money on the weekends.

I always loved going with Mamí to the doctors' home. They lived in a big, bright house out in the suburbs, with roomy staircases, shiny new kitchen appliances, beautiful framed photos of themselves on the walls, and a lush green backyard—the polar opposite of our older apartment in a two-family home back in the city. There was a little tan-skinned girl who lived downstairs and told me one day that her white stepdaddy called her "zebra." Once my parents found out, I wasn't allowed to go on my own to play downstairs anymore.

Visiting the suburbs, I thought people's lives there were more luxurious than ours, with their larger, newer-looking homes and multiple cars in the driveway. But what I assumed was a utopia, I'd learn, wasn't meant to be accessed by everybody.

The next time we'd go out to the suburbs, it was because I'd been invited to my first sleepover by Katie, my pre-K classmate. Her sleepover was a New Kids on the Block–themed slumber party, where we were all expected to wear baggy jean jackets and big New Kids on the Block fan buttons. Although Mamí didn't believe in sleepovers, a cardinal rule of overprotective Latina moms, she would make an exception for me because she knew Katie's mom from the daycare.

Katie's family lived out in another local suburb that was much farther than Mamí was used to driving. An anxious driver by nature who like a true New Yorker didn't get a license until adulthood, Mamí was driving that day because Daddy had twisted his knee playing street basketball and wore a cast. Suddenly we saw red flashing lights and heard a loudspeaker.

"PULL OVER!"

A hush fell over the car as Mamí pulled the car to the side of the road.

I peered through the window as a police officer approached Mamí's side of the car.

"License and registration," he said.

Mamí handed him her license and registration. Neither of my parents said anything to me, but I could feel the tension.

"Where are you headed?"

"We're taking our daughter to a sleepover nearby," Mamí replied with the voice she always used at work.

The police officer, a clean-shaven white man with brown hair, looked over Mamí's info, stone-faced. Then he looked at Daddy. I was scared—what had we done wrong?

"License," the officer said.

Daddy's face turned up in disgust.

"Why do you need his license if he isn't driving?" Mamí asked, careful but polite.

The police officer gruffly insisted Daddy hand it over. Daddy complied.

The policeman went back to his car. Mamí and Daddy whispered back and forth. Then out of nowhere, the officer returned. He gave my parents back their identifications and told Mamí to watch her speed and that we could go.

"Nah, we not coming back out here to get her tomorrow," Daddy told Mamí as soon as we pulled off.

Mamí turned to the backseat to look at me. I could not go to the party.

"But what am I going to tell Katie?" I protested.

"You tell her you thought you could stay over but you can't anymore."

It didn't make sense. We were just a few minutes from Katie's house.

My head hung as Mamí and I approached the well-kept multilevel suburban home, while Daddy sat in the car. We knocked. Katie's mom opened the door, and the faces of Katie and all my friends peered excitedly around her. I did my best to appear upbeat.

"We're so sorry! Unfortunately, Natasha's dad's not feeling great, and we won't be able to make it back out here tomorrow to pick her up, so she can't stay," Mamí said, feigning a smile. "But we did want to drop off a present!"

I handed over Katie's present to her, trying to hold back tears, my eyes scanning what I could see of the house and the other girls behind her. I could hear "You Got It (The Right Stuff)" playing on the TV in the background.

"Oh, we completely understand, although we'd love to have her still!" Katie's mom said.

"Thank you, we're so sorry, but we have to get going!" Mamí replied.

Mamí and I walked back to the car, and we all rode home as Daddy ranted about the officer. I wanted to cry, but I'd learned early that crying in front of both of my parents was met with alarm from Mamí and vexation from Daddy. And so, I learned to swallow my tears early on, allowing myself to shed them only in Mamí's presence, when I couldn't hold them anymore.

On Monday at school, Katie didn't seem to have much to say to me about my missing her party, but she did dish on all the highlights. I wanted to tell her it wasn't my fault, that I hadn't broken my word. But that didn't matter now.

The incident in the car illuminated the new rules of operation for our family going forward. The way Mamí looked and talked empowered her to fit in most everywhere she went. She could speak like the white people at the bank and on TV when she needed to do so. Her "look" allowed her to navigate worlds that seemed inaccessible to someone like Daddy.

Mamí served as a hall pass for me too. I was her browner daughter, but still *her* daughter—a good girl, with my clear and proper English, big eyes, and curly ringlets. But when Daddy was with us, we had to exercise more caution. There were places we didn't go all together. We did not go to restaurants often, as Daddy did not like being stared at. We limited the stores we went to, as Daddy always seemed to be followed. Daddy seemed to be not totally free, whereas Mamí could pass in any direction. Yes, I was their child, but the color lines had been drawn. No matter how much we saw each other as one family, this outside world did not see us the same way.

———

Later that year, while humming my favorite song as Mamí drove us home in "Betsy," our old hoopty, after babysitting for the doctors,

I took in the June breeze blowing through the window, which I'd rolled down with a hand crank. As I exhaled, I decided to instigate a conversation sparked by our latest visit to the suburbs.

"Mamí, I want to be white," I said with a smirk.

It wasn't an innocent remark—it was my five-year-old version of trolling. Although my statement also came from a real place of frustration, even as a kindergartner, I understood the power of provocation.

My mother's face tensed, and all traces of the smile she had held disappeared. "Why do you say that, Natasha?" she asked looking straight forward, both of her hands steady on the steering wheel.

"Because white people live in nice houses, and they have nice cars, and they have money too," I explained matter-of-factly. "White people always seem happy."

She was quiet, but I could tell that what I said unnerved her. Mamí had gone out of her way to buy me Black dolls and give me Black history flashcards, to boost my sense of self as a Black child, but I wasn't blind. Children perceive society's messages clearly, no matter how much spin adults try to put on the ugly truths. There were no Black presidents. No Black mayor on TV. I had no Black schoolteachers or principals yet. Upstate New York seemed to me a white world that we were only secondary characters in.

Of course I loved our Sunday-morning salsa cleaning sessions, Daddy's soul music blaring through the house while he worked, the smell of *pollo frito* and *tostones* crackling on the stove and how I got extra Christmas presents each year because of Dia de Los Reyes, getting to leave a little cardboard box for the Three Kings under my bed. I just wanted to know why some things seemed out of reach. It would be years before I encountered wealthy upper-class Black people in real life, and not just on *The Fresh Prince of Bel-Air*. As far as I was concerned, rich Black people were make-believe.

At a loss for words, Mamí did what many parents do when confronted with the uncomfortable: issue a warning. "You better not let your father hear you say that," she said sternly. She didn't look at me but kept her eyes on the road ahead, coldly staring straight. She was not equipped with the language to explain to her young child what her fresh eyes had picked up on.

The TV screen we shared as a family and snuggled in front of on Fridays together may have given me positive fictional worlds like *A Different World* and *Family Matters*—but the news fed a stream of images of a struggling Black America and Black diaspora—from the Rodney King riots to the 1991 coup of Jean Bertrand Aristide in Haiti to starvation in Sudan. I always saw "Save the Children" commercials, and the kids who needed saving came from Africa.

At my young age, it seemed struggle was synonymous with Blackness. And yet right on the other side of my brain I'd also picked up on a message that to be Puerto Rican was to struggle too.

History showed us Ricans were considered to be some of the most undesirable Americans from the day the United States "acquired" the island colonized by Spain. In the 1940s and '50s, during a wave of immigration to the mainland, some U.S. papers denigrated their new neighbors.

"Slums Are Heaven After Hungry Puerto Rico Swamps!" printed one New York newspaper. "Thousands of them are so poor, jobless, ignorant, and even diseased as to make their impact upon welfare and health authorities serious and inevitable; potential voters; of deep interest to communists," wrote one New York tabloid in 1947. There is another with a vintage photo of a woman standing with a child dressed in a KKK robe in front of a sign that reads NO NIGGERS, MEXICANS, PORTORICAN OR DOGS ALLOWED. To be compared with dogs was an intentional message. To be set apart from African Americans as a unique threat was another one. I came from two peoples who America considered to be a problem.

A couple years after that provocative car ride, Daddy declared that we were moving back to Syracuse. Crime had increased in the Rochester area, and after a prostitute was killed just down the street from us—with sex workers already living in the apartment downstairs in the home we rented—perhaps there was a deeper subconscious intervention taking place. The experiment in the Sister City was over.

Mamí was not happy with the decision to uproot us, and for three years my parents separated, leaving me living with her and my grandma and grandpa in the big yellow house Daddy and his siblings had grown up in. There I watched *The Price Is Right* on a big wooden TV with Grandma after school as Mamí hustled in her new teaching-assistant job, hoping for a shot to lead her own classroom one day. I'd grease my grandma's short black hair with Luster's Pink lotion, the sweet smell mixing with the cigarettes she smoked using her small, crinkled dark chocolate brown arthritis-ridden hands.

"Grandma, you know cigarettes are bad for you, right?" I said, concerned for my devoted grandma, who'd worked as long as her body could carry her.

"I know, baby, but hand me that Pepsi. And open it for me too, sugar," her sweet southern accent dripping on every word.

I did as I was told, listening daily while Grandma politely chatted on the phone and praised the Lord as she navigated difficult tasks like walking through the house or sitting on the bed. I noted that she and Grandpa kept separate bedrooms, his movements so quiet and in the background that it was easy to forget he lived there.

While I had no siblings, my cousin Mark was another frequent guest at Grandma and Grandpa's house, and he became like a brother to me as we played games of tag and watched BET and Nickelodeon. Seared in my mind is the memory of us sitting down in the living room to handwrite letters to his father, my uncle, who was serving time in prison, my mother helping us through the exercise. We both jumped with excitement when we got letters back, my uncle's smooth and clear writing telling us how he'd learned to play chess while away and promising to teach us when he was home, which he did.

My cousin Sheeda, the eldest daughter of my uncle Leonard, who was in the military, also came to visit the house on Garfield during stays in Syracuse, and we gleefully ran around the yard, both with our middle teeth missing, as we were just two weeks apart in birth and always in the same stage of growth. She'd try to teach me how to play double dutch, but I failed miserably, which gave me some existential Black girl angst.

All of my cousins, uncles, and aunts on Daddy's side were carbon copies of Grandma and Grandpa in skin tone—perfectly dark chocolate, with a smoothness that never betrayed their real age. When I was with the Alfords, I was the lightest one of the bunch. Now, at this stage of my life, living in Syracuse, I wanted nothing more than to blend in and look more like them.

Eventually Mamí got us our own apartment, and we said goodbye to the yellow house on Garfield Avenue, moving to the Valley, a once predominantly white enclave that had become more racially and economically mixed in recent years.

I was nine, and Grandpa had recently passed on, the first immediate family member I'd ever known to die. I'd seen him in the final days of his life, stomach cancer trapping him in a hospital bed, stillness something his hardworking body hadn't known nearly his entire life, through decades of walking and taking the bus to the steel factory. I kissed his cheek and braced for goodbye. In the aftermath of his death, I was a little less innocent, but still sheltered.

Although I started off in Catholic school on the mostly Puerto Rican West Side, getting my First Communion as any good Puerto Rican girl should, our move to the Valley allowed me to attend a new school—a public school called Meachem Elementary. I begged and pleaded to go to public school and be able to wear regular clothes, with a promise that I would keep my grades up.

Upon arriving at Meachem, I noticed right away that Black kids bused in together from the South Side and also stuck together in class, while the sprinkle of Black kids who lived in Nedrow and the Valley, like me, tended to mix with kids of all races. My best friends were an Irish boy named Jon, a Haitian American girl named Jessica, and a white girl name Jaycee.

I looked nothing like my friends, or anyone really, it seemed. My hair was a long, huge black ball of frizz compared with most of my Black girl classmates. I wore the nerdiest, thickest glasses, thanks

to my love of reading books at night and the limitations of our insurance. The baggy T-shirts handed down from our neighbor and
the off-brand sneakers Mamí bought me from Walmart made me an
oddball; Nikes and other name-brand sneakers seemed standard for
the kids I went to school with.

I'd met Jaycee in my band class, where she played clarinet and,
inspired by Lisa from *The Simpsons*, I played alto saxophone. When
Daddy, who had started to visit us again, found out about my friendship with Jaycee, he started to express concern.

I should be careful, he said, so I wouldn't get disappointed should
anything go awry. He'd once had a white best friend too, named Joey.
When Joey got jumped by some kids in the street who happened to
be Black, his mama accosted Daddy, yelling, "I knew you people
couldn't be trusted!"

I nodded along but dismissed Daddy's concerns. He came from
another era; he just didn't understand that times were different, and
kids at least, weren't caught up in race anymore like the old days. And
so on picture day I excitedly planned my outfit with Jaycee for the
friendship shot. We'd each find a vest, and I'd wear my hair straight
to match Jaycee's bone-straight blond hair. We cheesed for the photo,
and when the proofs came back, I excitedly took them home to show
my parents. We looked like an ad for diversity, ebony and ivory.

Mamí allowed me to get some small four-by-two wallets of me
and Jaycee, but Jaycee said her dad didn't have money to pay for our
friendship pics, just her solo ones. Soon I'd find out that Jaycee's dad
was mad that her sister had brought home a Black boyfriend.

By the time the next school year came around, there seemed
a natural gravitational pull away from each other, and I purpose-
fully sat with the Black table at lunch despite having friends of all
races at school. These were the unspoken rules. Placed in different
homerooms that September, seeing each other less and less, I con-
ceded that my and Jaycee's friendship had likely been interrupted
by something outside ourselves. And sad as it was, it was time to say
goodbye.

2

Mother Tongue

W hat are you?" Solana, the leader of a group of inquiring minds, asked me, the new girl. They were still trying to figure me out.

"That nose could be Arab," Solana said with a chuckle, her black box braids falling away from her perfectly smooth light-brown face. "You and Salim should go together, 'cause he got that nose too!" The group laughed playfully. Salim, a Pakistani American boy, was in fact very cute, and we would eventually "go together" for a month in true middle school fashion, but I clarified.

"Y'all play too much! No, I'm Puerto Rican and Black," I said, using the only words I had at the time to explain my identity in terms that made sense. I didn't intentionally mean to muddy the lines between race, ethnicity, and nationality by calling myself "Puerto Rican and Black." But at this point in my life "Black" was a term that equated to "African American"; "regular" Black folks were like the folks Daddy's side of the family had descended from in Florida and South Carolina. Sure, we used it for Black people who came from other places too, but around here, people knew what I meant when I said it.

"Ooooh, okay, I can see it now!" Solana said earnestly, the other kids nodding along as if their eyes had been magically opened.

Language mattered, and yet at this age no one had prepared us to explain who we were accurately. We used "Hispanic" and "Latino" interchangeably, but the two terms were not the same. "Hispanic" referred to people from Spain, or from countries colonized by Spain, or people who spoke Spanish. "*Latino*," on the other hand, meant people from any of the twenty-plus countries that made up Latin America, among them Brazil, Haiti, Martinique, and Saint Martin, where they spoke all kinds of languages like Portuguese, French, and Creole, although Spanish was the most common.

At times there were overlaps, and some countries, like Puerto Rico, Cuba, and Panama, fell within the umbrella terms of both Latino and Hispanic identities. But the preference for using one term over another would shift with the sands of society's understanding.

In my school and community, calling someone Spanish was clear enough. If you spoke the Spanish language or "looked Spanish"—mestiza or racially mixed and ethnically ambiguous, with tan skin and wavy or straight hair—that's what you were.

The older I became, the more questions I received about my heritage. Once while playing in a sandlot, a little girl, who was Black with chocolate skin, the same shade as Daddy's, started throwing particles of sand in my face as we built castles. When I asked why, she pointed at my parents, who were sitting far away on a bench, declaring her mommy didn't like "mixed people." Jarred as I ran to Mamí and Daddy's direction, I realized I'd never thought of myself that way. Mamí said mixing was how you described food ingredients, not human beings. I was not mixed—I was one hundred percent both of them.

But in the outside world, people always wanted to know just how Black or "Spanish" I was. Was I one of those mixed kids, who fancied themselves to be special? Did I speak Spanish, and if so, how well, and could I teach them how to say curse words?

When the questions came from adults, they seemed to carry even more judgment.

"Oh, that's a *shame* she doesn't know," one Latina woman remarked to my mother about me not speaking Spanish, when we were visiting Puerto Rican friends on the West Side. Mamí did her usual apologetic explaining about how it was her fault that I didn't speak Spanish, but it was me who felt the transference of energy and humiliation. The questions about my Spanish started to chafe more with time, widening the unspoken gap between how my mother and I were seen by the world.

I remember being about twelve, just before my facial features really started to transition from girlish chubbiness to slender and sculpted, when my mother entered me into a beauty pageant for the local Puerto Rican Day community festival.

I would be one of a few brown-skinned contestants but the only one who didn't speak Spanish fluently. I wore a peach-colored dress that Mamí had bought from the thrift store, and I shyly performed "The Star-Spangled Banner" on my saxophone during the talent portion, while all the other girls did perky dance routines or sang Spanish ballads. The entire pageant was hosted in Spanish from beginning to end, making me stand out when the emcee translated the question in English for me. So it was to my shock (and horror!) that I actually won first prize in my age category.

From the moment they placed the crown on my head, it felt wrong. I was starting to develop a complex about what it meant to be Latina. This was the early 2000's Latin pop craze era of JLo, Shakira, and Salma Hayek. For every girl I saw on TV or in magazines or even in children's books, none, not one, looked like me. So why now would I be deemed a *reina*, a beauty queen? Was it out of pity? I didn't want to be a token but smiled for the camera anyways.

Not long after the pageant, I received a letter in the mail, with an exclusive invite to a Saturday Academy for girls, put on by a local Black women's organization. It was signed by a woman named Mrs. Harper, a local principal who also ran the gifted and talented program I once attended.

I squealed with delight at the invitation, honored that these women would think to include me. Once I started attending, for the first time I found real fellowship with other Black girls in the city outside of my school. Together we learned everything from table etiquette to how to speak in public. Not only had Saturday Academy fostered sisterhood with other so-called at-risk girls in the city, it also provided a blueprint for Black womanhood, something I couldn't necessarily get from my own mother.

"Morenita, morenita men have named you . . . Not Latina. Morenita. Negrita chiquita de Estados Unidos," writes poet Tracie Morris. *"Morena"* is Spanish for "Black girl," sometimes referring specifically to medium-brown-skinned women of any Black ethnicity, including Afro-Latinas, or African American women specifically. It could be a compliment or a curse.

Mamí could not entirely help me interrogate my morena status in society, my negritude, as she did not fully understand her own. She hadn't learned much about slavery in Puerto Rico or the Black Puerto Rican leaders, like Marcos Xiorro, who had revolted and fought for freedom on the island. She just knew that she and we had African blood in our DNA. She knew that she had been called "negrita" by her own mother, supposedly a term of endearment, but one that marked her as the most Black-adjacent in her family, despite her mixedness.

It would be women like Auntie Cyn and Mrs. Harper from the Saturday Academy who would model Black womanhood for me. We spoke the same language.

Mrs. Harper was always put together. Pristine in presentation and confidence, she smelled good, and wore Afrocentric printed shawls and dresses that complemented her coiffed short salt-and-pepper hair. She bought me my first *Essence* magazine subscription as we sat in her office after Saturday Academy one day.

"Oh, you don't have *Essence* at home, sweetie? Write down your address."

Through Mrs. Harper's lessons, and the lessons of other women of Saturday Academy, such as Jackie Robinson, the first Black female news anchor in Syracuse, I would come to develop an idealized version of Black womanhood that equated to regality, community leadership, and wisdom.

And so, it would be no surprise that around this time in life as I turned thirteen, a primary ethnoracial identity started to form—a Black American one.

"I'm Black," I'd say defiantly, not interested in explaining myself to anyone anymore, or having to defend my multiethnic background.

"You are not *just* Black," Mamí snapped when she heard me refer to myself as such one day on a car ride, almost ten years after our last incendiary road trip. "I'm the one who gave birth to you. You are Puerto Rican *and* you are African American." Normally demure, she was now worked up.

"Well, people don't see me that way," I retorted stubbornly. "So I'm not trying to convince people about it." Our voices tangled and climbed over each other, leaving us both gasping for air during the argument.

"*Voy a dar te un puño.* . . . Don't get smart, Natasha!"

To me, saying I was Black was not about downplaying my Puerto Rican roots but about rejecting a system that seemed to have rejected me by default. I didn't look like the Latinos people expected to see in America—it seemed like everyone had gotten a clear memo. And not only was it fairer skin that made you Latino in America, but the ability to speak Spanish.

Back when I was in pre-K, my mother's friend had told her that I would struggle in school if she insisted on teaching me both Spanish and English. It was a wild claim with no scientific merit, but it was one that appealed directly to her greatest fears. Mamí struggled as a youth in school to keep up with the fast-moving English that my abuela didn't speak at home, and walked around carrying a dictionary. She didn't want that struggle for me. So Mamí left Spanish in my orbit, speaking it around and to me often, but English was king.

When she slipped into her mother tongue, I understood almost every word instinctively but replied in English. There was no correction or redirection, no insistence that I speak the language of my ancestors, as many first-generation immigrant families do. It was not what Daddy wanted for me, but he didn't possess the language to ensure I learned it, not to mention that it was easier to all speak the same language together as a family. As time passed, it became harder for me to take the risk of speaking Spanish. To add insult to injury, Mamí would tell me, "It's not too late, you can still learn!" As if the ball were now in my court. I saw the work required to catch up if I wanted to become fluent in a language I should've had a birthright to. To utter a grammatical error and have someone chuckle or have Mamí correct me again and again was an injustice I could not accept.

The more I encountered judgment in the world for not being fluent in Spanish, the more I resented that Mamí didn't teach it to me. How could I fully be my mother's daughter if there were conversations we could never have? I felt my mother had sent me into the world unprepared, unarmed. For every bit of pure love she'd poured into me, she didn't give me the one thing that she was best positioned to give me: her language.

There was almost a soft resignation, a sense that my assimilation as a kid growing up upstate would mean letting go. By releasing my mother tongue and mastering English, I would be let into "the American way"—a path that would surely set me up for a success that neither my father nor mother dreamed possible for themselves.

Never mind that both English and Spanish were languages forced on colonized peoples. To make it in this society, speaking with no foreign accent would indicate my belonging.

By this point, I was more than aware of the racially and ethnically drawn cliques forming at school. Syracuse was a real-life version of the famous book *Why Are All the Black Kids Sitting Together in the Cafeteria?* and it applied to Spanish-speaking kids too. I decided that I was going to be what everyone expected me to be: a Black girl—albeit with a "Spanish" mom.

Later in life, when I truly learned the difference between race, ethnicity, and nationality, I would come to understand that I wasn't wrong when I said I was Black. Race is about the physical features and characteristics that make a group of people similar. Although it's a social construct—that is, something that people have made up—it's generally based on visible attributes, and it has very real-world consequences. One could very well *feel* color blind, but if government policy dictates segregation by race, as it did in the United States during Jim Crow or South Africa during apartheid, race mattered.

Ethnically, I could be categorized as African American, Puerto Rican, even Latina—a descendant of my racially diverse island ancestors and enslaved African people in the continental United States—all at once. Ethnicity is about culture, a shared history, and customs; it's a way of speaking and being in the world. And I'd grown up in both cultures.

Then there was nationality. As an American, I watched Nickelodeon, loved greasy fast food, and was versed in both Notorious B.I.G. and Nirvana—a true '80s baby, a homegrown Discman-playing upstate New Yorker, a citizen of the United States. Although Puerto Ricans were technically U.S. citizens, even their concept of nationality was different.

Americanization may have been pushed on Puerto Ricans after 1898, but residents of the island originally known as "Borikén" by its indigenous ancestors already had their own unique national identity. Growing up in the continental United States made my experience different from that of my cousins, or *primas* as I called them, who were being raised on the island and speaking Spanish at home and school.

Research shows that many third-generation American kids from Spanish-speaking families struggle with learning Spanish because their parents refuse to teach them outright, hoping to improve their English, and therefore watch their Spanish fade away in Americanized environments and schools.

"English Only? For Mainland Puerto Ricans, the Answer Is Often 'Yes,'" blared the headline for a 2014 NPR piece on how a new generation of Puerto Ricans had lost its native tongue. In a survey cited by the article, Puerto Ricans outnumber other Latino groups in their preference for answering questions in English instead of Spanish. English and Spanish are both the official languages of Puerto Rico, although many Puerto Rican educators historically resisted the government's efforts to prioritize English, subversively using their positions on the front lines to emphasize Spanish with their students.

My abuela came from Puerto Rico in the 1950s knowing barely

any English, and she and her children spoke Spanish at home. Some educators in many Bronx schools in the 1960s commonly shamed Spanish-speaking kids like my mother when they made mistakes in English. Mamí wanted to be a teacher, but due to her Puerto Rican roots, her high school guidance counselor told her she should be a secretary. Secretary was seen as an aspirational vocation for Latinas at that time. Being a teacher? Well, that was shooting for the moon.

According to a 1975 article from the *Monthly Labor Review* titled "The Jobs Puerto Ricans Hold in New York City," fewer than 5 percent of Puerto Ricans held professional and technical positions, and fewer than 1 percent served as elementary and secondary school teachers. In the 1960s more than half of the Puerto Ricans who lived in New York City were utilized as low-wage workers in factories.

The U.S. has had a history of recruiting Puerto Ricans for contract labor and cheap pay since it took the island from Spain in 1898. Citizenship has not equaled equality. Mamí's decision to make our bilingual household into a 90 percent English household was not done in a vacuum.

Sociologists have long ago busted the myth that bilingual children suffer academically or have speech delays, and these days being bilingual is seen as an asset; increasingly, a privilege exclusive to the wealthiest and most educated American households. But a mother's fear is just as strong a motivator as a mother's love. Mamí made a choice for me, a choice that she hoped would give me more choices— more options in an English-speaking world.

Despite exposure as a newborn and toddler to regular Spanish from Mamí and my Puerto Rican babysitters, my Spanish faded over time. Somewhere in the recesses of my brain, deep in the pink and gray folds, there were still traces of my mother's mother tongue, foggy like warm rain on a window.

"Even Puerto Ricans who grow up here are not considered Boricua enough by some who live on the island, M'ija. We're like gringos to them too," Mamí would say to console me. *Ni de aqui, ni de alla . . .* "Neither from here nor from there."

But Mamí didn't understand my lack of fluency wasn't exactly the same as that of other third-generation Latino kids who looked like her but didn't speak Spanish. People still looked at them and *assumed* they were Latino. I was judged an outsider before even opening my mouth because I was Black.

Maybe it wasn't just my mother's mother tongue that I wanted so much as to unquestionably belong somewhere. And in the Black community, I belonged.

———

I was about nine years old when we took our first trip to Puerto Rico and I couldn't wait.

My last memories of my abuela were of her spinning six-year-old me around to merengue in the kitchen of my tío's house in Miami after his wedding, while I laughed giddily at her sassy shoulder shimmy. Puerto Rico itself was an abstraction. I needed to taste the food, walk the beaches, and smell the *fritura* crackling in oil to know this land was mine too.

With Mamí's queasy-faced whispered prayers and numerous signs of the cross on our flight there blessing our passage, we landed in San Juan to loud applause from passengers.

"Why are they clapping, Mamí?" I asked, stretching my neck to look at the other passengers.

"That's what they do here," Mamí said, now relieved. "Everybody is thanking God we made it safely."

I joined in the clapping with a cheesecake grin, eager to participate in the foreign ritual. After deplaning at Luis Muñoz Marin International Airport, Mamí and I grabbed our bags and took a car to my abuela's home, where she screamed, "NA-TA-CHA! *DIOS TE BENDIGA! MUAHH! VEN AQUI!*" I hugged her and quickly scanned the premises for my cousins Yamarys and Maxnina. My eyes landed on them, four and six years old respectively, with light tan skin, rosy cheeks, and straight, jet-black hair in bowl cuts. They looked nothing like me, I thought. They too were assessing me from behind Tío Max's long legs. I was their big American cousin, who had traveled all the way from the faster-paced land of New York. Their faces telegraphed both awe and a timid curiosity.

Abuela's home, a small yellow square stucco house with bars on the windows where tiny green lizards ran up and down, was like nothing I'd seen growing up in upstate New York. There was a drought on the island at the time, so we drank out of prepackaged water bottles, boiling water for warm baths, and not flushing toilet paper down the toilet due to unreliable plumbing. Despite the humble quarters, we were comfortable and love filled the home. Abuela had toiled and saved for this little house, still stocking shelves at a local grocery store in her older age to pay the mortgage.

Latinos, and Puerto Ricans in particular, are always portrayed as a family-centered culture. No differentiation to be made among us, no matter our appearance. These moments in Abuela's home were like a commercial for Puerto Rican identity, *la gran familia*—one of racial harmony—all of us equal and related in some way through our mix of Spaniard, Taino, and African blood.

But it wasn't lost on me that, unlike when I was with the Alfords, here with the Ortizes and Pagans, I was the darkest one in the room. That wasn't necessarily by accident. The Spanish Empire trafficked Africans to Puerto Rico by the tens of thousands by the mid-1500s. These enslaved Black people provided backbreaking labor in sugarcane fields and across society. Despite narratives that paint Puerto Rican slavery as "mild," it was a cruel institution that many Africans revolted against. Through rape and intermarriage with Spanish settlers, many of these African ancestors gave birth to new generations of mixed-race island residents. Even when slavery was abolished in 1873, the enslaved were forced to work three more years beyond that and sign labor contracts similar to those of my ancestors in South Carolina.

It took only a few generations for my Puerto Rican family to go from Black to white. My great-grandfather on my abuelo's side, Felix Sr., was Black, categorized as "*de color.*" It said so on his World

War II draft card, though he never fought in the war. His wife was considered white on the census, making their son, my abuelo Felix, mulatto. There was more blackness in Abuelo's bloodline, though. Abuelo Felix's grandparents were documented as *free pardos*, or free Black people, on their daughter Francisa's birth record.

Through intermarriage with mulatto or white spouses over five generations, the family eventually became mestizo, or racially mixed, a category of in-betweeness—neither white nor Black that came to characterize people's perceptions of most Puerto Ricans. And then that mestizo offspring, my abuelo Felix, married a "white" woman, my abuela Sonia.

On her side of things, by the time my abuela's parents gave birth to her, the family was already considered white, listed as such in the 1936 population schedule. My abuela's own grandmother was a mixed-race, or mestiza, woman, and she even had free pardo ancestors born in the 1800s. But these Black ancestors were now long gone according to the census. My Puerto Rican ancestors had become whiter—whether that choice was theirs, through racial mixing, or the choice of a census taker trying to lighten them up, I will never know. But they were white in the check of a box. This situation isn't unique to my family, and it's common enough that it has a name: *blanqueamiento*, or whitening.

The origins of *blanqueamiento* were not coincidental. In much of Latin America, and in Puerto Rico specifically, there was an intentional policy on the part of elite political leaders to whiten the population by encouraging mixing. The Spanish Empire encouraged and incentivized more European immigrants to come to the island in the hope that they would mix with African, island-born Black, indigenous, and other racially mixed people to create a whiter nation. The intention of *blanqueamiento* was rooted in the clear benefits: the whiter the nation, the more appealing it would be in the eyes of global powers; the Blacker the nation, the greater the threat.

Blanqueamiento wasn't just upheld through migration policies. It was also enforced in the personal and social interactions of Puerto Rican society and across Latin America. The common term *adelantar la raza* translates to "advance the race," a mandate that then translates to marrying a white or lighter partner.

This elevation of mestizaje wasn't just unique to Puerto Rico. Mexican philosopher Jose Vasconcelos, in a challenge to Social Darwinism, replicated racist ideologies with his theory of *"la raza cosmica,"* also known as "the cosmic race," or fifth race. Vasconcelos envisioned this mestizo or racially mixed population as being superior in every way because of its mixedness—more beautiful and enlightened, for not being purely "Old World races" like African and European.

The message of mixed being a preferred state of being was disseminated insidiously, policed by individual families through dinnertime conversations, mother-daughter chats in bedrooms, and the sizing up of prospective dating partners. Historically, people were forced to mix through rape and coercion. Others mixed by choice. But consistently, that *mestizaje*, or mixedness, had been used as a defense to accusations of racism. Surely a mixed people, ones who have long lost Black grandmothers and grandfathers, can't have race issues . . . right?

The famous poem *"¿Y Tu Abuela Donde Esta?"* by Puerto Rican poet Fortunato Vizcarrondo encapsulates this paradox. In the piece, a Black Puerto Rican man responds after a fair-skinned Puerto Rican man calls him big lipped and lobs racist insults. "And your grandmama, where she at?" the poet repeats after each stanza, alluding to the color-struck man's ancestor likely being Black herself. "You hide her in the kitchen because she's Black as Black can be."

Many Latinos have heartbreaking stories of realizing the consequences of being born as the Blackest one in their families—being told playfully or seriously that they had the so-called curse of *pelo malo* ("bad hair"), darker skin, or more African features than their siblings or parents. If they raised concerns, they were being too sensitive, divisive, or making much ado about nothing. It was a form of gaslighting in the name of national harmony that persists to this day.

But there were also Latinos who came from decidedly Black families who never accepted Blackness as a curse or a fate to escape. They existed in nearly every Latin American country including Puerto Rico, Panama, Colombia, Cuba, Venezuela, and Brazil. For these Afro-Latin Americans, to be Black was no novelty or question. Some still carried sacred traditions and spiritual practices directly from Africa and re-imagined them in their new homelands. They spoke Spanish influenced by the phonology of African languages. They even had recipes and food preparation that traced to the motherland, such as mashed plantain.

When I tried to learn more about these Black Puerto Rican pre-decessors, the family generations past who looked like me, Mamí had few details of their lives and origins—it had been washed away in the tides of ocean and time. When I spoke to her about my color being different from hers, she'd remind me of her grandfather in Puerto Rico whom she'd spent her summers with, of his beautiful short Afro, his brown skin that glistened in the sun just like mine as he tended to his chickens. She'd say lots of Puerto Ricans were my color. It was no big deal.

My mother had reversed the lightening and whitening that had inched our Latino family slowly up the ladder of racial caste by giving me a Black father. As a nine-year-old standing in my abuela's living room, I saw, standing there in my skin, the difference between my cousins and me, between my mom's brother and me, and the family that I belonged to.

That first night, I eagerly spread out the little palette Abuela had made for me and Mamí to sleep on, a fold-out mattress in a side bedroom. Mamí hung the mosquito net around us as the sweltering heat crept up my arms and legs. I looked out the barred window into the dark-blue sky, listening to the sound of the tiny tree frogs called coquis whistling through the trees they dotted, loving this beautiful island that had birthed half of me. "*Co-quiii, co-quiii, co-quiii,*" they sang sweetly as I fell asleep.

Just a few years later, Titi Nina and her whole family would move all the way north to Syracuse, giving me what felt like a second chance with my Puerto Rican family—a chance to create new mem-ories with the family I always wanted, and not just family I saw in pictures. Watching their acclimation to upstate New York, I saw the triumphs and struggles of being island Puerto Ricans in the north.

My cousins had to learn English, with Mamí and Titi fighting to keep them out of ESL programs even though they were being made fun of for the way they said certain words. Here, in this land, a Spanish accent was a mark of intellectual inferiority. People spoke down to you or even demanded that you "learn English" assuming that you didn't. I watched as Titi had to navigate a complex medical system for her own disabilities, Mamí helping each step of the way, translating complex bureaucracy and paperwork, which would've been impossible to navigate without language support.

Even with the basics—housing, food, and clothing—covered, this new upstate land was far, foreign, and in many ways inaccessible to them. There were still plenty of moments of joy and levity, watching these Boricua fish out of water. They had three Chihuahuas at any given time, and there was a constant ruckus in the house. Titi always welcomed me with a chilled Malta Goya drink and fresh pot of rice, and on special occasions, crispy *pernil* that she'd make just for me.

Unfortunately, an exchange between Titi and my daddy, which all started from a misunderstanding over the phone—language barriers—would lead to a nasty argument between everyone, when someone on Mamí's side of the family let the N-word fly at Daddy. It didn't matter that many Latinos used it all the time, especially in New York City, where they were from. Daddy wasn't having it and it would lead to a yearslong separation for my family yet again. It would mean just me and Mamí coming to visit our island family, while Daddy stayed home, symbolizing the duality of my worlds.

Despite the initial chaos of blending our families, their move gave me new empathy and gratitude for the move my abuela had made from Bayamón to New York City in the 1950s, all those decades before. Now I could see that even if I'd felt out of place there, they were out of place here too.

Rerooted as we all were, we all had hopes for something greater.

3

Pelo Bueno

After returning home from Puerto Rico, I found a new chapter of adolescence unfolding, quite literally, at the roots of my hair. Being a Black and "Spanish" girl—as my friends now referred to me—put me squarely at the intersection of the hair politics embedded within both communities. It was through hair that I would come to understand racial caste. I became acutely aware of where my hair's texture—beautiful to some, and less desirable to others—situated me.

My hair—the love child of Daddy's 4C Afro and Mamí's waves—required work, lots of product, and more work. My hair also curled when wet, but once dry, it would frizz up and become matted and tangled if I didn't constantly put in the work.

As I got older, *el doobie* became harder to maintain on me. Mamí's roller set rituals didn't work as well, and my hair became . . . bigger. It was the kind of fluff that couldn't be contained, like black cotton candy, the kind that would spoil in minutes in a Syracuse summer.

One day when I was about ten, a trip to Family Dollar changed everything for me. Walking through the hair aisle where Mamí would pick up containers of Blue Magic grease, I spotted the box. It was white, but in the center were two of the most beautiful Black girls I'd ever seen. They were not pretty like Moesha or Laura Winslow or any of the naturally beautiful girls I admired on TV. No, they were pretty like dolls—almost too perfect—with big eyes, Colgate-white teeth, and the longest, straightest hair I'd ever seen on girls my complexion.

Etched across the top of the box were three words I'd never forget: "Just for Me."

In an instant, I knew this box was, in fact, just for me.

I begged Mamí to buy it. Just for Me was a perm product, but I wasn't infatuated with it because it promised long hair that was detangled or easily maintained with a blow-dryer; I wanted that special, perfect sheen that only a relaxer could achieve. It was a fantasy in a box.

Despite some hesitation on her part, we gave "Just for Me" a try, but Mamí washed out the relaxer too early, and my first attempt was a bust.

We were back to square one, and it was time for a new plan. Mamí turned to one of her teaching coworkers, Ms. Johnson, a Black American woman who did hair as a side hustle, and she volunteered to come to our two-bedroom apartment to apply the relaxer herself.

Ms. Johnson started by lining my entire scalp and hairline in Vaseline, forming a barrier to the skin on my forehead, signaling that whatever was about to happen came with bodily risk, which made Mamí once again nervous. As she opened the jar of relaxer, the strong whiff of rotten eggs hit my nose—ammonia, the chemical used to break down the hair and make it submit.

"Okay, sweetie, when it starts to tickle and burn, you just let me know, okay?"

"Okay, Ms. Johnson," I said, nodding with a smile as she put the stinky pink glob on my hair, being careful not to rub it into my edges. It wouldn't take long before the tingling started, and within about fifteen minutes I was squirming to get free, squeezing my toes into the sole of my Payless sneakers, and clasping my hands together tightly between my knees. Ms. Johnson told me to wait five more minutes. Five more minutes felt like death, the burning like bee stings.

"Ms. Johnson, it's really hot!"

"Okay, sweetie, now!" she said, dipping my head under the sink and washing the potion out of my head carefully so it didn't get in my eyes. The water was my savior, but this was a baptism by fire that I never wanted to experience again.

After patting me down with a towel, Ms. Johnson smiled at the result. "Oooh girl, Natasha you look SO nice. SO nice, honey!"

"I want to be surprised and see it at the end," I said with a smile, scooting past every mirror in the house.

Ms. Johnson blasted my limp tresses with a blow-dryer. When she'd finished, she grabbed a round hand mirror and held it tight. "You ready to see it?" I nodded, eager for the grand reveal.

And there it was. The girl on the Just for Me box was staring back at me in the mirror. I no longer looked like the eleven-year-old nerd who played alto sax in jazz band, collecting Pogs and baseball cards. I looked polished and beautiful—like a grown young woman.

"It's so pretty, Natasha," Ms. Johnson said with a proud smile. "You have good hair, honey—beautiful hair." I vowed to perm my hair forever.

The message that my hair was something special, a sight to behold, always came from Black folks.

"You got good hair!" my classmates would proclaim whenever I wore my new permed hair blown out in long pressed styles. Upon meeting me, some girls would ask immediately if I was "mixed" to try to make sense of my long tresses—a reasonable but unfactual assumption based on myths that Black hair didn't grow long.

In truth, most brokenness or patchy baldness in Black hair historically was the result of external factors, such as the brutality of slavery. According to Ayana D. Byrd and Lori L. Tharps, the authors of *Hair Story: Untangling the Roots of Black Hair in America*, the kidnapping that took place during the transatlantic slave trade initially prevented Black women from practicing the sacred hair care rituals with the regularity they could in Africa. In their homeland many women valued hair as a form of kinship, status, and friendship. To attend to hair preslavery was a sacred job, and intricate braids, styles, and hair accessories were the ultimate symbols of self-pride.

After being stolen, dragged across the Atlantic Ocean, and put on the auction block, enslaved African women were forced to innovate and use tools meant to separate wool on plantations into combs.

Eventually, enslaved Black women started mixing a harsh chemical called lye to straighten their hair, tying rags over the top to protect their heads in the harsh sun and lay their hair flat. The practice could result in hair breakage.

By the formal end of slavery, new Black hair maintenance traditions had developed, as did improvements in treatments. But Black American people learned quickly that straight hair was the standard of beauty in the United States.

Colorism and texturism also went hand in hand.

The straighter the hair, and the lighter the body, the more it was perceived to be "good."

My first weeks of my new middle school, I was sitting at lunch with two girls named Tessy, who had the same medium-brown skin I had with short black permed hair, and Vanessa, a light-skinned girl with light-brown permed hair pulled back in a ponytail. Both Tessy and Vanessa ironically lived in the South Side–Valley border as I did and welcomed me with open arms despite my being the new girl.

Suddenly another student came and approached our table. I remembered her name from social studies class for its uniqueness, and the fact that it didn't sound like anyone else's—Tykeisha.

Her dad's name was Tyrone and her mom's name was Keisha, so it was a one-of-a-kind name just like the names of my *primas* Yamarys and Maxnina. Tykeisha had the smoothest medium brown skin, a few shades darker than mine, pretty almond-shaped eyes, the kind of plump lips girls pay for these days, and a perfectly white smile. But what stood out most, in addition to her cute FUBU skirt set, was her exquisite hair. While the rest of us had clearly home-done styles, Tykeisha had a fresh updo, with crisp black pin curls that made a tower on her head.

"I like your hair!" I exclaimed.

"Thank you," she said, smiling warmly yet cool, calm, and collected, as if she were used to compliments. "My mom did it, she's a hairstylist."

Over cold turkey sandwiches and cafeteria pasta, we'd learn that

Tykeisha's mom did hair out of a studio in her house on the South Side, like a lot of local hairstylists, and she was quite popular.

It took no time for me and Tykeisha to become best friends— she was smart like me, with a love for social studies and writing, an undercover nerd who knew how to navigate the minefield of fitting in at a predominantly Black school where most kids had known each other since kindergarten or lived on the better-looking East Side, whereas we lived on the South Side and in the Valley. Not only did Ty's mom start doing my hair, she would also use a razor blade to shape and sculpt my bushy dark eyebrows—a life-altering beauty improvement for a hairy Black Puerto Rican girl like myself.

Soon all the girls at school took notice of my hair. It was a *thing*. At recess, a girl named Carmaysia approached me to ask a question.

"You'll let me braid your hair?"

Just weeks before I'd had a run-in with Carmaysia and another girl named Chanice when we were outside playing kickball. Carmaysia and Chanice were like beauty and the beast, with Carmaysia being beautiful with the flyest clothes and sneakers, and Chanice having bucked teeth, oversized gums, a brittle tiny ponytail, and deep insecurities that she masked by acting like she was Carmaysia's tough bodyguard.

Memory escapes me as to what irked Carmaysia and Chanice, whether I hadn't run fast enough or cost the team a point, but I remember Chanice calling me out in front of everybody.

"Is you getting smart with me, Natasha?! Cause you can get punched in the face!" she yelled across the grass.

Despite my middle school's reputation for supposedly being a better magnet school, I'd already witnessed girls get into vicious fights, complete with hair pulling and pummeling, usually instigated by an eye roll or passing comment. I lived in dread of getting jumped daily—I wanted to be friends with everybody and was not a tested fighter despite Daddy giving me a few quick attic boxing lessons. But I also knew if I didn't stand up for myself now, Carmaysia and Chanice would terrorize me for the rest of my time at middle school, assuming I was a punk because I did well in class.

"Whatever, Chanice!" I yelled back, giving my best attempt at looking unbothered. "Just play the game."

Chanice looked stunned that I dared speak back to her.

"Yeah, whatever little girl!" she responded before going back to the base to make another run, while Carmaysia laughed and co-signed.

I breathed a deep sigh of relief when I realized that I would not be thrashed that day, and I tried to avoid them both going forward.

So now here I was, sitting near Carmaysia on the playground, some sort of respect clearly earned, when she extended the olive branch of braiding my hair.

"Sure! I don't care!" I told her, trying to act nonchalant as I watched her face light up while she pulled a comb out of her bag.

I sat on a big rock adjacent to the playground in the park while Carmaysia, Chanice, and the rest of the crew who worshipped them sat around me and played with my hair like I was a human baby doll.

"You got good hair. You don't even really need a perm, to be honest," Carmaysia said while braiding it, gum smacking in her mouth. "You mixed?"

I thought hard before answering this question. I knew what she meant when she said mixed—mixed like white and Black. My momma wasn't white and I didn't want to fit into that box of an in-betweener, somebody who wasn't enough of one thing or the other. "My mom is Puerto Rican, and my daddy is Black."

"Ohhhh okay! That's why your hair look like this."

I didn't dare argue. I was just happy to be making friends. And I knew that the ideas Carmaysia was espousing weren't unique. My favorite movie was a Spike Lee film Daddy bought me called *Crooklyn*, which had a scene where a bunch of girls are sitting on a Brooklyn stoop in the 1970s. "She got Peter-Rican hair," a dark-skinned Black girl exclaims while running her fingers through the loose, wavy brown hair of a racially ambiguous younger girl named Minnie. "Ay, *dejame!* Stop touching me, ugly!" Minnie snaps back, pulling her body away, repulsed at the petting, before the bigger Black girl issues a threat of a beatdown. "You think you so cute, later for you Minnie!" another Black girl chimes in.

The whole exchange exemplified the treacherous terrain of hair politics, but also how much Puerto Ricanness was associated with mixedness—girls with hair like Minnie's had "Puerto Rican" hair, not the kind of hair I had, even in the eyes of Black American folks.

But it overlooked that there were Puerto Ricans and Latinos of all nationalities who had Afros, locs, and 4C textures too—their African ancestors from the same continent as the ancestors whose DNA we carried in the mainland U.S. We'd all been victims of the propagation of *mestizaje* being the face of all Latinidad.

Once I got access to heat tools and a chemical-laden hair spray called Pump It Up, I got my master's degree in Black Girl Hair University and began sculpting my own hair. I practiced updos with crisp pin curls crowning my head. Clouds of hair spray made it hard to breathe while turning my hair into immovable pieces of plastic. Waterfalls of crunchy crimps would sprout from my scalp, making me look like a real-life Cabbage Patch doll. I started to love the coil and volume of my Black hair for its versatility. Tykeisha even taught me how to cornrow and I experimented with adding in hair tracks and weave ponytails.

I faithfully read *Hype Hair* magazine, picking up a fresh copy from the grocery store checkout line every time I shopped with Mamí. The magazine was a compilation of hair model photos flaunting trending so-called urban styles, with plenty of advertising of products in between. At this time, Mary J. Blige was hugely popular, and her newest style was a bob that flipped outward, almost like an upside-down chandelier. I went to Tykeisha, excitedly showing her the look I wanted.

"This! This is what I want done on my hair!" I told her, holding up the magazine.

Ty nodded. "Oh, my mom could do that for you, no problem."

I went to Ty's mother's kitchen salon, where I sat still and watched as she braided up my real hair underneath, then glued pieces of weave to my head before cutting and blow-drying the bob. The last step was spraying the hair with the poisonous Pump It Up spray, followed by a hot curling iron to achieve the bob's outward hair flip. When I looked in the mirror, I was pleased, thinking I looked pretty close to Mary J. Blige, if I did say so myself.

At school the next day, I sat down at the table of girls I always sat with, which included my cousin Sheeda.

"Ooh girl, that hairstyle is cute! Who did that?" said Imani, a short, witty, pug-faced girl who was known for doing everyone's braids at school. Doing hair was one of the few ways to make good money at that age, and the best hair braiders had a reputation for making so much that they always had a new pair of Jordans when they came out.

"Tykeisha's mom!" I said, beaming with pride, turning my head each way so the table could get a look.

I left early to head to class and proceeded about my day. When I got back to my locker, I had a note from Sheeda waiting for me in the locker, writing and passing notes being a regular pastime for us back in the early 2000s.

"Girl . . . I just wanted to let you know that as soon as you left, Imani and everybody was talking about your hair, making fun of you. I had to check them, but you should know."

Apparently, to Imani, my Mary J. Blige bob looked more like a high-sitting mushroom stuck to the top of my head, one that didn't flatter my hawkish nose or skinny face. I felt the heat of embarrassment flush me, then a spark of heat. Why were mean girls so duplicitous?

As soon as I got home, I wanted the hair out. I sat under the shower, ripping the glued hair out piece by piece, with no care to protect my own natural hair underneath.

I didn't want to look like a girl who was "trying," and decided I would stick with the rivers and lakes I was used to: permed, pressed, and straight, with the occasional Alicia Keys–inspired cornrows for warmer days.

Nevertheless, I still was floating in the liminal space between hair cultures throughout high school. Although my non-Hispanic Black girlfriends exoticized my hair, thinking that my "Spanish" roots made it so long, when I picked up copies of *Latina* magazine or saw "Spanish" video vixens in hip-hop music videos, their hair looked nothing like mine. Every Latina star's hair was characterized by either bone-straightness or waves that required nothing more than a light mousse to run out the door.

My *primas* had the kind of hair that was considered "Latina," long manes that flowed down to their butts. Their ponytails were full and swung as they walked or perfectly filled the slicked buns they wore high or low, no extensions needed.

My kind of hair, requiring steps to reach its straightness, was nowhere to be found in mainstream representations. Mine wasn't a 4C Afro like my Dad's, which was considered *pelo malo*, or bad hair, but its thickness and proneness to frizz didn't exactly make it *pelo bueno*—good hair—either.

Beyond so-called *pelo malo*, Latin America and the Caribbean had plenty of stories where beautifully coiffed and maintained natural hair styles could cause a student to be suspended from school for violating dress code. Natural hair in the workplace was not perceived as professional and people could face employment discrimination if they did not conform to straightened hair standards. Despite all its so-called racial mixedness, they were guilty of the same kind of discriminations that happened in the U.S.

The *pelo malo* standard was so strict that even curls could fall into that camp. Mamí, with her long, wavy hair with body and no 4C texture, had been occasionally told she had *pelo malo*, demonstrating the depth of the obsession with Eurocentric beauty ideals. *Pelo malo* was a reminder that no matter how much Spanish some Latinas spoke, their ancestors came from Africa. In order to move up the racial totem pole in the colonial era, many Afro-descendant women in Latin America perfected the art of straightening their hair, creating looks that helped distance them from their Blackness.

The rare occasions I wore my hair curly and wet, I was universally told by family, friends, and strangers alike that it was "cute," an infantilizing compliment I cringe at to this day. No one ever said my curls were "professional," "sexy," or "polished." Only straight hair got that reaction.

By the time I was a high schooler, I had killed all semblance of my natural curl pattern with perms. It was gone; the most my hair could do was offer up a limp wave pattern when wet, like overboiled ramen noodles. The healthy, bouncy curls of my girlhood had long been permed and pressed away. I was fully a member of the creamy crack club, despite never really needing it.

Imagine the cognitive dissonance when you realize that in one culture, you have "good hair," and in another, your natural hair is too wild, in need of taming. And yet both of these cultures are supposed to be yours.

Still, the reality was that both cultures policed hair. Mastery of transforming natural hair was something African American and Afro-Latinas shared in common, and language barrier aside, we'd all heard the message loud and clear about which hair type was supposedly the best.

I remember one boy in my middle school named Ziggy, who came from a Rastafarian family; the only boy with dreadlocks in class. Despite being a vibrant personality, a kind boy who treated everyone nicely, Ziggy with his brown skin and bright smile was teased mercilessly by some of my fellow classmates. They threw anything that would stick into his hair, calling him an "African booty scratcher"—even though he wasn't African and they were Black too—bullying him the entire year.

One day Ziggy walked into school with all his locs shaved off, his hair in a short cut. Most of us were speechless. Although he maintained his smile, with not much to say about his hair, I felt sorrow for him. Sorrow that a better world didn't exist, where Ziggy's hair— where all our hair—could be just as God made it.

4
Quinceañera

I sat in the living room, my heart racing as I waited to see the consequences of my actions. I heard Daddy's feet speeding up in pace as he approached, and I counted down. This was it, the end of my life. Whatever had made me think I could cuss at Daddy from a couple rooms over and he would somehow *not* hear it? It was a typical teenage miscalculation. Naïveté. Foolery. Plain stupidity.

As Daddy approached me with a swat from his big arm, I threw my breakfast tray down and cowered for protection, going from fourteen years old to four in an instant. "I'm sorry! I'm SORRY!"

After a few swats and my incessant blocks, Daddy stopped, looked at me with distaste, then turned around and left.

To get hit wasn't good, but the fact that he didn't say anything to me afterward meant I was in *real* trouble.

I hadn't gotten a spanking since I was two years old, when Mamí, with social work training and childcare experience under her belt, explained to Daddy that although they'd been raised with beatings, *their* child would not be hit or endure the risk of being snatched up by child protective services.

With both my parents coming from households where they had to get switches off trees or threatened to hold their hands over open flames, Mamí and Daddy made a pact when I was a small child that they would discipline me differently. But now I was a teenager, and Mamí frequently joked that they'd created a monster—an opinionated, book-smart girl child who was starting to question everything around her, including them, a dynamic that chafed their instincts and cultural norms.

Black kids don't talk back to their parents.

Puerto Rican kids get a chancleta—a flip-flop—to the head for getting smart.

I'd heard all these claims, and yet sometimes my mouth opened before my brain could step in to avert disaster.

At the root of my missteps with my dad was that he'd recently moved back in with us after his separation from Mamí. Although he'd kept in touch, with letters and custom-made cassette playlists that he MCed with inspiring messages just for me, he was coming back smack-dab in the middle of my transition from little girl to preteen. There were pros, like him answering some of the deeper questions I had about the trials of being Black in America. But I also saw the difference the presence of a man in the house could bring.

It was no longer Mamí and me, negotiating our lives together, and me manipulating her to get what I wanted, whether it was more TV time or Domino's pizza for dinner. Now our revamped trio had a strong captain at the helm, a military man with very particular rules that made our *casita* feel more rigid.

Each week, it seemed I was learning something new Daddy didn't like. My tone of voice. My facial expressions. Not cleaning the bathroom or dishes well enough—I would have to reclean or rewash until I got it right. Forgetting to turn the lights off or pick up after myself, after years of being babied by Mamí, who cleaned everything instantly, like a human vacuum.

Perhaps there was an adjustment for Daddy too. The little girl he'd lived with just a few years before was no longer a little girl but a preteen coming into her own. Or rather, just a preteen being a preteen, something Daddy had no healthy model for how to handle with his drill-sergeant style of discipline.

I'd gone regularly to church for years, invited by my school friend Vanessa, and tried my hardest to be a "good girl." Vanessa's church was a new world for me. Some of the most active Black leaders in the community, attorneys and doctors, attended. Many of them lived outside the city of Syracuse, in the suburbs, but they drove in weekly for service.

These were the Black people I dreamed of growing up to become. They were polished, educated, and well spoken. They had nice homes with big lawns, and two cars in the driveway to match their two-parent households. Their dads went to church with their moms. They'd graduated from HBCUs—historically Black colleges and universities—and other good schools. Some of them even took trips to Martha's Vineyard—though I never knew what that was until I finally asked a church friend what the black dog stood for on the sweatshirt he always wore.

I wanted so badly to make it in life so I could have a life resembling theirs. I wished I went to church with a mom and dad, like some of the families who'd been in the church for years. But it would just be Mamí who came occasionally, and sometimes me all alone after Mamí dropped off on going to mass after I left Catholic school and started to ask questions about why all the people in the stained-glass windows were white. (Me and my questions about race had to have stressed that poor woman out. Her new favorite response became "Ask your father!") My world at church and my world at home seemed to be worlds apart. At church I was an esteemed adopted daughter of sorts—not raised there, but always welcome. At home, I sometimes felt like a problem child.

Each infraction from Daddy met with yelling or a warning from his cutting eyes. "Take that lip gloss off!" he would order, to which I internally deep-sighed. "You think you know so much, that's your problem now!" he'd tell me when I went too far in expressing my point of view. I feared my father in these preteen years, which presented as respect—but deep down I carried simultaneous resentment and a desire for his approval.

Little did I know it was the same pattern that had played out with him and his own father. The barking and orders I endured were nothing compared to the cutting down he'd survived at the hands of his father, a former deacon. Daddy would defy the strict house rules and accept his beatings later, a true rebel to the core. "You and your father are so much alike, that's why you butt heads,"

Mamí would say exhaustedly to me every time there was a new tiff. "He's only like that because of what he went through. When you're older, you'll understand."

The latest incident—the swatting from Daddy—had started over him yelling at me to turn the TV down. In response and typical teenage rebellious fashion, I mumbled a string of obscenities under my breath at him, imitating the reckless talk and f-bombs I heard on the bus and in hallways of school. Little did I know he had heard me.

As I sat on the floor, picking up my splayed utensils and pieces of pancake off the carpet in the aftermath, tears held back by the shock that he'd let me survive, I heard the door unlock downstairs. *Dammit.* It was Mamí. I heard her trudge up the stairs slowly, the exhaustion of the day in each step. I knew it wouldn't make sense to plead my case, so I went into my room and sat on the bed to await my punishment.

I could hear the tense voices of my parents talking back and forth down the short hallway of our two-bedroom upstairs apartment. And then she came to my room and opened the door gravely, as if someone had died. The truth was, someone had. It was me. I was dead to my father.

"I don't know what made you think you could talk to your father that way, Natasha. But you are in TROUBLE, you hear me? *Malcriada. . . . .* He's not even coming to your quince anymore!"

A lump formed in my throat. My quince. The day I'd been waiting for and counting down until for the past three years.

Quinceañeras were for good girls, something I had mostly been up until then. But it seemed I had ruined everything. *Malcriada. Malcriada. Malcriada.*

———

Mamí first mentioned the idea of a quinceañera to me when I was eight or nine. We'd just gotten a batch of new photos mailed to us from my tío Jose in Miami, and one showed his daughter, my cousin Liz, in a gorgeous white fluffy ball gown. She had her arms outstretched, doing a waltz with Tió, while a group of boys her age wore tuxes and danced around her in the silver-and-black ballroom.

"What's that, Mamí?" I inquired.

"That's your *prima*'s quinceañera, Natasha. Her sweet-fifteen birthday party."

Mamí explained it was the day a girl celebrated becoming a woman, an important milestone of Hispanic and some Latino cultures. Unlike the traditional American sweet sixteen or debutante ball, quinceañera celebrations happened at age fifteen, drawing on cultural traditions tied to this age. Historically, quince (fifteen) was the age a girl was ready to be courted by suitors, bear children, and assume her role as woman of the house, despite being just a few years after she'd started her period.

The celebration's origins are believed to be Mexican, the hybridization of indigenous Mesoamerican coming-of-age traditions and religious practices of the Spanish Empire. But quinceañeras now take place throughout Hispanic and Latin American countries, from Panama to Puerto Rico. They started as very modest and serious affairs, with a simple church service, or a girl in a plain white dress gathered with her family to mark the occasion. Quince rituals—like being handed your last baby doll and having your father change your flat shoes to heels—symbolize the transition into womanhood. But in modern times a quinceañera symbolizes the granting of contemporary teenage privileges, like wearing makeup or getting your eyebrows or nails done. The quinceañera party industry is a multimillion-dollar business, sometimes overshadowing the actual meaning associated with the quinceañera.

While modern quince celebrations may look very different from earlier iterations, they are still opportunities for sharing and reconnecting with heritage. As Julia Alvarez wrote in her book *Once Upon a Quinceañera*, the celebrations "become exquisite performances of our ethnicities within the larger host culture while at the same time affirming that we are not 'them' by connecting us, if only in spirit, to our roots."

And to this only child, only daughter, the only negra of the family, a quinceañera—its pageantry, its promise of transformative power, its magic—sounded spectacular. It was the one thing that it seemed no one could take from me as a birthright.

I'd thought about the oddity of it many times: how strange it might be to see my little brown self climbing into a big white dress with a crown, to be debuted in a Latina tradition, far up north in Syracuse. I looked nothing like the Latina girls I'd seen featured in *Quinceañera! The Essential Guide*, a book I'd found in the local library, from which I started planning. But I wanted something that uniquely bonded me to Mamí. *Our* heritage.

Funnily enough, Mamí never had a quince.

"I didn't want Abuela spending all that money," she told me one day as we were sitting in the car, talking about planning mine. She was a typical eldest daughter, responsible with a dash of martyrdom. "But I want you to have one if you want it, M'ija. You could always get a car too—but you have to choose," she said. The quince was my choice.

A few years before my own celebration, Mamí took me to her co-worker's daughter's quinceañera. Seeing the girl walk into the ballroom of the American Legion in a beautiful white dress, a tiara on her head, I saw a Puerto Rican princess. I wanted the same moment.

And so Mamí scraped and saved and planned, plotting out the entire perfect day. My quinceañera wouldn't take place in a Catholic church, as was tradition, but instead at the predominantly Black Syracuse Baptist Church, where I attended youth group Bible study regularly. Our party DJ would need to be bilingual and have a catalog of both Spanish music, old-school jams, and hip-hop of the 2000s. And with most of my friends being Black American, all of them would need to take classes with us to learn the salsa group dance we'd be doing.

My girls separately would be learning bomba, an African-inspired Puerto Rican dance and music style, and with it using the African-inspired movements that we all knew well from homecoming dances and basement parties, in tribute to my Black ancestors from Puerto Rico. This is how my quince would be my own.

But just one month before the party, we had this problem. Daddy was still not speaking to me over the swearing incident, and his silent treatment felt worse than a single beating, which would've worn off by then. Each day he would come home from work and go straight to his room, the door closed behind him.

I tried to be a dutiful daughter to win back his affection—picking up after myself, cleaning where I could, and keeping the TV volume down, mindful of the source of our tiff. I did my homework and kept my grades up, still going into work on the weekends at McDonald's, where I ran the cash register to save up for sneaker money. But each time I checked in with Mamí to see if his heart had softened, the answer was the same.

"No, M'ija," she'd say sorrowfully. "He's still not going."

I was crushed but learning a valuable lesson, that opening my mouth had consequences. All my life my father had seemed untouchable, a monument of strength. He faithfully went to work daily, ironing his uniform, cleaning toilets for white-collar workers who sometimes barely bothered to acknowledge his presence. But his strength also formed a fortress I found myself left outside of when he thought it necessary to teach me a lesson. Our family dynamic was again on shaky ground.

Now it felt like it was just Mamí and me all over again, as it had been when Daddy moved out. Mamí and I against the world. She was the only one able to deal with my ugliness and insolence and still come back each day to care for me hands-on, no matter what. Fathers, it seemed, could opt out.

Meanwhile I would soon be dealing with a different kind of drama back at school. It all came to a head one Tuesday in the halls of Nottingham High.

"Yeah, I been hearing Lil James took your virginity a while ago—you didn't know that?" a gossipy girl named Sinclair said as Ty and me stood at our lockers chatting in between classes.

"WHAT?!" I yelled, both stunned and outraged at the accusation. Ty looked down at her feet.

"Girl, that rumor is so old, everybody been knew about it," she replied with a scoff and some pity.

"Well it's NOT TRUE, so I don't care how long it's been around! Who told you that?" Tears were starting to well in my eyes, something I hated about myself when I got angry.

"I mean, apparently he didn't deny it," Sinclair said, deflecting. "But I think you should confront him. Just ask him directly!" she continued, riling me up like the true hypewoman she was.

"Oh, I will, RIGHT NOW," I said, marching down the hall, Ty and Sinclair trailing me as I searched for Lil James in the crowd.

James was a senior football player I'd innocently become friends with during my freshman year. Short in stature—hence the "Lil" moniker—brown-skinned with a raspy voice and dark lips from smoking too many blunts, James spent time after school with me (then a cheerleader on our pitifully small squad of four), chopping it up before football practice, chatting on the phone, and heaping endless praise on me for being such a smart, cute, mature freshman girl.

He was intrigued by my being "Spanish and Black," something that would be a common theme with Black boys throughout my life. "You know how to speak Spanish? Say something in Spanish!" was something they often asked me. Lil James was sweet to me; I even held his hand when he grabbed mine while walking down the hallway one day. But after weeks of hanging and after reluctantly realizing that my plans to "wait" until marriage were real, Lil James lost interest, fading into the busyness of football practice but still managing to stay amicable with me.

Now, a whole semester later, here we were with Lil James in the hot seat, and me seething over this apparent betrayal. I found him sitting in the hallway chatting with some girls, as expected.

"I need to speak with you," I said curtly.

He stood up and walked a few steps away with me.

"You told people you took my virginity? Why would you lie?"

"Wait, wait, what? What are you talking about? Who told you somethin' like that?"

"Apparently *everyone*. Everyone has been saying you took my virginity, and you know that's not true."

Virginity was like a fresh pair of Air Force Ones. One scuff was enough to ruin your reputation as a girl. I didn't make the rules, I just knew how they worked.

"I NEVER said that," Lil James replied with concern and outrage. "I swear on my *daughter*, I never said that."

Lil James did in fact have a daughter to swear on. Teenage parenthood had become a rare but not wholly shocking reality for some kids at our high school. I stared into his eyes, trying to decide if he was lying or telling the truth. What hurt most about this rumor was that I'd never even seen a boy naked. I naively thought I could've stopped the rumor, had I known it existed—but now it was too late. The whole thing felt like yet another gross injustice for being a girl.

After the confrontation, I huffed away and walked into the only place I knew to go: the classroom of Mrs. Murphy, my favorite writing and journalism teacher. Short in stature, with a round face, red hair, and gray eyes, she was a white lady from the outskirts of the city who stood out like a sore thumb in our school of mostly Black pupils, but she was a tough cookie who didn't let her height get in the way of commanding a room.

"What's wrong?" Mrs. Murphy asked before I could even open my mouth.

The dam of tears broke. She let me cry on her desk, as I explained what happened through tiny sobs.

"Oh dear, my dear Natasha," she said soothingly. "You have to understand that boys like that are just trying to keep you in your place. You are smart and destined for greatness. A rumor about your virginity is all they have to work with."

I looked up, wiping the tears that covered my face.

"Sometimes people think if they can ruin your reputation, they can ruin your self-esteem. And the thing about you—the light in you that shines so bright—it makes them insecure. They want it dimmed, so you won't continue to make yourself better than them.

"But you will meet far better men outside of high school. You just have to get to college."

Not knowing better, I nodded, trying to shake off the embarrassment as the injustice of it all sank in. I was coming close to my quince to celebrate my womanhood, but too much about being a woman seemed unfair. Virgins had targets on our backs for "conquering" a sexualization process that had started early.

Meanwhile girls without experience were called prudish, expected to learn the art of sexiness and seduction somehow. Girls with experience were trashed by boys and girls alike for exploits that never managed to stay private. Half of the words both the boys and girls used in school to describe women sexually were derogatory: whores, hoes, rollers, jump-offs, sluts, and hoochies, just to name a few. Boys didn't have to worry about losing their virginity.

Back when Daddy was actually acknowledging my existence, I'd walked by him in the living room when he suddenly handed me a book by author and journalist Nathan McCall titled *Makes Me Wanna Holler.*

"Read this," he said. "It's a good book. You need to read it."

I took it my room, completely unaware of what I was about to be exposed to. Inside, a chapter called "Trains" had been folded down and highlighted for me to read. I read in horror, digesting as McCall detailed the brutal gang rape of a neighborhood girl. The thirteen-year-old girl was an acquaintance of McCall's, beautiful and quiet, who found herself trapped in a back room of a house, thinking she was there to meet a friend, only to be coerced into having sex with twelve boys. McCall himself took part in the "train."

My stomach dropped with disgust at the end. At that point in my young life, I couldn't understand how a friend could do that to another friend, and I felt terrible for the girl. Was this Daddy's warning to me that good girls could get "ruined" too with one bad choice? We never talked about boyfriends, healthy relationships, or what to expect. But this was a clear message he wanted me to absorb.

All these messages felt contradictory. As much as I'd tried to conform by playing by the rules, somehow the system seemed flawed. I was trying not to internalize the sexism I saw everywhere but it seemed almost unconquerable.

"We can go to whoever told you this right now, and I'll tell them it isn't true," Lil James said, giving an Oscar-worthy attempt at defending my honor.

I looked around at the cafeteria full of kids who I imagined all knew this rumor, and the hallway, where a few nosy eyes and ears were listening in on our conversation. It dawned on me that this was pointless. By virtue of being a girl, a freshmen girl at that, and an only child without brothers or boy cousins at school to defend my honor, I would never win the purity battle, no matter how hard I tried.

I shook my head as Lil James looked at me. "Whatever," I said. "I don't even care anymore." And I walked off.

———

With Daddy still ignoring me and boys at school being a disappointment, I threw myself into dance practice with my quince court for distraction. Mamí persuaded her coworker and fellow Boricua Janellys to teach us the steps in the gym of a local daycare.

"Forward, middle, back! Forward, middle, back!" Janellys would yell out in a strong Spanish accent to us kids as we giggled and tried to nail salsa in place of our chickenhead and Harlem Shake dance moves.

Quinceañeras were about friendship, and sisterhood, specifically. Choosing your court was about who you wanted by your side on your big day. Those friends who wouldn't mind putting on the same *dama* dress so you could stand out and be the princess for the day. Friends who would not complain about skipping an evening of surfing AOL, watching *TRL*, loitering in the mall food centers. I picked my closest friends for my court—Vanessa, Tessy, Solana, and Howard from Syracuse Baptist, Ty, my cousin Sheeda, and other friends from middle school. We probably looked like we were attending a debutante ball, not a quince.

Like quinces, Black debutante balls had a deeper meaning for African Americans than just putting their daughters in frilly dresses. These balls and cotilions traced back to the late 1700s and provided well-to-do and upwardly mobile Black families a chance to present their daughters—often called debs—to society, showing off their good manners, social training, and etiquette. The balls also came to showcase debs' educational achievements and career aspirations. The image of the debutante was a direct response to every degrading racist image of young Black women that undermined our beauty, intelligence, and contributions to the world.

Even with debutante balls' rich history, we couldn't find a debutante or quinceañera cake topper that featured a brown girl, so Mamí bought brown paint, and one of my art teachers kindly painted over the tan-pink face of the topper. I knew enough to know that anyone selling quince products probably wasn't thinking of a Black Latina. I was grateful, but I hated that we had to paint my cake topper. It was not a perfect match to my walnut-colored skin.

Little did I know I had yet another conundrum developing, this time within my court. Solana was a close friend at school and a preacher's daughter, who was always left home alone while her mama and daddy volunteered at the church. She was smart and had even gotten into a summer college program for inner-city kids with potential.

But lately during the fittings for our quinceañera dresses, Solana's dress was getting tighter every time. Her secret was one that none of us would fully understand until months later.

"I gotta stop eating all these Hot Cheetos!" she said with an embarrassed giggle, throwing me a smile with her super-white teeth and box braids swinging as she shimmied into the dress.

We were children in growing bodies. Good girls with secret

worlds. Our mothers had emphasized closed legs, "waiting for marriage," "respecting ourselves," and other vague commandments, while boys called our landlines when our parents were asleep. With this in mind, Mamí rarely let me out of her sight. Still, my girlfriends found ways to get from under their parents' purview, and their stories became a whole separate education for me.

Solana was bright eyed, beautiful, brown, and had long, full black hair down her back. She was funny and charismatic, and fell for a boy from the East Side who gave her the love and affirmation she craved. I listened as Solana told me of her escapades right in her mama's house after school. Now Solana's secret was forming in her womb, soon undeniable.

But the real humiliation should've been worn by those who'd left her—left us all—unprepared for the myriad ways the world would use and abuse us as girls, and who made our very ability to produce life a source of contempt. While we were getting to play dress-up and have parties like the quince, we were growing into much more pressing issues to attend to as women.

Perhaps this was the greatest lesson of my quinceañera era: not the custom-made dress, or the practicing of salsa with my court of friends, or the selection of napkin colors, cake flavors, and food menus, but the fact that becoming a young woman meant becoming more desirable and at the same time more vulnerable, in every way.

I knew this because the past year I'd been quietly logging into AOL Instant Messenger as LilMamacita15, chatting with a cute college junior named Luke from an Ivy League university. Six-two, with medium chocolate skin and short cropped hair, he played baseball and lived four states away. Despite the age gap—I was just fourteen, and he was twenty—Luke and I chatted about random things like TV shows, school, and sports.

"What's your address? I wanna send you something," Luke wrote to me one evening. Pushing past my initial hesitation, I typed my address and pressed enter to send it right over. Within one week, I got a small package with a Tommy Hilfiger change purse and a little

handwritten note with words I can't remember, except for the promise to visit and chat in person one day soon.

It wouldn't occur to me until years later that I could've easily been
in grave danger by giving Luke my address. His interest in me was
confirmation that I was interesting and smart enough to command
the attention of older (and presumably more sophisticated) young
men. Older "boys" hung around us high school girls all the time. It
was as normal as the city bus pulling up at 4:00 p.m. to take us back
to the South Side.

I'd been prepared for Luke's attention because in eighth grade
I met a twenty-three-year-old named Darryl. Darryl had graduated
from Nottingham, the high school where I was headed, and was a
star football player who'd even gotten into college out of state. But
Darryl was taking a break from school. He would drive by Percy
Hughes Middle School regularly to chat us all up after school. He
was a god to us because he had a car and would offer to give us rides
wherever we needed to go.

After trading numbers, Darryl kept in touch with me, and he
knew when I had an early dismissal. "You wanna hang out for a little?" he asked after pulling up at school that day.

I calculated the risk. As a teacher, Mamí knew the half days and
school calendar as well as anyone else. But she might be late, maybe
to tidy the classroom or catch up with coworkers.

"Sure!" I said, my heart racing as I got into the car. The male gaze
is a powerful thing, like a magnet; the closer you lean into it out of
curiosity, desire, or validation, the easier it is to get sucked in. When
I got into Darryl's car, I saw how dusty and messy it was. The shin-
iness of his tall brown frame hanging through the window was a lot
less shiny from inside. We drove to the cluster of slightly run-down
apartment buildings just two blocks from the school where he lived.

"My mom is home, but we're just gonna walk down the hall to
my room," he instructed me. I followed, every alarm bell in my head
going off. It suddenly felt like a mistake to not know exactly what
"hanging out" entailed; I had just wanted to go for some ice cream

or late lunch or to do something fun. But I hadn't developed a voice to say that yet.

As soon as we got to Darryl's room, I saw how deeply unimpressive it was. His bedsheets were wrinkled, and there were random sticks of deodorant atop his dresser and half-opened sneaker boxes and hats everywhere.

Within just a few minutes he was on top of me, trying to kiss my face, pressed against me as I sank into the bed. I looked up at the ceiling uncomfortably while his heavy weight pressed against my skinny girlish frame. His slobbery kisses felt like a puppy licking my face. I calculated that if I was still enough, he would be bored and lose interest. And sure enough, after twenty-five minutes—which seemed like hours—Darryl gave up. "All right," he said, "I can drop you home if you want."

"Yeah, I better get back before my mom gets home."

We drove in silence.

"Drop me right here at the corner," I told Darryl, not wanting him to know where I lived.

I speed-walked down the street, ready to run up the porch stairs. There Mamí was, standing in the driveway, hand on her hips, a steam of rage bubbling out of her nostrils and eyes.

"Where have you been??"

"I was at Ty's house!" I said, picking the friend Mamí would have a harder time getting hold of to verify and trying to keep my eyes from wandering.

"Are you lying to me? Why are you so late getting home? You got out more than two hours ago!" she said, clearly knowing that her only child was in fact lying.

"I swear, I was at Ty's house! I *just* got dropped off and her mom had to go!" I said, my heart skipping a beat as I tried to evaluate how believable my deception was, and praying Mamí didn't call Ty's mom.

"If you ever lie to me, you are going to have a problem—you hear me? *Coño!*"

"I hear you!" I said, bounding up the stairs and out of sight,

thanking God I'd escaped two run-ins and promising to never have
to ask for forgiveness on this subject again.

———

I looked at myself in the mirror at my latest quince dress fitting,
evaluating every inch of my face and body, while a little Puerto Rican seamstress with a lazy eye measured my barely-there bust and
waist and tried to evaluate how I really measured up. I knew I was
too skinny. It was something nearly everyone, including Daddy, lovingly teased me about. "You bony! You need to eat a sandwich or
something!" Compared to the video girls we consumed on BET's
106 & Park after school, immortalized in the latest Hype Williams
or Director X music video, my frame was thin, with no plump booty
or D-cup breasts. I wanted to be thick, like the girls who got the
most attention at school, but it wasn't in the cards for me.

"You should be grateful you're skinny!" Mamí would lament every
time I complained. "Abuela used to make me wear a girdle in fifth grade
because I was too fat! I struggled my whole life. You're blessed, M'ija!"

Standing in front of the mirror at the dress fitting, I didn't exactly see the blessings, although I was glad I had no mother forcing
me into a girdle. But staring back at me were the two discolored
veneers on my front teeth I'd foolishly agreed to get to cover up my
fluoride-stained teeth back in middle school. They were still there,
causing me to cover my smile with my hand each time life naturally
parted my mouth for joy, because they didn't match the rest of my
chompers. Then I had this nose—this curve-shaped centerpiece on
my face that didn't look like anyone else's at school.

"You'd be pretty if it wasn't for that damn nose!" I remember
my coworker at McDonald's saying with a guffaw, a scruffy guy a
couple years older than me named Sy, who was also at Nottingham
High. The verbal assault came out of nowhere, a drive-by attempt
to shoot down my self-esteem, but Sy wasn't the first to imply that
my unique features made me less attractive. Once a group of senior

girls at school reveled in loudly talking about my awkward face a few tables over in the library.

In the mirror at the quince seamstress's place, I assessed myself soberly, with the precision of an attorney. Sy was right. I had a couple things going for me, but I wasn't pretty like the Black or Spanish girls who were most popular around our city. This might present a challenge in finding a suitable partner for my quince. He needed to be cute, cool, rhythmic enough to learn to dance salsa and pose in pictures with me, while also finding me cute enough to agree to the job.

For most of the school year I thought the son of Mamí's coworker Ms. Johnson, who'd done my perm, would fill in. But he was a basketball star at school and had missed every salsa practice up until now due to practices and away games. After two months of missed practices, it started to dawn on us that he probably would never show.

Mamí worked her magic again, recruiting another son of a different coworker to be my quince partner—a Puerto Rican boy named Angel, who was ironically one of the cutest guys at school. Angel had piercing black eyes, fair skin, cropped hair, and a lot of city-boy swagger. His mother was a Black Latina, with dark-brown skin and long jet-black hair, and his father, whom he took after, was a near-white light-skinned mestizo with green eyes. Latino boys, especially fine ones like Angel, never seemed to notice me, so I understood from jump that this was strictly a favor for my mom and expected nothing of it.

Although we never spoke before our moms arranged the pairing, Angel and I became cool in the final weeks leading up to my quince. He knew how to salsa, so it didn't matter that he'd missed all the practices.

Things were looking up.

At home, Daddy had slowly begun to acknowledge my presence, either asking when my mother was coming home or telling me to do random errands around the house. There were no apologies in our home, ever. No makeup conversations or unpacking of emotions in the overstuffed suitcases they sat within. Life was not an after-school special.

Forgiveness came like the change of seasons, with small indications that the old things had passed away and been replaced with new air and soil. An offer of scrambled eggs. Holding a door open so you could pass through with bags. Asking what had been on the news. That's how I learned to say sorry in life, and to know when a truce had been made.

Despite not having spoken to me in months and actually coming down with a bad cold, Daddy pulled out his tuxedo rental just a week before letting us know without words in the final hour that he would in fact attend the party.

The day of my quince, Friday, June 8, 2001, the sun seemed to shine brighter than it ever had at the top of Syracuse in June.

After putting on my dress, I stood in front of the mirror of my bedroom, the wall covered in honor roll certificates and Daddy's homemade plaques, feeling like I was crossing the finish line of an exhausting race I'd been running for the past year.

One by one our immediate family arrived at the house: Cousin Sheeda, dressed in her Communion-wine-purple *dama* dress, Abuela in a sherbet-orange lace dress with poofy sheer sleeves, and my nine-year-old prima Yamarys.

"She look like a queen, Ronnie," Abuela declared proudly to Daddy. "Natasha look like a queen!"

"It's Natasha's quin-za," Daddy said, recording with his big camcorder, mangling the Spanish word but saying it with reverence.

The limo was white, gleaming in the sun. "Is this the bride?" the limo driver asked.

Both Mamí and Daddy jumped in fast. "Oh, she's not a bride, she's turning fifteen," Mamí said quickly.

"It's her *fifteenth* birthday," Daddy chimed in for good measure.

I got into the car to head to Syracuse Baptist Church for a brief service. When we arrived, I was escorted down the church aisle by both my parents as a prerecorded version of "Glory to Your Name" played on the speaker with a rousing guitar underneath. I sat and listened as my friends Ty, Vanessa, and Howard serenaded me with a soulful rendition of the gospel song "Jesus You Are."

After the service we exited the church, me and my court laughing as cars sped by, beeping, then took photos by Syracuse University before we went to the Genesee Inn hotel, on the nice side of town, for the party.

Walking into that ballroom, I felt like a caramel-colored Cinderella in a fairy tale I'd written for myself.

"Azúcar, azúcar negra / Ay, cuanto me gusta y me alegra . . ." Celia Cruz's holy and gritty vocals sang on top of blaring salsa trumpets. The choice to play Celia—an Afro-Cuban musical pioneer and the most famous Black Latina singer I knew—belting a song about being Black and proud was as intentional as every other aspect of the party. Celia's very presence validated my existence. Her brown skin, broad nose, big hair, and full lips affirmed that the Blackness of my quince was both normal and authentic. In homage to her, I lifted up the skirt of my poofy white dress and stuck out my barely-there hips with confidence, completing a salsa spin, praying I wasn't offbeat.

"Baila, Natacha, Baila!" Abuela cheered from the crowd, squealing with approval.

The other women—all Puerto Rican women, mainly friends of my mother—were cheering my name with *wepas* of pride, welcoming me into a new stage.

"Rumba, Natacha!"

The excited parents of my friends looked on with wonder; for most this was their first quinceañera. My entire court got into a line formation, from dancing in couples to moving as one unit, and we were on beat.

I could see Solana much more clearly now than I had before, dress pulled tightly at the belly, five months pregnant, struggling to breathe and keep up with the turns and spins but trying her best to show up for me. Soon she'd be holding her baby in her arms and fighting for her right to raise it against the wishes of pushy adults, defying the odds and graduating high school, even though her mama sent her far away to the suburbs after the baby was born. We were all becoming women in our own ways, insisting, pleading with a world around us to let us be.

We'd skipped the traditional opening father-daughter dance, considering that Daddy had only just started speaking to me, and he wasn't really one to play along with what was expected. Instead I danced salsa with Mamí, her eyes beaming at me, looking overjoyed in the cream-colored sleeveless dress she'd worn for the occasion. It was the proudest I'd ever seen her.

After our introductory dance, we moved into our Afro–Puerto Rican–inspired choreographed bomba, with my *damas* in head wraps and long, flowing skirts. I felt the drums in my chest, I was free, floating on gusts of wind that blew from Bayamón to the ballroom of this hotel. Once the dances were done, I breathed a sigh of relief. The presentation of myself as a young woman was complete. Now it was time to party.

My friends and I turned up to Lil' Mo and Fabolous's hit song "Superwoman," Jay-Z's "Give It to Me," and of course my favorite song since it hit the airwaves in 1998, "Still Not a Player" by Big Pun. It was the only song where I got to hear the words "Boricua" and "Morena" on the same track, and I'd point to myself each time Pun and Joe alternated between the words in the chorus. Abuela Sonia joined us in the middle of the dance floor, giving us a taste of perreo and sending everyone into a frenzy of laughter and cheers.

"Go Abuelllla! Go Abuelllla! Go Abuelllla!" we chanted.

Later that night I'd realize that while my parents once had their wedding in a YMCA gymnasium with homemade favors, we now could afford to rent out the Genesee Inn just for my quince. Mamí going from a day-care worker to a teaching assistant to a full-on teacher had really changed our lives. Our family was advancing in this northern land of American dreams.

And this had to have been the Blackest, most American—but still very Puerto Rican—quinceañera to ever hit the 315. That *azúcar negra* Celia Cruz sang about—I could finally taste it.

5

Gifted

I don't mean to discourage you, but your SAT scores aren't exactly Harvard-level. It's just not standard for people to get in with a score like this," Mrs. Murphy said to me as she sat back in her chair. I looked into her gray eyes and straightened myself in my seat at the other side of her desk, trying my hardest to mask the disappointment of my favorite high school teacher knocking down my Ivy League dream like it was a piñata.

It was a gentle knock. While it didn't quite spill everything out of me, I began to feel like I should've never hoisted my dream so high.

"I just don't want you to be disappointed," Mrs. Murphy insisted quietly.

"Oh yeah, I know," I replied nonchalantly, sneaking a peek down at my butter-tan Timbs, pointing my toes so they wouldn't crease. Disappointment implied that my expectations didn't match reality. Harvard was a reach school. Wasn't the point of a reach school to stretch a student's faith in their abilities? I knew I was reaching. Did I need to be reminded?

"I was planning to retake it anyways. I'm sure I'll do better next time, since my mom is putting me in a prep class—I'll keep you posted," I said as I hurried off to my next class, which I suddenly couldn't wait to get to. *1600. 1600. 1600.* My 1160 PSAT score wasn't perfect, but I had received a letter in the mail, informing me that mine was on the higher end for Black students nationally. I thought I'd done well. Apparently, it wasn't good enough.

What was normally a private number was now public knowledge: my score, along with all of my grades, had been published across Onondaga County in a newspaper series called "The Junior Journey," a special monthly full-page Sunday story that profiled college-bound students during this critical junior year. Mamí had gotten a call from Mr. Jones—a city school district superintendent who knew of her teaching work—who asked if I would agree to represent the city school district. It was an honor to be considered, and of course I said yes.

The paper would follow one junior each from a suburban, rural, and city school for the entire school year—preparing for SATs, going to classes, activities, and prom, and ultimately applying and (hopefully) getting into college. I was, of course, the only brown face of the three students featured. Being in the paper was a big deal—especially in the days before social media, where the newspaper was the main standard of who and what was worthy to be covered.

"That's great they thought of you, M'ija," Mamí said. "But that's a lot of attention. Just don't tell too much of your business." Mamí had never been comfortable with the spotlight. She told me often that I got my speaking ability from Daddy's side. To me this was just another one of her many warnings about life to ignore.

"Ma, I'll be fine. Just let me have my moment, *por favor!*" I said before putting my nose back in a book while nestled in the couch. To the outside world, it sounded like we were bickering, but this is really how we talked.

I hadn't thought twice about accepting Mr. Alicea's invitation, because ever since I could remember I had always been identified as a "bright" student—a poster child for my classroom and schools, exemplary of what was possible in an underfunded school district, defying the odds with grades, prizes, and achievements.

That dream of attending Harvard had begun forming when I won a youth scholarship for the Saturday Academy I attended weekly. The honor meant I was required to send information to fill the printed program for the awards dinner:

PLEASE PROVIDE A SHORT BIO AND LIST YOUR DREAM
COLLEGE OR SCHOOL. PROVIDE A HEADSHOT.

Mrs. Harper, my instructor at Saturday Academy, had gone to
Spelman College her freshman year, the esteemed all-girls HBCU
founded in 1881 by Baptist missionaries in Atlanta. It had produced
famous alumni such as Alice Walker, Marian Wright Edelman, Ber-
nice King, and Stacey Abrams. The school's colors were a pretty baby-
blue-and-white combo and their tagline was "A Choice to Change the
World." I didn't know there were all-Black schools for girls, let alone
colleges, but Spelman sounded glorious. Listening to Mrs. Harper
speak of her alma mater, I dreamed of an educational utopia of other
smart Black girls whom I'd learn with side by side. Naturally I wanted
to follow in her footsteps so I listed Spelman as my top choice. But
something in me told me to add another school to the program's form.
I racked my brain thinking of what schools had a strong reputation. I
wanted to go to a place that had the best of the best resources. Everyone always said "Harvard" and "smart" in the same sentence on TV
and in movies and supposedly, it was where brainiacs went, so . . .
SPELMAN COLLEGE OR HARVARD UNIVERSITY, I typed.
The very act of typing it out loud felt audacious. How dare I insist that I, a bright but certainly regular public-school kid from the
city, belonged at the number one school in the country? It felt like
I was somehow breaking an unspoken rule by saying aloud I was
good enough to aim for admission there. I didn't know a thing about
Harvard but I figured I had nothing to lose.

Later at the scholarship dinner, I sat with a corsage on my satin
dress, my hair pressed and my eyes sparkling. I was asked to stand
in front of the three hundred people gathered as they read my bio
from the podium.

". . . And Natasha would like to attend Spelman College or Harvard University one day—that's right, young lady!" said the speaker,
an older Black woman who helped run Saturday Academy.

The whole room erupted with applause and oohs and ahhs,

smiles on brown faces of every shade, eyes wide with excitement, as if I had already gotten in. I wanted that feeling for real. Now I had something to strive for.

My grooming to be an overachiever had started long before that dinner. Daddy bought me a set of encyclopedias before I could crawl. At five years old I flipped through old copies of *LIFE* magazine in my bedroom library, being exposed to images I probably had no business seeing, like the iconic 1972 napalm girl photo from the Vietnam War and the 1962 shooting of activist James Meredith by a white bystander as he marched for voting rights in Mississippi. Daddy even took me on a school tour of every public school he'd attended, including Percy Hughes, which he helped integrate in the 1960s, facing down some screaming white parents as he entered the building. All this early exposure to education made me crave learning.

After bringing home my first straight-A report card in kindergarten, I saw Daddy's face light up, as it did when his team was winning basketball on TV.

"Good job, Boonky, this is what we like to see!" Daddy said, invoking my childhood nickname. "That's how Alfords do. Go get you anything you want from Toys 'R' Us," he said, grinning and giving me a hug in the living room before he went off to his custodian night shift at McDonald's.

Doing well in school appeared to have a double payoff: it made Daddy happy and earned me rewards. That night at Toys "R" Us, I selected a Cabbage Patch doll with crimpable hair—the hottest girl toy of the early '90s—as my prize, and I was sold on getting straight As moving forward.

But the next semester, when I brought home another straight-A report card, the reaction was different, somewhat muted. Mamí and Daddy sat me down, looking at each other with trepidation, and broke the news.

"We are very proud of you, Natasha," Mamí said gently. "But we want you to know that you don't get a toy each time you get good grades."

No prize? My shoulders slumped slightly as I took in their speech.

"That's right, Ratty-Roo," Daddy chimed in. "You do good in school for yourself, not for us. This is so you'll go far in life."

I nodded in response, but they couldn't fool me. I remembered the look on Daddy's face when I brought home the report card and the way my teachers reacted when talking about my work at school. Being good at school was a *good* thing.

On the Black side of my family, we had actual college grads, even if Daddy wasn't one of them. I remembered the photos and large oil paintings on Grandma and Grandpa's living-room wall at the yellow house on Garfield. They were of my uncles and my aunt in their graduation and military uniforms, service that funded their college dreams.

That may not have been the same for Mamí's Puerto Rican family, with her being the first to actually go to college and graduate, the rest of our immediate family being working-class laborers. One uncle served in the National Guard, but there was enough of a standard set by my parents that I knew getting at least a high school degree was expected.

The more near-perfect report cards I brought home, the more achievement became a core part of my identity. I watched with envy as my friends who got B-pluses got toys and PlayStations as rewards. But it didn't matter; I'd now internalized that to be me was to get good grades and perform well in school, regardless of how my parents reacted.

I devoured books above my grade level like they were oxygen, reading so much I would get scolded for not putting the book down when it was time to eat dinner. Books took me away from my lonely only-child life, in the city of Syracuse with its cold winters and slower pace, to the creepy world of R. L. Stine's Goosebumps series, or the gritty drug-dealing streets of Omar Tyree's *Flyy Girl* or Sistah Souljah's *Coldest Winter Ever.*

At around ten years old I left the supposedly safer world of Catholic school and persuaded Mamí to send me to public school in fourth grade so I could wear regular clothes and "express myself." At Meachem Elementary, my fast reading and clear handwriting got me immediately identified as one of only a few Black students among a larger group selected for the gifted-and-talented program. Every Wednesday I would board a yellow bus with a group of Meachem kids to enter a world of wonder and academic exploration.

"Gifted," as they called it, was my safe haven, my happy place. The program was the one day in the week where I was truly challenged in an academic environment, not bored out of my mind or resisting the urge to raise my hand and share the answer, for fear of taking the wind out of other kids' sails.

At Gifted I was surrounded by kids of all races across the school district who loved to learn, and we were given a ton of unstructured time to do so unconventionally, from building homemade water filtration systems in science class to using Microsoft Paint to draw or playing *Oregon Trail* on computers.

At Gifted there were hardly ever fights or behavioral disruptions; students talking back to teachers wasn't a thing. Gifted was a five-star luxury hotel—once you've stayed in a five-star, do you ever really want to go back to what you're used to?

What I didn't realize was just how lucky I was to be seen as gifted. Historically, the abilities of African American and Latino kids of all races have been underidentified for gifted-and-talented programs. Low-income kids were too. Selection was about way more than objective criteria like grades and test scores; it was about the choosers—the selectors—seeing you as worthy. And these programs were key to setting you on a college-bound path. I was lucky not only to be smart but also to be chosen.

"You think you so smart cause you go to Gifted? Don't nobody care!" my classmate LaToya snapped at me one Wednesday in the lunchroom as I made my way out to the Gifted bus.

It was all a misunderstanding, the details of what had triggered her murky, but the look of annoyance on LaToya's face and the shock on mine were enough to say it all. I thought we were friends.

"No . . . I don't!" was all I could muster saying before heading to the bus, trying to diffuse the tension. Saying kids do not like you for being good at school—especially if you're Black—is a cliché, a controversial trope long critiqued by scholars like Karolyn Tyson, William Darity Jr., and Domini R. Castellini, who argue it's not just "a Black thing" when kids get heat for being high achievers or even called "white-acting" for doing well. Their research shows that students of all races can face heat for being "nerds" but when it's racialized, it's usually tied to systemic inequalities.

"In a society categorized by patterns of race and class privilege, the charge of acting white is loaded with the resentment (misdirected) of the less privileged, toward the few individuals among them who receive the coveted rewards by those bestowed with power," they write.*

Indeed, it was the special privileges that seemed to be a problem—salt in the wound. Other students wanted to know why they, too, couldn't go to Gifted. Didn't someone see their potential?

Grappling with these difficult feelings of guilt over being a chosen one had to take a pause, though. Before I knew it, just one year into my time at Gifted, we got devastating news from Mrs. Harper herself, who then ran the program: Gifted was being shut down. There wasn't enough money in the district's budget. I went back to my regular classes and continued to get good grades.

Upon graduating from elementary school, Mamí made an intervention. "You're not going to Clary."

"But *whyyyyy*, Mamí, that's where all my friends are going!" I whined, grimacing and hoping my pouting would guilt her into changing her mind.

She was unmoved. "All kids do is fight there. There are disruptions to learning. You're not going there, and I'm talking to Mr. DeMarco, the vice principal, to see if you can get on the waiting list at Percy Hughes. You'd be on track for Nottingham."

---

* Karolyn Tyson, William Darity Jr., and Domini R. Castellino, "It's Not 'a Black Thing': Understanding the Burden of Acting White and Other Dilemmas of High Achievement," *American Sociological Review*, 70, no. 4 (August 2005): 600.

Mamí wasn't wrong. Clary Middle School, my zone school, bused in kids from the South Side and the Valley, and operated as only a seventh- and eighth-grade school, which many preteens had a field day with. Percy Hughes, the K–8 school Daddy once racially integrated as a first grader, was now considered a magnet program, with Spanish-language and science opportunities that set it apart. It was also close to Syracuse University, drawing a more racially mixed, economically diverse student population.

Just in time for the start of school, Mr. DeMarco called with the good news: a spot had opened up, and I was off the wait list at Percy Hughes. I begrudgingly boarded the yellow school bus daily, traveling to the edge of the East Side in a neighborhood I didn't live in for this so-called better educational opportunity.

But it was at Percy Hughes that I would meet a lifesaver in human form—Mr. Freeland, the first Black male teacher I ever had. Mr. Freeland was a social studies teacher on paper, but really Superman to us students, with suit, tie, cropped military haircut, and glasses to match.

Freeland, as we called him, had the audacity to teach us mostly Black seventh graders the philosophies of John Locke, Martin Luther King Jr., Malcolm X, Gandhi, and Hiawatha, when some might argue we didn't have the capacity to understand them.

Freeland also addressed each of us by our last names as a sign of respect, even during something as simple as roll call.

"Mr. Davis?"

"Here!"

"Mr. Rodriguez?"

"Here!"

"Ms. Alford?"

"Here, Mr. Freeland!"

"NOTHING DISTURBS THE LEARNING!" was Freeland's frequent refrain whenever we kids were chatting and not listening, or bickering among ourselves. "They engineered the hood," he would preach, pointing out how in Syracuse, just blocks away from wealthy colleges and neighborhoods, you could always find a housing project like The Bricks. "How is that possible if it's not nefariously done? Racism is when you can create poverty. And the North is damn good at that." He would also rail on frequently about new-age rappers and their destructive effects on society, including a new raspy-voiced rapper from Yonkers who was climbing the charts.

"This nonsense is demonic!" he yelled, holding up the cover of DMX's latest album, *Flesh of My Flesh, Blood of My Blood*, on which DMX was pictured covered in blood. "They want you to listen to this crap and have you conditioned to go to jail before you even turn eighteen. The music industry doesn't care about y'all. Remember, 'He who controls the media, controls the mind!'" "Freeland so crazy!" kids would joke, half in awe, half amused.

I'd already memorized all the lyrics to "Ruff Ryders' Anthem," but I understood where he was coming from.

Despite Freeland's monologues about rap and media, he wasn't a king of respectability politics. He wasn't all that impressed with some of the Black bourgeosie of the city, who he charged with preserving the status quo to maintain their privilege. "The real gatekeeper is not always the gatekeeper who you think it is," he warned. In fact, little did we know then that he had his own power struggles with some school administrators, the educational guard of the city school district, who preferred he didn't stir up revolutionary thinking. But two women admins—one Black and one white, protected Freeland against critics and told him to teach in the spirit of his own last name.

Freeland had come from to Syracuse from Albany after getting out of the navy, with a dream of establishing himself and his family. I suspected that's why he taught with such fury and determination. He'd run a Boys and Girls Club, and earned his master's degree at Cortland University. Specializing in American history, Freeland recalled the lessons he learned in his education. "If anybody ever tells you the Civil War wasn't fought over slavery, they're telling a debilitating, deliberate lie to mask how much Black people were actually worth at that particular time," Freeland recounted. "But if you can steal labor then you can steal labor now. If you educate people you have to pay, you have to give them jobs and you're going to have to compete with them." Freeland wanted us to be able to compete.

I soared in Freeland's class, picking up books like *The Souls of Black Folk* at twelve years old, trying to make sense of the text. After reading my essay comparing W. E. B. Du Bois and Booker T. Washington's strategies for Black liberation, he wrote on my paper: "Natasha, you're a future voice that will be strong. Many will try to make you lose focus. Please don't ever lose focus—Mr. Freeland."

And because Freeland said it, I felt chosen, in a good way. He made it clear that during my next stop—high school—there was an entire system designed to derail and ultimately fail Black, and particularly Black girl, students.

Once I entered the halls of Nottingham High, I saw exactly what Freeland meant.

Nottingham was hailed as a beacon of diversity during the time I attended. Founded in 1953 on the East Side near Syracuse University, it was a place where Black and white American kids now went in almost equal numbers, along with immigrant kids from countries around the world like Bosnia and Somalia.

We had an excellent theater program, a good mix of AP and honors classes, and a great basketball team. We also had a program for differently abled students, providing them a path to graduation in a nonconventional setting that met their needs. Nottingham was simply one of the best public high schools the city school district had to offer.

But for all of its diversity, my high school was a tale of three schools: a school with kids on track for college, others tracked to vocational school, and everyone else.

The Syracuse City School District was one of the Big 5 districts in the state, along with Buffalo, Rochester, Yonkers, and New York City. It was considered to be under-resourced and high-need—59 percent of students were eligible for free lunch. Just outside the city sat sprawling, gorgeous, and wealthy suburban school districts, funded by strong tax bases. Syracuse had done the opposite of, say, school districts like Wake County, North Carolina, which in 1976 unified city with suburban districts. As scholar and Syracuse native Gerald Grant wrote in the book *Hope and Despair in the American City: Why There Are No Bad Schools in Raleigh*, the merging of districts meant racial balancing and eventually socioeconomic balancing. But up in the "good North" we built highways like I-81 that bolstered white flight and kept our school districts strictly separate.

With poverty more concentrated in the neighborhoods we came from, there were a few kids in our schools who had a daddy who was a lawyer, or a mom who was a doctor—but many of those families had moved to the suburbs. Our buildings lacked investment, and depending on what school you went to, textbooks fell apart.

I remember once doing an exchange program to promote racial dialogue with kids out in the neighboring Fayetteville Manlius suburb and being blown away by their new football field, gigantic campus building, and science labs. When they—nearly all white kids—came to see our school building for the day, it was a little embarrassing how ours looked stuck in the 1960s and '70s compared to theirs.

Despite having majority-Black students in the district, most of our teachers were white, with Black people plentiful in staff roles like hall monitors, coaches, lunch aides, and custodians. There are always exceptions to the rule, but the rule sent an interesting but quiet message. For the most dedicated teachers, this work was a calling, and they gave their all despite what the district lacked. For a select few, they often misunderstood the culture of the kids they taught, like one teacher who complained that her school had started a gospel choir.

I had managed to do well even within this environment, my mother's status as a teacher in the district surely helping me, but not all of my friends were able to do the same. Our freshmen year, we were gathered in an auditorium and told, "Look left and look right. Half of you won't be here in four years." Harsh as the message was, the graduation rate for the Syracuse City School district was 53 percent. Summer schools were full of Black students and other students of color, trying to make up for that one failed class that kept them from graduating.

We were victims of the "resegregation" of America: although *Brown v. Board* said students couldn't be separate and unequal, inequality was everywhere. Even with these strong and divisive forces, many of us still managed to make friends across color lines. We didn't break into physical fights over race. We could talk and joke and dance with each other at parties, and our homecoming courts managed to look as diverse as the student body. But school was often where those friendships were contained. In our senior class photo from high school, you see a diverse student body, but smaller friend groups mostly separated by color.

Most Spanish-speaking Latino kids went to Fowler High School on the West Side, where Mamí taught, far away from the more affluent East Side. It was a common joke that the pregnant high school girls, often Latina, went there for school. But a small number of those kids who came straight from Puerto Rico and other Latin American countries also went to Nottingham, and would be sent into ESL programs if they didn't know English fluently. I never had classes with them, but I did notice they stuck together.

I could understand the clique mentality as Latinos of all shades were still a minority compared to Black American kids in my high school. It never occurred to me to try to fit in with them. There was a boy who ran around school claiming to be half–Puerto Rican, wearing Puerto Rican flags at every turn, even using a Spanish accent for his English, but as soon as he turned his back, people mocked him as a wannabe. The last thing I wanted was to seem like I was trying too hard, so I didn't.

The language barrier between me and the "Spanish" kids would be yet another factor that made it easy for me to be just Black in high school—to be seen and think of myself as a Black kid with a "Spanish" mom, not as someone with two ethnic identities.

My entire high school experience changed when I was introduced to a program sponsored by the NAACP, called ACT-SO, which stood for Afro-Academic, Cultural, Technological and Scientific Olympics. ACT-SO had over twenty categories for Black high school students to compete in, from photography to poetry to playwriting. Local winners went on to national competitions around the country during NAACP conventions each year.

When I saw "oratory" on the ACT-SO program flyer during high school orientation, I knew I wanted to join. I didn't have a traditional talent like other kids who could sing or dance, but I knew I could read, write, and speak well, having won an oratory competition at nine years old at the community college by reciting a Shel Silverstein poem. ACT-SO could not only give me a forum to develop this talent but also provide a community of other Black students who liked school as I did. To us, there would be nothing inherent in Blackness that made school or achievement unattractive. In the program, it was quite the opposite. Our achievement was tied to our Blackness—a continuation of the legacy of our ancestors, a way to make our people proud.

To prepare for ACT-SO, Mamí said it would be good practice to do another oratory competition sponsored by the American Legion Dunbar Post, a historically Black chapter of the organization for military veterans. Competitors had to deliver a ten-minute speech on the Constitution with no script or papers, and then be prepared to improvise another speech on one of three constitutional amendments judges would pull from a hat. The winner would get a couple thousand dollars in scholarship money and advance to the county, then region, state, then national competition.

I was terrified. How had I agreed to speak in front of a live audience, from a memorized speech about, of all things, the U.S. Constitution?

The answer came in the form of Daddy, who a few days before the competition knocked on my bedroom door with two cassette tapes in hand. One had a photo of MLK on it, the other, Malcolm X. "This might help you for your competition," he said offhandedly.

I listened to the grainy tapes one at a time, the power of Malcolm's and Martin's words filling my tiny bedroom on Garfield Avenue, and then I got to writing. It was a speech about voting rights and the importance of embracing the ballot in realizing the promise of the Fourteenth Amendment: "No state shall . . . deprive any person of life, liberty, or property, without due process of law; nor deny to any person within its jurisdiction the equal protection of the laws."

Most fourteen-year-olds probably weren't spending their Saturday nights writing about the Constitution, but this is really how I spent my free time. I was enthralled by the rare opportunity to force adults to listen to a kid for a change, to be heard in a society that routinely demanded quiet submission from its youth and talked down to us.

On competition day I took the stage sporting chunky, clunky black heels and an ill-fitting navy-blue suit from JCPenney. I had self-cut bangs with an unintentional slant in them and probably looked like a young televangelist, but inside I was trembling, terrified. Still, competition forced me through the fear.

I took to the stage, ironically in Clary's school auditorium, took a deep breath, and raised my voice to the mic.

"Good evening, ladies and gentlemen. Let me bring your mind to thoughts about freedom," I began. "There are many different aspects and levels to mental freedom. Physical freedom. But today, I would like you to think about our political freedom. . . . Voting enables us with a great power. Yet it is up to us to take advantage of it and seize the opportunity."

I compared voting to a remote control. "Many of us let other people have that remote control. . . . So let's not just vote. Let's run for office. We can be senators. We can be presidents. We can be anything!"

I was feeling the energy from the crowd, and it fed my confidence like oxygen to fire.

"Exercise the right to vote. Not only for me, the under-eighteen group who can't represent themselves . . . but the future of America a future that is so bright and so promising that you can't afford to miss the opportunity to stand up and be heard!"

I walked offstage to rousing applause, the cheers filling the auditorium, and sat patiently as the other competitors delivered their speeches, relieved to have tasted the thrill of a live audience. The second portion of the competition was an extemporaneous speech, where a veteran pulled one of three constitutional amendments out of a hat, and competitors had to speak on it for three minutes. I swallowed my nerves and got through it, then went backstage to wait again.

I'd go on to win that competition, much to my surprise. Even more remarkable was seeing an article about the win in our local paper, the *Post-Standard*, a few days later. A reporter had been in the audience, and she wrote an inspirational story about the power of giving youth a stage, citing my speech. That article took me from being invisible to seen, a higher standard emerging before me.

The reaction to that story affected my entire trajectory, and my foray in oratory would eventually make me somewhat of a small-town celebrity. I would win other awards, two state titles for the American Legion oratorical—the first Black/Puerto Rican student to do so—and the first from the city. After years of my being a nerdy smart kid, it felt good to be known for something more.

But even with all my wins, I had a weak spot.

I have never felt comfortable improvising. Words were so precious, the audience's time so sacred, that I only wanted to utter the most carefully selected phrases and sentences. I was also just scared shitless of talking off the top of my head. Extemporaneous speech always felt to me like flying a plane without knowing where I'd land.

To get around my impediment, I wrote not just one prepared speech but *also one speech for each extemporaneous topic that could be called.* It was four times the work, but it was my safety net, and it made me feel protected from fumbling around onstage looking for words.

This strategy got me far: multiple county competitions, regional competitions, and even the state. But on my way to becoming the first African American or Puerto Rican oratorical winner in the state, my weakness was exposed.

I was standing on the school auditorium stage, looking out at an audience of more than a hundred people during the extemporaneous portion of the competition. Lights glared in my face as the clock ticked, and I tried to find the words to one of the speeches I had prepared for this moment. My heart beat faster with my realization that they weren't there.

The realization was like a fog that descended over every hour of practice, every minute of drilling, that I had put into preparing in the weeks before. I dared to investigate the faces of the people sitting in the seats. Some grimaced, feeling my pain. Others gave me warm smiles, hoping their positive vibes would float onstage to comfort me. I watched the father of the boy who in the last few rounds had always come in third place nudge his wife in the ribs with a smirk.

Finally she's losing.

We got her weakness.

She's not as good as they say she is—not compared to our boy.

I began again, "This amendment calls upon us to consider . . . to consider . . ."

I made up three more lines and then said "Thank you" before quickly exiting the stage.

I knew I'd already lost and went backstage to sit in silence.

"I'm so sorry, are you okay?" John asked me, genuinely concerned, more a friend than his competitive dad.

"I'm okay, thank you," I replied, keeping my tears at bay. "I don't know what happened out there, but I'm glad it's over now."

After a pep talk from Mamí, I wiped away my quiet and slow-flowing tears and took a deep breath to cool my flushed face. We waited about twenty-five minutes as the judges deliberated, and I counted down to when I could be home again, in Syracuse, eating Burger King on our living room couch, watching TV to decompress.

"We have a decision! Please line up," said a man in a blue hat covered with American Legion pins of his military service, and we all quickly moved into line, then filed out onstage to applause from the crowd.

I half listened, preparing my smile for when they called me for last place. But after they called third and second place, my heart started to beat faster.

"In first place for high school, representing Syracuse, New York . . . Natasha Alford!"

The room stood, applause filling the auditorium. John's father's face turned cold, and I was flanked by American Legion vets who handed me a plaque and posed next to me for pictures. I was frozen in disbelief, but I smiled through it all.

A short white man with a dark brown mustache and beard walked up to me afterward. "Your speech was exceptional," he said, and it turned out he was a judge. "It didn't matter that you'd fallen short on the extemporaneous piece. You had such high scores on your prepared speech, you were going to win anyway. I just want you to know." He patted me on the back.

"Great job, Natasha, congratulations," John whispered to me before being whisked away by his parents.

I thought back to how onstage I had wanted to turn around and run, but I didn't. Too often we back away from challenges, never realizing how close we are to knowing what we are truly capable of—how close we are to realizing our power. I had been lucky to be considered gifted, but now I had finally found my *gift*.

———

Despite my wins in oratory, Daddy rarely attended my speeches, usually due to his work or workout schedule, which he was strict about. But Mamí was there for all of them. "So proud of you, M'ija," Mamí said after my win. "Just stay humble."

It was advice she would repeat after every win, advice I accepted but eventually it started to chafe. Whenever people would compliment me on my grades or wins or recent press, Mamí would blush and reply, almost embarrassed, "Aww, well, we tell her to stay humble. She's no better than anyone else."

My mother's words sent a message that I needed to appear aware of my luck at all times, never overconfident. To do so made you a target for correction—and the worst thing you could be, where I was from, was stuck up. Thanks to my small-town local fame, I was self-conscious about counteracting both concerns before I spoke a word.

"Don't leave Syracuse and be like those people who never come back, you hear me?" a well-meaning local activist told me when visiting our school. He was speaking to the reality of the brain drain in rust belt cities like ours, where people came, amassed intellectual and social capital from local universities, then left for greener pastures.

I promised him, no matter where I went, I would plan to come home.

Once when I was walking downtown with Vanessa, who'd taken over the best-friend slot from Tykeisha—who had started hanging with a different group of girls, saying she was a "bad girl" at heart who didn't want to be so "goody-goody" all the time with me—we encountered a stranger who recognized me from the newspaper.

"Are you Natasha Alford, that young lady from the paper?" said an older white woman with gray hair. "My goodness, I am so proud of you!" the woman declared, her hand shooting out to shake mine vigorously.

"Thank you so much, I truly appreciate that!" I responded with a smile blushing.

"You keep up the good work, young lady. We need more youth who are focused the way you are."

We exchanged pleasantries briefly, and I resumed walking with Vanessa.

"Why did she have to kiss your ass like that?" she said with a snicker and an eye roll.

The comment felt like a sucker punch, coming from my best friend. Being an only child meant my friends were my chosen family. I was starting to get the sinking feeling that my closest friends didn't always have my back, and even resented all the attention I was getting. Maybe Vanessa was right, though. Perhaps the excessive praise was off. They knew I was just a regular kid, just like them. What *was* the big deal?

Still, I vowed to use my newfound talent for speaking as much as possible, doing everything from participating in Toastmasters meetings to American Legion conventions. Once, as part of the superintendent's student cabinet, I had the opportunity to help plan what would be the district's first ever hip-hop summit. In partnership with Syracuse University and Russell Simmons's Hip-Hop Action Network, the summit promised to bring music artists to our often-overlooked upstate New York town for a day of dialogue and political activism to encourage teens to vote. The summit had gotten mixed reactions in the city, as critics slammed it for being a wasted school day that us city kids should be using for learning the skills we lacked, *not* some problematic hip-hop.

I was asked to deliver a speech, and for weeks I wrestled with what to say at the Carrier Dome, which would be full of my peers from across Syracuse high schools. I loved hip-hop, but sometimes it didn't feel like it loved me or other girls. I thought of all the music videos I'd seen on BET and VH1, the messages our 2000s generation received regularly from artfully shot music videos with girls in the background, mere decorative pieces. I also noticed how so-called foreign-looking and Spanish video girls were considered "exotic," and rapped about as such. Hip-hop had color lines too.

While often I just wanted to enjoy the beat, too often the words that came out of my mouth while singing along to the hits of the day felt degrading. What I went through freshman year with Lil James had laid the groundwork for a constant feeling of being on guard with boys, having to prove myself and my friends worthy of respect.

So when I took the stage, dressed in a custom airbrushed T-shirt with my name on it, matching gold nameplate earrings, and the green contacts that were my signature look at the time, the awkwardness of my elementary-school fashion fails far behind me, I decided to take my moment in front of the stars present that day, including Fabolous, Doug E. Fresh, the Rev. Run, Raz-B, and Russell, to call out what I saw as misogyny in hip-hop.

"Girl, you wanna come to my hotel / Baby, I'll give you my room key / But did he tell you he doesn't care if you get pregnant or get left with an STD?" I rhymed onstage as my schoolmates clapped and cheered with "Oooohs." A CNN producer was present in the audience that day, and she gave me her business card, to use if I ever ended up pursuing journalism. We exchanged messages once but never spoke again.

———

The culmination of the pressures of this entire high-achiever dynamic came my junior year, when Mrs. Murphy whispered that warning about SAT scores.

When I saw the score, it was more than just a score for me. It represented the village of people I couldn't fail and the city I felt I was representing. I attended a basic SAT weekend course at Onondaga Community College (OCC) with a goal of boosting my score, a course that paled in comparison to what other Ivy League applicants had probably taken. Although I'd told Mrs. Murphy that I would retake the exam, her words planted a seed of doubt that represented so many other moments when I'd already questioned myself.

Researchers describe the trade-offs or lost opportunities that high-achieving Black students make to succeed academically as "racial opportunity cost." The term can refer to psychological stresses, like a fear of failure that inhibits the very growth mindset we need to succeed. People learn from making mistakes, and yet many high-achieving Black kids feel they can't afford to.

Researchers suggest that racial opportunity cost is also tied to representation, where high-achieving Black students feel like show ponies, who are praised for being smart as if it were an anomaly for them to be Black and smart. They are trotted out as evidence that a school system isn't failing its students of color: *See—she's got great grades!* Token success stories can let school systems off the hook for the rest of the unengaged student body. They can also be weaponized to blame other young people for their academic struggles.

I begrudged the use of my poster kid status to make other kids feel like they were not doing enough—that they weren't enough—when I knew many of them were just as capable.

Researchers also note that racial opportunity cost affects communities as well. What it takes to succeed at school, in an educational system where whiteness is associated with intelligence, sometimes makes you feel like an outsider in your own community. You may have to forfeit opportunities to bond with your own people, if your school system was structured like mine, where the majority of kids in my honors and AP classes were non-Black and non-Hispanic.

I was studying different topics, having different discussions, and working on group projects with a different set of kids than the ones I rode home from school with. Opportunities to mix groups academically happened only in spaces like gym or art class. The sorting and categorizing of a Black achiever as somehow "different" was an oddly placed burden to carry in my backpack along with everything else I was sorting through as a teen.

The pressure to be excellent seemed relentless and began to affect me even beyond my academic life. The morning of my driver's permit test, as I looked at a photographer from the newspaper awaiting me, I felt sick to my stomach. He was there to document the outcome of my test for the "Junior Journey" series, but what if I failed in front of the entire city? Could I afford not to be perfect? Would people revel in that failure? I passed, but I felt like I'd faint the entire time.

Mamí had also grown prickly at the fact that newspaper articles described me only as Black or "the African American student to win" the competitions. "You're Puerto Rican too. They need to mention that!"

I didn't get the big deal—if people didn't see me as Puerto Rican and constantly had to ask if I was, did it even count?

Pressure aside, acting out was not a privilege I had. We, the so-called gifted Black kids, watched as hall monitors and principals and deans ran down hallways to break up fights, calm emotions, and

defend teachers who were getting cussed out by unruly students—
things many of the kids who acted out knew better than to do at
home. We, as the select chosen ones, needed to continue playing our
part, which required not ever breaking character.

We would learn to smile when we ached inside.

To be polite when we wanted to rage outside.

To downplay our needs because there were clearly kids with
bigger issues for the adults in our lives to attend to.

We could not afford to not be put together.

Yet people assumed our good grades meant we were emotionally and physically safe at home. Our mental health was taken for
granted. We needed room to make mistakes.

I had not yet learned that perfectionism is a cage, a response to
traumas of all kinds, generational and personal. Naturally I would
have moments of breaking free from that cage, my humanness pok-
ing through.

In my senior year, I was at the NAACP ACT-SO rehearsal, the
final competition I'd ever get to do. I sweated in the auditorium seat,
back at Clary Middle School, where they held our first rehearsal.
Although I'd taken home a national medal in oratory the summer
before, making the entire city proud, my oration for this year was
not fully drafted yet.

I'd been so caught up trying to keep up in calculus and fulfill all
my extracurricular responsibilities, but more truthfully I was burnt
out. I didn't know what to say anymore to the world, and my mental
drought manifested as a blank speech page.

"Natasha Alford, you're up!"

I sat staring ahead.

"I said Natasha Alford, you're up!"

I took a deep breath, stood up, and turned around.

"I . . . don't have it ready yet."

Mrs. Cooley, the program director, shook her head and then
launched into a sermon fit for a congregation in front of the entire
auditorium of coaches, mentors, and students. "If you represent this

city, you need to be prepared! You cannot just wing it. This is serious business, and all of these people have taken time out of their day to support you when they could be anywhere else."

I felt the seething vexation building up inside of me. I wondered if white children had to be talked to like soldiers in the army when they made mistakes, every misstep some grand failure that would shame their ancestors. I wondered why we couldn't just have an off day. I wondered whether her speech was so sharp because some of the coaches in the audience were white.

I refused to look Mrs. Cooley in the face as she spoke, her voice only getting louder as she realized I would not turn to face her.

"Natasha, do you *hear* me?!"

I would not be subjected to a verbal tirade, when I knew there were kids giving their teachers and parents hell. I was a *good* kid.

I stood up sharply, stone-faced, feeling the sting of two dozen eyeballs on my back, and walked out of the auditorium in front of everybody.

Once in the hallway, I went into the bathroom and sobbed in a stall, dialing Mamí on my small Trac cellular phone, barely able to get out words between breaths.

"Ma-mi—[*sob*] please come [*sob*] get [*sob*] me . . . NOW!"

"What happened, M'ija?!"

"Just [*sob*] come, Mamí, please!"

Mamí was there in five minutes flat. Before I knew it, she was wiping my face so I could exit the bathroom with dignity and go home.

As we were preparing to leave, one of the ACT-SO coaches, a Black man with long locs, a local professional in the area I'd never met before in my life, was passing by. "She has so much potential," he said to Mamí. "Such a smart girl, but she has to fix that attitude."

I rolled my eyes and then wiped them, as Mamí walked me down the hallway to go home.

6

Golden Ticket

I stood in front of my bedroom mirror, looking my outfit up and down. I'd pressed my hair extra flat, and once again I was wearing a JCPenney clearance-section pinstripe suit. It had become somewhat of a uniform for me, a symbol of professionalism and polish that I needed to give off to the world. Today I was going to meet a man who could change my life, and I needed to look the part.

The week before, Mr. Feinberg, the school guidance counselor, had called me into his office to talk. I had begun to roam Nottingham's halls, skipping my economics class, during my senior fall semester. I was bored, but more than anything, I was ready to get on to college. For all the begging Mamí had done to get me to apply to Syracuse University, I held my ground, knowing that if I went far away, I could finally do what I wanted, when I wanted. ("It's right down the street, M'ija!" was not the selling point she thought it was.)

"Natasha! You still interested in Harvard, right?" Mr. Feinberg said. "We've got their rep in my office as we speak. Come over to the conference room."

I couldn't believe how easily fate had intervened—I'd forgotten all about the visit Feinberg said would happen. Just one turn down the other hallway would've meant missing the visit.

When I walked into the small conference room adjacent to Mr. Feinberg's office, the first thing I saw was the Harvard rep—and her dark-chocolate skin, short Afro, and glasses. I did a double take. Black people really went to Harvard?

"Welcome, come right in," the Harvard rep said softly as I scoped the room for my competition. There were seven students, three of them white, one Black, one a mestiza Latina, one Asian, and me.

The rep was an alum turned recruiter, and her job was to spread the gospel of what the university had to offer. I liked that she seemed like a regular Black woman and not the stuck-up image many associated the school with. I wondered why she was in a place like Syracuse, recruiting.

Syracuse always felt overlooked—the underdog, the city people passed through to get somewhere larger, whether it was music concerts or political conventions. Nothing big happened here. Who knew Harvard thought we were worth making time for?

The rep spoke about the school's incredible resources, extracurricular offerings, and historic campus, founded in 1636. But I remembered what Mrs. Murphy had said about my SAT scores. They weren't high enough, according to her.

As if she could read my mind, the rep said, "We look at more than just perfect scores or perfect grades. I know people might expect that, but it's really about how well rounded you are. Your full story. That's what we care about, in addition to knowing you can handle the workload."

I nodded heavily. This meant I still had a chance.

After the meeting, I ran up to Mr. Feinberg's desk. "Do you think I could get in?"

"Yes, definitely," he said. "There was a time long ago when this school sent at least two or three kids a year there. You've got a good shot."

If Feinberg believed in me, then I would apply. He knew the odds and handled everyone's college applications. I stayed on my best behavior in every class, no attitude or talking back, so I could ask my teachers—all white women and one white man—to write me recommendations. Precalculus was a struggle, but I hoped Harvard admissions would overlook my average grade. I would include the newspaper articles about my public speaking to boost my application.

For my essays, I sat after school in Mrs. Murphy's class on her computer and carefully typed, making my case. If Harvard gave me a shot, I would make the most of my opportunity and become a broadcast journalist or a politician. I wanted a job where I could influence the world for the better, much as how the local journalists who'd written about me changed my trajectory.

I wrote about the American Legion's Girls State program I attended the summer before, a mock government made up of fictional counties, where attendees learned the legislative process. How even though I was different—a Black Puerto Rican girl from the city of Syracuse—the mostly white girls in my county, from rural areas and the suburbs, had nominated me to run for the top spot of governor of this fictional state. I told the story of how even though I tried to fade into the background, to not vie for a leadership spot, they persuaded me to run and helped me campaign so I would win. I explained that the experience was democracy in action and showed the power voters had in shaping our government.

Much like my campaign for "governor," I did my best with my essays. I showed them to Mrs. Murphy and Mrs. Ladd, my math teacher, and then left my fate in the hands of the admissions committee.

By the time senior spring came around, I'd forgotten about Harvard, having turned my eyes back toward Spelman College.

One day during fall semester Mr. Feinberg called me into his office again.

"Ms. Alford, I have important news for you," he began. "There is a Harvard alumnus who is meeting with a select couple of students for lunch this Saturday . . ."

I immediately understood the subtext: an alum could put in a good word for me at the college. It was the edge I needed to make my application stand out and make up for my SAT scores. "This alum was supposed to meet with Tim O'Malley and Robert Murphy . . . but Robert has a soccer championship game this weekend he can't miss. So that means a slot has opened up for you." His sly grin said it all. He thought this was my opportunity. *The* opportunity. This lunch would get me in. I smiled and nodded graciously, but inside I felt the sting of truth: I was a fill-in. A backup plan.

The alum wasn't even expecting to see me. Still, I would gladly take Robert's slot with the fancy person, and I'd make sure not to disappoint Feinberg, who was obviously looking out for me. "I'll be there, no problem!" I said, though my heart was still with Spelman College or Howard University, the beloved co-ed HBCU in Washington, DC, that I'd also applied to for admission. Now that I knew I still had a chance to boost my reach-school application, the survivor/competitor in me shifted, and I wanted to know what it would take to win. "Is it like an interview?"

"Just consider it an important lunch meeting. Be yourself, and you'll be fine," Feinberg said with his usual wink and a smile.

The alum was a respected doctor who had retired to the Nottingham, a suburban nursing home in the neighboring white town of DeWitt. Mamí and I pulled up to the place; it looked like a private lodge, with lush green bushes and a large circular driveway. The Nottingham was nothing like Loretto, the nursing home in the city where some of my classmates worked part-time on weekends, serving food and doing cleaning and kitchen work. If Loretto was the Walmart of nursing homes, then the Nottingham was Nordstrom.

I walked with Mamí into the beautiful lobby, lit by chandeliers, with fireplaces and upscale furniture, ornate wallpaper and bookshelves hugging the walls. We were directed by an employee to a window-filled dining room that looked like a five-star restaurant. There were linen tablecloths, flowered vases, and number placards in the center of the tables, with senior citizens in bustling conversation from their wheelchairs. At the Nottingham most of the kitchen and waitstaff were young and Black; nearly all of the residents white.

"We're here to see Dr. Max Katzbach," Mamí told one of the staff.

An attendant brought us over to the table, where to my surprise, I saw a little old man with white hair on a large head that made him look like a bobblehead doll wearing thin glasses, surrounded by four other older white men and women.

"You must be Natasha," Dr. Katzbach said warmly, reaching for my hand.

"It's a pleasure to meet you, Dr. Katzbach," I said, greeting him back, my code-switching in full effect. When I was with friends, my speech was relaxed, with an upstate city twang and a melodic cadence. When I spoke with professional people like Dr. Katzbach, or the many adults who could affect my future, I enunciated every word, projected my voice, and appeared pleasant. I'd learned from watching Mamí that women who were nice, who didn't bark when they spoke, who acted almost as if they were scared to bother you, were responded to pleasantly. People wanted to help them. I wanted people to help me.

"And who is this young lady?" he asked, looking at Mamí.

"I'm Natasha's mother. It's nice to meet you. I just came to drop her off, but I'll come back in about an hour," Mamí said sheepishly.

Dr. Katzbach wasn't having it. "Oh, please stay. We have plenty of room. Let's bring over a chair!"

He requested the staff to rearrange the table to get us seated, and I saw two young Black boys my age in staff uniforms across the way giving me long, curious glances as I sat down at the table of old white folk.

Dr. Katzbach introduced his friends one by one, sharing the Ivy League schools they'd all graduated from and their professional achievements before retirement: these old white men and women were retired doctors, lawyers, professors, and more.

I sat at attention, channeling every bit of home and church training I could muster: eyes on each person who spoke, a smile, a nod, a look of wonderment and gratitude.

What transpired over the next hour would be a blur.

There, in the dining room of the Nottingham, Dr. Katzbach and his friends started to very casually but intentionally grill me about almost every aspect of my life.

Where had I grown up? What activities did I do? What were my career aspirations? Why did I want to go to Harvard? What did I plan to study?

I tried to answer each question like Serena Williams at Wimbledon, swinging hard every time I got a chance to speak, fully aware that I was onstage and that my success depended upon me, sprinkling in humor and turning on the charm when needed.

The Nottingham had a robust menu; anything we wanted, we could get. Grilled chicken. Sandwiches. Hamburgers. A bowl of salad and the bread plate next to the main plate. Multiple utensils to choose from.

I looked down at the multiple forks and spoons in front of me, trying to remember every lesson I'd learned at Saturday Academy on how to eat properly at a dinner table. The women who ran the program wanted us Black girls to be ready for moments like this, but I still couldn't remember if the outermost fork was for the salad or the main meal. I was nervous that this little move would out me.

So much of my life had become about acting like I knew the rules to places I was the first from my family to walk into. I peeked out of the corner of my eyes, watching which forks my elderly hosts grabbed first, and copied their moves. Mamí did the same as I did, keeping a pleasant look on her face, making her shoulders small as if not to take up space. I wiped my mouth every five seconds and listened in.

I learned that Dr. Katzbach was Jewish and graduated from Harvard College in 1932 and Harvard Medical School in 1936. He flew to England and served in World War II afterward as a U.S. Army medic. It was there he met his wife, who was a nurse. She'd died before him, but he spoke of her as if she were the most beautiful woman still living. As a Jew, he went to Harvard around the time the university had a quota on Jewish students, a result of backlash against "too many" Jews being admitted.

His stories were like tornados of information to listen to as I tried to understand his slightly stilted speech while absorbing the history he recalled about running a medical practice in Syracuse, organizing sports teams over in England during the war, and his life as a retiree at the Nottingham.

When the lunch was over, I felt relieved. I'd worried whether I'd done a good enough job listening, if there was anything I wished I hadn't said, if they knew I was nervous the entire time.

"You should be so proud of her," Dr. Katzbach said to Mamí as we stood up.

"Oh, we tell her just to keep humble, she's just a regular kid, but thank you," Mamí said, blushing with her eyes down. I smiled through my frown.

After hugging and shaking hands with each person at the table, I gave Dr. Katzbach a warm and careful embrace and thanked him. His wrinkled cheeks were soft and warm. I held him like glass, terrified of doing anything to harm his fragile, nearly-hundred-year-old frame. "Come back anytime to visit, dear," he said. "You'll do well at Harvard." When he said that, my heart leaped. Did this mean that he'd put in a good word for me with the school? I wanted to skip back to the car. I couldn't wait to share the good news with Mr. Feinberg.

———

I got the news I'd been dreaming of. A thick baby-blue-and-white envelope came in the mail that my mom revealed when I came home from school. I had been accepted to Spelman College, the historically Black all-girls school in Atlanta.

But once my acceptance letter came back with a financial aid package that provided a modest scholarship, yet nothing close to full tuition, Mamí shut down any dream I had of attending my beloved Spelman. To attend an HBCU like Spelman would be continuing the legacy of the Black women who'd mentored and nurtured me in Syracuse. It would mean immersing myself in the Black culture that Daddy cloaked our household in, the movies, music, and history that I absorbed on Garfield Avenue. But Mamí was practical.

"They didn't give you enough money, Tasha," she said, looking at the stack of papers disapprovingly. "Too expensive."

I knew nothing about the inner workings of FAFSA and financial aid, but just trusted that Mamí knew what she was talking about. It never occurred to me to call the school or make my case for more scholarship money. Instead, I licked my wounds and enthusiastically set my sights on Howard University instead. Howard was one of the most famous HBCUs, known for producing talent like Congressman Elijah Cummings, Justice Thurgood Marshall, Toni Morrison, Zora Neale Hurston, Phylicia Rashad, Ta-Nehisi Coates, and Omar Tyree, the author of my then-favorite book, *Flyy Girl*. Howard had a history of producing changemakers, leading research in science, technology, engineering, and mathematics. Its law school was one of the best in the country and its medical school was respected globally, creating doctors who didn't just practice medicine but also focused on community uplift.

I had heard amazing things about the school located in the Chocolate City of Washington, DC, from Señora Martinez, Mamí's Colombian coworker whose son, Santiago, DJ'ed my quinceañera and attended Howard after graduation. When I was accepted to the school with a full-tuition scholarship, I had every reason to believe it was a sign from God that HU was where I belonged, and I jumped up and down in the living room on Garfield Avenue at the news.

Not needing to visit to make a decision, I sent off my intent to attend in the fall on a tiny little navy-blue card with a Bison logo on it. I was going to The Mecca.

One morning in English, as Mr. Tony rambled on about Shakespeare, my best friend Lance whispered over: "I didn't get into Harvard, Tash," he said, shaking his head. "Did you check to see if you did?"

It was April of our senior spring. Graduation was just two and a half months away, and I assumed that since I hadn't heard anything yet, I probably hadn't gotten in.

"Dang, I'm sorry," I whispered, feeling genuinely terrible for Lance. "I didn't check—I forgot it was even coming out."

A light went off in my head. I'd applied regular decision and clicked "email decision," so of course I hadn't gotten anything in the mail yet. I needed to get out of class, so I lied and asked my teacher if I could go to the bathroom. Instead I ran down the hall to the school office and knocked on the vice principal's door. "Can I use your computer, Ms. Maggio? I just want to check if I got into a college." "Go ahead dear, you can sit right here, I'll give you some privacy."

I logged in with lighting speed. And there it was at the top of my inbox:

CONGRATULATIONS! WE ARE PLEASED TO OFFER YOU ADMISSIONS TO THE HARVARD COLLEGE CLASS OF 2008!

An intense wave of warmth hit my entire body. I stared at the screen in disbelief.

Nothing will ever be the same after this.

This was long before the days of smartphones and recorded gatherings of kids surrounded by throngs of family and friends to see if they'd gotten into their school of choice, who jumped and screamed, hugged and fell over each other to celebrate. No one was there to see the moment my entire life changed but me. I walked out of the office stunned. Lance, who'd managed to sneak out of class too, was standing there with Ms. Maggio, Ms. Randall, another vice principal, and all the office secretaries.

"Did you get in?" Ms. Randall asked.

"I . . . got in . . ." I said in a near daze.

The room erupted in screams and cheers as Lance threw his arms around to hug me and Ms. Randall ran over to the school announcement speaker as the class-change bell rang. The guilt I felt at getting in while Lance celebrated me had already started to settle in. Why couldn't both of us make it in? Everything felt like a competition, me against everyone else, even when I wasn't trying to compete with anyone.

"If you see Natasha Alford in the hallway, congratulate her for getting into HARVARD UNIVERSITY!" Ms. Randall said over the loudspeaker. I cringed at the well-meaning announcement, but everywhere I walked in the hallway, people who knew me congratulated me, giving me head nods or dapping me up, from the athletes to the d-boys who skipped all classes. I had finally gotten the equivalent of hitting the championship-game-winning shot for my team—the city-school kids from real Syracuse.

"Okay Ms. Harvard!" a guy shouted out at me as I walked by.

When I'd made it down to the math corridor, I saw my precalculus teacher, Mrs. Ladd, her eyes glistening.

"I didn't want to tell you, but I secretly wrote you a recommendation to ease any concerns about your math grade," she said, her hands clasped together in shock and joy. "When you showed me your college essay about Girl's State, it brought me to tears. I wanted you to get in. We were all rooting for you to get in."

I listened in disbelief and then hugged Mrs. Ladd, something I'd never done before, only managing to get "Thank you so much" out again and again. It seemed the entire universe had conspired for my success.

After school, I headed to our house on Garfield Avenue. "I got in . . . I got in . . . I got in," I repeated to myself, trying to make it feel real. The high of the news was still fresh on my ears, the disbelief just as strong.

Daddy was sitting in the rocking chair underneath our family photos in the living room, watching TV, when I got home. I prepared myself to tell news that can be delivered only once. "DADDY!" I said, the words jockeying and pushing each other down to get out of my mouth.

"What?" he asked slightly annoyed at the interruption.

"I got into Harvard!" I was breathless, beaming with pride.

Daddy paused for a second, slanted his head to the side, and looked at me, his dark sunglasses covering his eyes.

"Harvard?" His face twisted up like he'd just tasted a cup of rancid milk. "Why the hell would you want to go there?"

My excitement crashed and evaporated into a thousand small pieces, like a plate of china knocked off a table. I should've known

Daddy was unimpressed by these institutions. Despite all his encouragement to get an education, he was also still holding out hope
I'd join the military as he had.

"It's the number one school in the country, Daddy. It's *really* hard
to get in. It was my reach school!"

"Oh, okay. . . . Well that's good," he muttered and went back to
watching TV.

I was zero for one, but I still had one more shot with Mamí.
Maybe as a college-educated woman who'd helped me fill out the
FAFSA and taken me to Saturday Academy, she would understand
just how big a deal this was.

About an hour later I heard the wooden door creak, signaling
she was home.

"Mamí, I got into HARVARD! I got in!"

She looked at me with the exhausted eyes of a woman who'd
worked a long day, carrying too many bags that were too heavy with
not enough help, still trying to figure out what she'd order for dinner
that night.

"That's good, Tasha, but if they don't give you the money, you
can't go. We'll just see what happens," she said, dropping her big
purse onto the chair.

"*Moooooooom!*" I protested. "Really?!"

"Tasha, that's great, but I just got home from work. Let me take
a look at everything first."

I quietly stomped off to my room. Unlike with Daddy, it was safe
to be mad at Mamí. To *show* her I was mad. Some people can never
live up to their parents' expectations. In my case, I had exceeded
expectations, and it didn't seem to make a difference either way. Yet
I was still deeply torn. What about Howard? Did it even matter that
I still wanted to go?

"You're not seriously going to turn down Harvard, right? What
decision is there to make?" asked Mr. Little, my favorite AP History teacher, who didn't sugarcoat anything and said exactly what he
thought at all times. Mr. Little had worked in Syracuse schools for-

ever and was a graduate of them too. He knew what this admission represented, and how it defied the low expectations people often had of city-school grads, no matter the color of their skin.

"I mean, I may still go to Howard," I said, digging in. "It's a good school, and I got a full ride." I didn't like the implication that because I'd gotten into a richer school—a whiter school—it was somehow better. Or better for me. My HBCU dream was soul deep, a chance to be affirmed in ways that I hadn't been thus far in my entire education in this snowy, segregated town. But as I looked at Mr. Little's bewildered face, his unfiltered words pierced the defense I'd put up.

He was right, I figured. People like me could never turn down an opportunity to go to a place like Harvard. I'd gotten a golden ticket like the one Charlie wanted so badly for Willy Wonka's chocolate factory. There were some people, like Veruca Salt, who could easily have bought their golden ticket into college (and did). Some people, like Violet, with their accolades and perfect test scores, had the resources to increase their chances. Kids like Augustus Gloop had everything given to them, so a college admission was just another delicacy. And some, like Mike Teavee, with their smarts, knew the ins and outs of places like these with ease. I was no poor kid without shoes on my feet, like Charlie, but it did seem I had extremely good luck. Not taking this admission seat seemed ungrateful. If I wanted to change my and my family's life, I didn't have a *right* to turn it down.

"You're doing all you do for you—not for us," was still Mamí's frequent refrain, and I was sure to hear it come back up in our negotiations about what came after high school. She still would much rather me go to Syracuse University and be a five-minute drive away, close to family in the spirit of Latino cultures, despite her own example of moving far away. It was at this point in life that I started to tune out my mother's advice, for better or worse. If I had listened to her, I reasoned, I wouldn't have gone as far as I wanted—literally and figuratively.

Daddy, to his credit, had come around, and had the nerve to tell folks at work that I was going to that college up in Cambridge. "Oh, did she get an athletic scholarship?" they inquired, shocked. "What sport does she play?" Daddy, indignant as always, set them straight. "NO. She's *not* an athlete. She just got in."

A couple months later, we visited Aunt Cyn's church in Buffalo, our whole family gathered for a rare group outing that even Daddy managed to go to. Aunt Cyn showed me around the church, introducing me with pride to every person she could. "This is my niece from Syracuse, she's going to HAR-VARD," she'd say, cheesecake grin flashing, her big blue church hat perfectly crowned like a sculpture on her Jheri-curled short black hair.

I offered up my usual big smile with a blush and shook hands and made eye contact with every person I met, like I was running for town mayor.

When Auntie Cyn had me stand in front of the congregation as a visitor, she didn't hesitate to again bring up where I was matriculating in the fall.

"Oh, that's big-time!" her pastor replied with a sly smile. "Just don't go there and forget where you came from, now!" he continued, chuckling loudly, over people's applause. My face turned red as a brown face could turn, and I laughed along with the crowd, so they knew I could take a joke. But inside, I couldn't wait to leave church that day.

Even at my home church in Syracuse, there was some concern about my college admission, namely from Pastor Jake, the young white former football player who'd made his home among the predominantly Black parishioners at Syracuse Baptist.

"Natasha, I'm glad for you getting into college. But you should know that schools like that are liberal. You'll have to be careful. It's not going to be easy to find a true godly church out there . . . They let women be pastors," he warned.

I took heed of the advice, genuinely concerned. I was honestly always conflicted about the "no women pastors" mandate at my church, not buying the story that the fall of man was really Eve's fault. She was just trying to gain knowledge with that apple bite, after all! But I surely didn't want to stray from God in pursuit of my education. I thanked Pastor Jake, vowing to keep my eyes open to find a place that my church leaders at home would approve of.

Meanwhile, when we told Abuela I'd gotten in, a look of genuine confusion crossed her face.

"*Qué es eso?*" she asked quizzically.

"Yes, Mamí, that's a really good college for her," Mamí chimed in, explaining what and where Harvard was in Spanish.

"*Ayyy! Que bueno!*" Abuela said, drumming up excitement for a place that in her sixty years of living she had never needed to know existed, by fate or by design. "Thas good. *Dios te bendiga*, Natacha!" she said, before going back to crocheting.

My closest friends, it seemed, were all staying close to home. Lance went to Syracuse University with a generous full-tuition scholarship. Vanessa was going to OCC. And Ty was headed out to Buffalo State even though she really wanted to open her own hair-dressing business (college-bound kids were not allowed to take vo-cational classes). We'd beaten the odds that we wouldn't graduate high school.

Daddy would explain many years later that it wasn't that he didn't feel happy for me getting into college, but he was concerned. Why would I want to go somewhere where I'd be a minority? What if I encountered racism? How would I handle whatever fantasy of a rich, white, elite school he had imagined? And what if I changed?

Weeks later, after learning how robust the school's financial aid program was for working-class families like ours, Mamí realized that in combination with my oratory scholarship dollars, my edu-cational costs would be manageable, so she changed her tune about the school up in Cambridge.

"You won't have to use credit cards to go to college like I did, M'ija. GOOD job!" she said, breathing a sigh of relief.

For once, it seemed, Mamí was truly impressed with me.

7

Black and Crimson

Walking up to Harvard Yard, I saw the words inscribed at the towering entrance of Dexter Gate: "Enter to grow in wisdom." Armed with my bag of dirty sneakers, old T-shirts, and sweatpants, I was in awe of the grandiosity of the promise. But first I had business to attend to.

I had arrived two weeks earlier than my classmates to clean toilets as part of Harvard College's dorm crew program. It was Mamí's idea for me to earn some money first, and since cleaning was honorable work in our family, something I'd done the summer before at the state fair for money to buy Jordans, the proposition of scrubbing toilets for my classmates wasn't odd at all to her or Daddy.

"Wow, they payin' good money!" Daddy remarked in awe once he found out about the fifteen-dollar-an-hour wage. I knew nothing to contradict his assessment. Surely I would grow in wisdom through it all.

My family looked around at the lush, grassy Yard enclosed by historic brick buildings as we unloaded our green van at the drop-off area, but my mind was ten steps ahead, thinking about all the people I was planning to see that week.

My class, the class of 2008, had been part of the ultimate social experiment—the first incoming freshmen class to have access to a little website called TheFacebook, which you could only sign into with a college email address. Because of TheFacebook and a very lively visiting weekend during our senior year of high school, I already knew who many of my classmates were.

A squad of older Black Harvard kids had rolled out the red carpet for us visiting prefrosh, as we were called, personally escorting us to everything from BBQs and spades games at Quincy House to a "Get Your Jollies" dining hall party in Dunster House, where we danced on tables and sweated so hard it literally dripped down the walls, as that Lil Jon song said it would.

A group of well-meaning older girls pulled us aside for a special Association of Black Harvard Women (ABHW) preview meeting, donning black and purple shirts in the tradition of the organization, dishing on how to stay safe that weekend and watch our drinks around some guys who might be hoping to take advantage of any naïveté or our rookie alcohol tolerance.

But even with the warnings, the prefrosh weekend mood was light, and our Harvard hosts were proud ambassadors of the Ivy playground they'd learned to traverse. They wore Nikes and T-shirts and nondescript labels too—nothing like the Polo shirts and blazers with boat shoes I'd imagined Harvard kids would wear 24/7. As I danced in the steamy dark basement of an unknown dorm, my long black crimps fresh with Pump It Up, hanging over the leather Rocawear jacket that I wore with jeans and slim women's wedge Timbs, I realized that despite my early assumptions, these were regular college kids.

It hadn't always been fun and games to be Black at Harvard, though. The book *The Black Guide to Life at Harvard* was given out every year to frosh and students alike, and I devoured the guide right before I got to campus, hanging on to every piece of its rich history with swelling pride.

I didn't know Black people had been at Harvard since its founding in 1636, albeit not as students. They were laborers, servants, and staff to the white men who came to the university to become preachers. These Black people cleaned toilets and maintained the grounds, a much-harsher version of what I had the choice of doing for fifteen bucks an hour.

According to the *Black Guide*, three Black students first enrolled at Harvard Medical School in 1850 but were voted out after more than half of the white student body refused to take classes with them. One of the three students, Martin Delaney, would go on to become an abolitionist, journalist, and Pan-Africanist who coined the term "Africa for Africans." That was also the year Congress passed the Fugitive Slave Act, which forced escaped Black people back to their so-called owners, a policy Delaney forcefully condemned, advocating that the formerly enslaved fight to the death to resist if necessary.

The next Black Harvard student wouldn't appear until twenty years later, in 1870, and his name was Richard T. Greener. Greener worked for a white jeweler who thought it a worthwhile experiment to groom his employee for higher education. Greener turned out to be an accomplished orator who succeeded in spite of the isolation and racism of Harvard and went on to become the first Black graduate of the college, a professor who opened a law practice, and eventually the dean of Howard Law School.

Other brilliant Black minds would enter the halls of the university, including W. E. B. Du Bois, the famous intellectual and co-founder of the NAACP, who was the first Black person to receive a Harvard PhD, in 1895. Alberta V. Scott would be the first Black woman to graduate from Radcliffe, Harvard's adjacent women's college, building an accomplished career as an educator. She was invited by Booker T. Washington to teach at the Tuskegee Institute but had her promising life tragically cut short by illness at age twenty-six.

In the early days, Black students could be subjected to insults like "nigger" openly and had their intellectual abilities constantly downplayed and questioned by fellow students and staff alike. In 1922 some white Harvard students even formed their own chapter of the Ku Klux Klan, showing that the northern cities of Cambridge and Boston were far from perfect havens of freedom and equality for Black people and Jews.

The trickle in of Black Harvard students became more of a flow in the 1960s and '70s. Many became campus activists, fighting against the racism they saw playing out and demanding that the university divest from oil stocks in African countries under colonial rule, include Black construction workers on local projects, hire Black tenured professors, and, most importantly, recruit more Black students.

Black Harvard students were so active that they took over University Hall in 1969, not long after the assassination of Dr. Martin Luther King Jr., demanding an African American studies department. After Dr. King's assassination, the number of Black Harvard students doubled to 121, the university caving to the pressure and guilt for not directing enough recruiting efforts to Black communities. A year later, Harvard would persuade a Black American Arkansas native, an engineer who worked on the moon landing, David L. Evans, to join the admissions team. Evans would revolutionize admissions, staying for fifty years, recruiting thousands of Black students from across the country, in his signature bow tie and suit.

The 1970s saw a slight shift from protest to a push to create space for the Black student experience on campus, with the formation of organizations like the Black Students Association (BSA), replacing the earlier Association of African and Afro-American Students at Harvard and Radcliffe (AFRO); the ABHW; the Kuumba Singers gospel choir, and even the short-lived Third World Society, which included Puerto Rican students.

The 1990s were considered a golden era for Black Harvard. Most Black students lived all together in the Radcliffe Quadrangle, enjoying a Black and Crimson comradery and community that most previous Harvard graduates had only dreamed of. Many of these students were also politically active, protesting apartheid in South Africa and demanding appointments for Black professors on campus in the struggling Department of Afro-American Studies, which still lacked investment from the billion-dollar-endowed school. And in this era, Black intellectual powerhouses would come to Harvard to teach at the department, among them Henry Louis "Skip" Gates Jr., Evelyn Higginbotham, Cornel West, Lawrence Bobo, and Kwame

Appiah, overcoming tremendous challenges to form an intellectual dream team that made the school a premier destination for scholars of Black issues and a draw for students like me. I arrived on campus with a dog-eared copy of Dr. Gates's memoir, *Colored People*.

I would become a beneficiary of all these struggles and fights for justice and, like many of my Black classmates, took the legacy I inherited very seriously. We didn't count on seeing portraits and sculptures of Black folks posted up next to the many white men honored on campus—but I could tell, from how well organized Black Harvard was during our orientation, that we had a place here.

I thought back to that essay I'd written in seventh grade in Mr. Freeland's class about Du Bois and his theory of the Talented Tenth, a controversial bourgeois theory not everyone embraced. Maybe there was no such thing as a select few Black folks chosen to uplift their entire race, but I was literally part of a tenth—the historic 10.3 percent of Black people who had been admitted to this place of higher learning in the year 2004, the highest number in the university's history. "All men cannot go to college but some men must," Du Bois argued. Surely, I had to find a way to live up to the great expectations set before us.

———

I stared out of the window of my new Thayer Hall dorm room, the grass and trees reminding me of Syracuse, save for the tourists who hung out by the "John Harvard" statute snapping photos. College in Cambridge was like living in a museum. After eighteen long years as an only child, and hugging and kissing Mamí and Daddy goodbye in a prolonged exchange ("Mamí, you don't have to unpack every box, please Mamí!" I begged), I was finally on my own.

In the two weeks before the official start of school, I cleaned athletes' dirty bathrooms, wiped off ledges, and mopped floors. I wasn't the only one: there were quite a few of us kids who needed or chose to make money by coming early. No race was exempt—everyone from Black to mestizo Mexican to white American kids had picked up sponges for dorm crew.

That eased most of my self-consciousness about needing the job for money, but some of it lingered, especially once everyone else got to campus. I qualified for the Student Events Fund, money set aside for low-income students to get free tickets to campus events, which required discreetly picking up your tickets before the event. Not every Black student had to do this—and discovering who did or didn't was a fascinating new dynamic.

In just a few weeks I saw that the simple ways of labeling and compartmentalizing people I had learned back in Syracuse were much more complicated at college, especially regarding ethnicity.

"Are you Habesha?" a petite, dark-eyed girl with long black hair and medium-brown skin asked me as a group of us walked through the Yard, headed to a Freshman Black Table (FBT) meeting, a Black Harvard tradition that brought Black frosh together for weekly discussion, step team rehearsals, and electing a representative for the class on the Black Students Association board.

I had no idea what Habesha was, but it sounded like an identifier, a group I didn't belong to.

"Oh no, sorry," I replied shyly.

"Really? What are you, if you don't mind me asking?"

"I'm Puerto Rican and Black."

Here in college, I was about to learn that "Black" was so much more.

"Wow! I still can't believe it. You look *just* like one of my cousins. I could've sworn you were from Ethiopia or Eritrea. It might be worth looking into," she insisted.

I smiled at the suggestion as I looked into her face. She had a point. We both had the same skin tone, long eyelashes, prominent foreheads, and slight curves in our noses. She wouldn't be the last person to ask me if I was Habesha that week, or in my life going forward. But in this moment I felt almost a protective instinct kick in—I didn't want to be mistaken. I assumed this girl's and my cultural experiences had to be completely different, no matter how similar we looked. I wondered what people were assuming about me if they thought I wasn't *Black*-Black American.

In the early months of school, I quickly became best friends with two girls: Adaora, who was Nigerian American and from the Bronx, and Veronica, who was African American and from New Jersey. Adaora had uptown cool, combined with the sane maturity of the middle child, and wore long microbraids down to her waist wherever she went. She was naturally caring, studious, and the daughter of pastors, so we shared knowledge and love of God.

Veronica was hilariously witty and a gifted writer. A fellow only child, she had similar quirks: she counted brownies as dinner, sported long, pretty, pressed black hair, and binged TV shows from *South Park* to *Sex and the City* by the seasons, back when Netflix only mailed out DVDs. She kept us rolling with laughter all the time, her brilliant observations about the absurdities of society and our college life ensuring that we never took where we were too seriously or doubted our sanity and abilities.

Our core group of three expanded to seven as we bonded with another group of fun, down-to-earth girls who were also from the New Jersey and New York area, the only Black girls I knew who played rugby like real badasses. It was the era of Jill Scott's "Golden" hit song, and we jokingly called ourselves GOLDEN: Goal-Oriented Ladies Determined to be Esteemed Nationwide. The name stuck. Our sisterhood went deeper than our collective love of low-rise jeans, shiny hoop earrings, and *America's Next Top Model*—to be Black women at this school brought us closer together.

Harvard's randomized housing system meant that sophomore year, all students had to find a "blocking group" to belong to, ensuring they'd live together no matter where the Hogwarts-like housing lottery sent them across campus, an impetus for friend groups to find their people and stick together.

It was no surprise, then, that Black kids often formed blocking groups with each other, clinging together to ensure some racial diversity in their living arrangements. While certainly not the rule, it was fascinating that even within Black blocking groups, specifically among Black girls, a few mirrored the kind of color separation you'd see in a Spike Lee joint, à la *School Daze*, an unspoken division between light skin and darker skin.

When I looked at my blocking group, we were all brown-skinned girls, Veronica and I being the lightest, with our medium-brown complexion. It never occurred to me to wonder how this subtle separation happened; I just knew I was always comfortable with Black women who looked like Aunt Cyn or the women who'd mentored me at Saturday Academy.

We GOLDEN girls were also every flavor of the Black diasporic rainbow: from Nigerian American to Jamaican American, Haitian Jamaican, and African American. Our Black ethnic diversity exposed me to new things—like understanding that Adaora was Igbo, which was different from the Yoruba tribe, or that Lucy's dad spoke both English and Creole, a language she longed to master just as I longed to master Spanish. Our differences were interesting, exciting even, but never a roadblock to friendship.

Me and the GOLDEN girls sat at the same table every day for lunch in Annenberg Hall, the cathedral-like dining hall for freshmen. Although I hadn't decided to go to an HBCU, I saw quickly that there were enough Black kids at Harvard that I didn't feel alone.

Not only were the GOLDEN girls and my other classmates fun and down-to-earth; they were also gifted. Miles, a tall and spunky mathematician, brought his saxophone with him wherever he went on campus, along with a speaker to play Jersey club music, hip-hop mashups of hits from the rap collective Dipset. Tisha had score-perfect SATs and was already on the pre-med path to become a doctor. And Lloyd had been training for the Olympics for track and won national awards.

Affirmative action be damned, I thought. These were the most qualified young, gifted, and Black kids I'd ever come across, a direct challenge to the myth that affirmative action meant "unqualified" people got a boost.

"None of you are mistakes," was the frequent refrain of Dr. S. Allen Counter, a legendary Black professor of neurology who ran the Harvard Foundation for Intercultural and Race Relations, an office that supported students of color on campus. "We meticulously and deliberatively chose you. Over twenty-two thousand apply, half are qualified and half are highly qualified—and we take an even smaller number than that. You are supposed to be here," he lovingly insisted in his signature polished voice and suit.

In truth, the policy of affirmative action was introduced by the JFK administration and implemented in 1965 by the Johnson administration to address employment discrimination in race, color, religion, and national origin. Then the policy expanded to other places like schools and universities, and to other marginalized groups, like women.

I knew from the *Black Guide* that earlier generations of Black students had dealt with blowback from some white classmates who believed they didn't deserve their spots. But why should we feel guilty if our race was one of many considerations in our overall application, when surely it affected our lives? Gender had also been a factor in affirmative action—women of all races, including white and Asian women, benefited greatly from it, and as a gender, women's numbers at the college increased in the wake of the policy.

There were all kinds of unofficial forms of affirmative action at work in American higher education, favoring athletes, kids whose parents donated to the college, the children of professors and staff, and legacy status kids, under the policy that if a family member had attended the college, your application might get a small "tip" of favor.

Now knowing all the ways the invisible hands of privilege worked to position my peers for success, why would I feel bad that the school considered how my race, and the enslavement of my ancestor Beachmon Alford, might have affected my life trajectory just a *tad* bit? Or how remarkable it was that I and my other classmates from marginalized groups thrived in spite of our complex histories?

While many Black Harvard kids were similar to me in being high achievers, not everyone's trajectory in getting there was the same.

I looked around Adaora's perfectly set up dorm room, with her neatly arranged books, precisely sized plastic organizing bins, and notebook labels for EC 10 a contrast to my cluttered and chaotic room. There was a photo of her in all white, with other girls, dressed in white too.

"What's this from?" I asked curiously.

"Oh, that's from high school graduation! Choate Rosemary Hall!"

I stared curiously at the photo, surprised at the lack of caps and gowns, and noticing that in addition to Harvard paraphernalia, Adaora had a hoodie with "Choate" on it too.

Choate was an elite boarding school, and although Adaora came from a working-class family similar to mine, she shared a commonality with other Black kids who had gone through prestigious programs like Prep for Prep or A Better Chance, which plucked their high-achieving selves from underrepresented communities and low-income areas and sent them off to boarding schools away from home for a once-in-a-lifetime education, and into the pipeline of Ivy League recruiting.

At these boarding schools with funny names that sounded like museums—Exeter, Choate, Deerfield Academy—they lived independently with roommates, managed demanding coursework, and had incredible extracurricular experiences, the pricey tuition often paid for by financial aid.

The concept of growing up outside the watchful eye of my overbearing Boricua mother was so foreign to me. I couldn't fathom the idea of Mamí ever letting me go away to a boarding school while in high school. She still hadn't even let me attend sleepovers all those years or have my own car, let alone live away at school. "Sleepover? Cha-cha!" she'd say. "I don't know those parents! You can't trust people anyway," she'd yell over her shoulder, crushing my dreams as she folded clothes.

But now, looking at how well it seemed Adaora was transitioning to the college atmosphere, I wondered if maybe going away would have been good for me.

There were rich Black Harvard kids whose parents could foot the bills at any of these boarding schools or private schools, though. Some of them were legacy Black kids. These kids didn't necessarily walk around saying they were legacy, but you'd hear whispers about how their older sister or mother or father had gone to Harvard and had a prestigious board position or job. Some of them just *looked* like legacy—or at least what I imagined a legacy to be. Well kept. Unstressed. Labels like Prada, Hermès, and Chanel naturally lived on the bags they owned or the shoes they wore. Their spring break vacations weren't to Miami—they had passports and flew to St. Tropez and Italy. And you couldn't forget the two or three kids in any given class who cosplayed like they were from the hood, while the actual kids from the hood probably would've loved nothing more than to trade places with their rich selves. I quietly dreamed of the day my future Black children would finally have a rare moment of privilege from birth, applying as legacies should they want to go here. But I knew it would mean getting through this place and actually becoming successful, as a person and a parent. As Mr. David L. Evans joked, "Being the child of an alum can heal the sick, but it can't raise the dead!"

There were also the "incogs," which stood for "incog-Negroes," an unflattering label given to those who expressly did not hang with Black people and didn't associate with the Black community at large. They didn't return the head nod on campus when you passed them, let alone make eye contact.

But the greatest observation was that Black people from across the African diaspora appeared to outnumber African Americans, or "JBs" (which stood for "just Black"). For the first time I was meeting high numbers of students with African names or Caribbean accents.

Beyond Black immigrants and first- and second-generation kids, I met Black people from other faraway places—such as Britain and Cape Verde, a country I'd never heard of until getting to Boston, where there was a significant Cape Verdean population.

There were also, finally, Black people like me, with a Spanish-speaking parent or two—the so-called Black Latinos. There was Gabriela from New York City, who was Bahamian and Dominican; Stacey from North Carolina, who was Colombian and African American; and Katrina from Connecticut, who was Puerto Rican and African American. Despite our decent numbers, it never occurred to me to organize or gather on account of our Blackness and Latinidad.

So many of us found our homes in the Black community and in Black organizations, even when we connected—or attempted to connect—with the other side of ourselves.

"Do you like Latino culture?!" a perky Latino Club ambassador asked my friend Gabriela, who was brown-skinned and Dominican, at the extracurricular activities fair.

"I didn't feel like explaining that my mom was Dominican and I spoke Spanish since birth," Gabriela confided in me later over dinner, "but I had to at that point."

"Ugh! That is SO annoying," I said. "Like why even assume that you weren't Latina to begin with? Based on what?"

"Well you know, we don't fit the 'look.' But honestly, it just turned me off, and I don't even feel like going to future meetings," she said with a sigh of resignation.

Gabriela's experience encapsulated the odd feeling that I'd had when I went to one Latino Club meeting on campus.

As I looked around the room, I saw a mostly fair-skinned and tanned group of students, people who looked no different than Titi or some of the Latino kids on the West Side back home. I stuck out like a sore thumb. But I felt guilty. I'd promised myself that in college, I would do my best to be a better representative of *both* my cultures, to not further antagonize Mamí by saying I was just "Black" but to make an earnest effort to learn Spanish and immerse myself in Latino-focused organizations as well as the Black ones. Once-thriving groups like La O, or La Organización de Puertorriqueños en Harvard, didn't have an overwhelming presence anymore.

FUERZA was a pan-Latino group, welcoming to people of all Latin American countries. It was founded by ten Dominican students back in the 1990s as FUERZA Quisqueya, *quisqueya* being a Taino word meaning "cradle of life" and a nod to the island's original inhabitants.

Looking back, I can see that FUERZA had everything I would've loved to do or had interest in—the Candela hip-hop dance group and the salsa club; a special food event celebrating Latino cuisine, with trips to Izzy's Puerto Rican restaurant in Boston; even meetings about Puerto Rico's colonial situation and the fight for independence.

Not every Black Latino at Harvard experienced isolation from the Latino community, either. There were girls like Katrina and Stacey, who were more than comfortable attending meetings, joining campus salsa clubs, and finding belonging in groups like FUERZA. Both Katrina and Stacey had Latina moms and African American dads like me. I wondered whether, if I saw myself more as Mamí's daughter and less as Daddy's, I too would've found more of a home in Latino orgs on campus.

Perhaps it was just a matter of time; I had only so much time in a day to do extracurriculars, and already found myself overbooked in the early weeks. But perhaps it was also psychological. Walking into meetings with fewer Black people reminded me of the otherness I felt as a child in all-Latino circles with Mamí, where I was the darkest and couldn't participate in conversation.

The color line was embodied in the title of one of the campus Latino study groups, about political alliances between African Americans and Latino voters: "Black and Brown Together Forever?"

That phrase—"Black and Brown"—always felt odd to me. How was it that Black represented African Americans, Africans, and everything under the Black diaspora, when so-called brown people, who were Latino, could be just as Black too? Were we calling Celia

Cruz "brown" because she spoke Spanish, when she was Black as day? Was Roberto Clemente "brown," with his 4C Afro hair? How was it that Latinos defaulted to brown, when so many of us were not?

Similarly for Black folks in the U.S., many of us were light-skinned too, and not always due to a white parent. Plenty of African Americans of all shades could be easily assumed to be Latino if you plopped them down in a new country and vice versa.

The desire for clean and simple categorizing of people seemed rife with contradiction and weird rules.

I knew there were plenty of "brown" people in the world—people who looked like my tíos and Titi Nina. They weren't exactly white or Black. It wouldn't have been accurate to say they were either.

But to assign brownness to *all* Latinos sent a subconscious message that mestizaje—the state of being brown, mixed, not part of any binary—was the default for Latinidad.

But even some Latinos at college who fit the expected Latino phenotype, with lighter skin and wavy hair, preferred to hang with the Black community. Many of them grew up in hoods and cities right alongside working-class African Americans and were often Puerto Ricans and Dominicans. Class mattered as much as race.

Just as wealthy African American, African, and West Indian kids existed, there were wealthy Latinos of all flavors. In fact, college was my first experience meeting Latinos who came from well-to-do families. It was also my first time meeting Latinos who were literally white—not Anglo in origin, but white, from Spain, Venezuela, Colombia, and even Puerto Rico. If not for their Spanish surnames, you'd think they were like any other WASP.

My friend Rafael was a Latino who hung mainly with Black folks. A fair-skinned Dominican from Brooklyn, he sported baggy clothes, wore his hair in long cornrows, and had a strong New York accent. He was so dedicated to the Black community and Black causes that he even won an award at a campus celebration of Black men for Most Involved Freshman.

"Tash, can I ask you something?" Rafael messaged me one morning. "Was there something wrong in me getting the award? Did I do something wrong, like I was steppin' on people's toes? Have you heard stuff like I'm too involved in the Black community, and that's dumb cuz I'm not Black?"

My heart ached for him. It felt like a no-win situation. He was just hanging with people who more generally felt like home—a place that felt authentic, and very much was in the Northeast. The scenario reflected just how truly inclusive the Black Crimson community was on campus, as were Black people in general. We welcomed all kinds of folks, handing out invitations to the theoretical cookout thoughtfully. But Rafael's winning struck a nerve with some Black folks in that it indirectly sent a message that an actual Black man wasn't worthy of the award.

I tried to soften Rafael's concern that he deserved the award and should feel no shame, but I still wrestled with the complexities of the situation. Just how far did the borders of community extend?

EVEN THOUGH I MYSELF WASN'T SURE EXACTLY WHERE I FIT INTO the Latino community at Harvard, there was one group of Latinos who could help me with the single most important personal issue a Black student in a new college needed to handle: her hair. Thanks to the *Black Guide*, I learned that Dominican salons were famous for being able to press hair of any texture straight for forty dollars.

On my first visit to the local salon, I entered with a slight mix of anxiety and shame. The hairdressers looked at me, and I could tell they were trying to decide if I was Latina like them or Black like them.

I listened to the women greet me and ask what I wanted in broken English, hating that I put them in that position, when I could surely understand them in Spanish.

I sat in the chair and stealthily listened to them chat about my hair while bachata music blasted through speakers in the background and a hairdresser put my hair in big curlers, as Mamí had all those years before.

Over an hour later when the hairdresser took my hair down and blew it out—the heat so hot it nearly burned my ears off—I had a perfectly straight, shiny blowout. I vowed to come back to Dominican stylists forever.

Nevertheless, these visits to the Dominican salons coincided with the natural hair movement that swept through college campuses in the early 2000s. Black women who had permed their hair their entire lives were now realizing that they'd never seen their actual hair texture up close—and when they let it grow, they saw it was beautiful. Young women were starting to move away from the harsh chemicals of relaxers and toward natural hair products that held their curls and kept them moisturized. But the first step toward natural hair freedom required the Big Chop: cutting off all of one's damaged permed hair, after letting it grow out a bit so there'd be some natural hair left to start a new crop, untouched by chemical straighteners.

I wasn't ready for that just yet. I stared in the mirror at my long, blown-out style, the slight smell of burnt hair lingering in the air. I wasn't ready to look like anyone but the girl staring back in the mirror at me just now. I blended in perfectly.

———

I loved my new college environment. I was parentless and soaring in my independence. I also felt fully accepted. In this rich, diverse world, there seemed to be space to be understood as African American and Puerto Rican without being questioned. There were also lots of multiethnic people at school, which took some of the spectacle out of it.

This didn't mean that there were no conflicts or tensions about Harvard's Black diversity. Diaspora wars had broken out on our email listserv, such as when a news article came out stating that Ivy Leagues had more "non-native" Black people than "native" Black people—descendants of chattel slavery. My classmates matched intellectual wits with essay-long emails about why so many Black admits were African or West Indian, and whether their experiences being Black would have been different if they'd grown up in the same hoods and broken school systems as some African Americans grew up with. We also got real about the stereotypes that persisted about generational African Americans that people used to justify dismissing us. One of my ABHW sisters who'd gone on a bus trip with fellow Black Caribbean students listened as some of our class-mates slandered African Americans, throwing around stereotypes about our so-called laziness. They did not realize one of her parents was African American. Another ABHW sister recalled one African student group meeting that was expressly clear about being only for Africans. It was tragic to me that African Americans weren't consid-ered "model" minorities by some, including our own Black people, despite the miracle of our survival in this land. Our justice struggle historically produced benefits that weren't exclusive to us.

One of my fellow step team members argued the university should be more transparent about how many African Americans were actu-ally admitted, since it was the hard-fought legacy of the civil rights movement, inspired by our ancestors' oppression, that led to poli-cies that made the university admit more Black students in the first place. The 10.3 percent of the class that was Black had become majority African and Caribbean, although the university touted the number as a reflection of its diversity. Should generational African Americans—descendants of chattel slavery—be treated as an inter-est group with targeted recruiting from the university?

That seemed not only reasonable but perfectly doable in my eyes.

I didn't respond to the debate on the list, my discomfort and desire to see unity apparent. But Adaora jumped in with a similar sentiment that only confirmed why she was my best friend, even with her being Nigerian and me being what I was.

"We need to unite and counter oppression!" she pleaded, noting that it was a problem that African American kids were in the mi-nority in more ways than one at the university. "We can all eat a piece of the pie. But we have to counter the structures that make it so that everyone is not."

The community had done such a good job uniting us under the umbrella of Blackness at Harvard that some of these conversations felt deeply uncomfortable, as if they had the power to turn neighbor against neighbor. But ultimately, they were healthy and fair debates.

These were the kinds of issues we young minds pondered, but this was in-group family business.

No matter our differences, overall we were brought together by the sense that we must be united, in this place.

My short time at school had confirmed that racism and a system of colonialism, imperialism, and white supremacist ideologies had led to the race-based slave trade and colonization of the various countries most of us originated from. The fact that we all went by different names was in part because many of us (although not all) were ripped from our homelands and scattered across the globe.

In fact the transatlantic slave trade helped make Harvard. Enslaved Africans in Antigua and the West Indies provided the labor that New Englanders invested in and used to buy land for the university. The land used for Harvard Law School was funded by a white man named Isaac Royall Jr., deemed "the largest slaveholder in 18th-century Massachusetts," who got his money from the slave trade.

We walked the classroom hallways and campus buildings with the ghosts of enslaved Africans all around us. According to a Presidential Committee report, *Harvard and the Legacy of Slavery*, university professors and staff owned seventy enslaved Black people before 1783, including one girl named Cicely, owned by a Harvard tutor and professor named William Brattle, who was buried in the cemetery across from the university's famous Johnston Gate. I walked Brattle Street to go to the movie theater all the time, passing the cemetery, never knowing but constantly surrounded by tributes to colonizing men, long dead and gone.

One was Professor Louis Agassiz, a scientist whose family name was inscribed around campus. Agassiz believed that the races were in fact separate species, with Blacks being socially and intellectually inferior. He was the kind of dead man whose aura hung over the buildings I needed to show up in with confidence.

It seemed a great tragedy that the Black Harvard guide had not included the story of Pedro Albizu Campos. Campos was an Afro-Latino who arrived at Cambridge from Ponce, Puerto Rico, the son of a Black domestic worker mother and Spanish merchant father. With the fortune of coming from a good family, Campos ended up at Harvard Law School, the first Puerto Rican to ever be admitted. He was a brilliant orator, spoke seven languages, and went off to fight in World War I in the army while at school.

When Campos returned to law school, he became a respected student leader and was set to be class valedictorian. Racist professors wouldn't endure the humiliation of a Black Latino valedictorian, though, and they conspired to delay his exams so he couldn't graduate with his class. Instead of giving a commencement speech, he'd return to Puerto Rico in 1921 to finish his exams at home and have his degree shipped to him.

Despite his academic promise, Campos would die from a stroke shortly after being released from federal prison. He'd been arrested multiple times, most recently after Puerto Rican independence activists fired guns into the U.S. Congress in 1954. Albizu Campos alleged that the U.S. prison conducted radiation experiments on him while he was incarcerated.

That Campos had been academically gifted but still denied a moment in the sun because of his Puerto Rican heritage—his Blackness and foreignness too offensive—could've been a freeing realization for me at the time. This ancestor of *la isla* could've shown me that all of these standards and supposedly merit-based milestones I was trying to reach were created at the hands of flawed men. Campos was a reminder that Black people weren't originally meant to be at this university—as students, anyway.

Occasionally we got real-time reminders too. Once, after organizing a fun field day between the girls of ABHW and guys of the Black

Men's Forum, we found ourselves being pulled aside by the Harvard Police Department in the middle of a kickball game. Despite our clearly uniformed ABHW and BMF T-shirts, someone had called the police on us, claiming "kids from off campus" were on Harvard property trespassing. The callers were very likely our own classmates.

———

By the end of my freshman year, I got a call that would shake me out of the euphoria of college life. My grandma, Daddy's mama, whose edges I lovingly greased after school, had passed away after battling Alzheimer's. I flew back home to Syracuse for the funeral and came back to Cambridge in a fog of grief, feeling that yet another link to my past had been cut from me. But the return to campus made me realize the process that was beginning—that school was, in fact, my new home, the Black community specifically being the place I felt safest. I burrowed further into campus life. At Caribbean Club dance parties I was learning the beauty of the African diaspora, something I didn't get much of all the way up in Syracuse, New York, outside of the reggaeton I'd played on my CD player. I loved going to the heart-pumping, euphoria-inducing marathons in the Mather Dining Hall where my classmates would sing, hop, and wave their flags.

"You make meeee wannaaaaa . . ." *Thump-thump-thump-thump-thump* . . . The speakers vibrated nearly the entire dining hall. "Jump around di place! Jump and pelt my waist!" the singer said over the beat.

So much of this fast-paced music, which I'd learned was called soca, reminded me of the merengue I'd danced to with Abuela as a kid, or the salsa chants we sang in the kitchen on Sundays with Mamí. The plantains and rice we ate at special events reminded me of home. The pride in my classmates from countries and islands that were predominately Black—Trinidad, Barbados, Jamaica, Nigeria, Ghana, and Kenya—sent small pangs of longing through my heart.

I still didn't know where my African American people originated *from*-from, I just knew we built the country we were in right now, a country where we still had to fight to be respected as full citizens. We'd created a culture of our own, so influential that it touched and inspired the world, and yet people often weaponized the stars and stripes as if they weren't soaked in our blood.

After the party, inside the window of my dorm room in Thayer Hall, I hung the one flag I did have with me to take pride in—my towel-size red, blue, and white Puerto Rican flag, as Mamí did around our home back in Syracuse. The flag had a history of its own, telling the story of people who had given their lives in the name of freedom and independence from outside empires, ours included. To many of them, they preferred their Boricua flag in black and white.

One day I'd come to understand that there was a whole legacy waiting to be inherited in connection to this flag too, far beyond flag-waving, dancing, homecooked meals, and parades—a history I was destined to learn as I listened to that small voice that whispered, "There's more to it than what you've been told."

8

Hispaniola

Subject: Your Mamí

Natasha I just received the letter that you are on probation
because of the D you received.

I am suggesting that you focus only on books and 1 social activity
if you want to graduate from Harvard. The letter made it sound that
if your grades do not go up you might not be able to continue there.
You have made it for 2 years, so I know you can make it for 2 more.
But college is hard and you just cannot do everything. You must
spend 99% studying and the other 1% for social. Especially at a hard
school like that.

You are there and I am not. But a mother's advice, because when
you apply for grad school, no school will want you if you have grades
lower than B's. So see what activities you can drop because this is
your career, and that is more important. I would take that letter
seriously because you do not want to fail at something you wanted
so much. So see what you can do. Call me later, I keep calling and no
answer.

love Mamí

My stomach sank. I thought I could get away with being put
on academic probation and handle it quietly myself, not
realizing that the college notified a student's parents with a letter.
The older I got, the less Daddy called and the less I called him;

these emails from Mamí served as communication for both of them. But I knew he wasn't pleased either.

A lot had changed since I got to Cambridge that sweltering August of 2004. The great W. E. B. Du Bois may have written that he was in Harvard and not of it, but I was in Harvard and having the time of my life. For the first time ever, I was not being defined as a straight-A student, and it was freeing. I quickly surmised that being all about academics would require so much of my time that I would miss out on what the university offered that I really wanted: a social life.

I'd been drinking out of a firehose of social activities: performing at the BSA Talent Show with the Expressions hip-hop dance club, acting in plays like *The Colored Museum*, produced by BlackCAST, sampling my first amaretto sours at the First Friday happy hours put on by the Association of Black Harvard Women, and "punching" (also known as being recruited) for Harvard's finals clubs.

Finals clubs were social clubs that were both visible and secretive at the same time. The multimillion-dollar properties were built into Harvard's campus landscape and provided members-only perks, like private parties, chefs, and networks with some of the most powerful alumni at the college. Getting in was an invitation-only "punch" process that took place sophomore year, and there was no rushing or soliciting for membership. Critics of the clubs blasted them for the elitism they represented within an already-elite space, as well as for incidents of sexual assault and underage drinking.

Harvard as a college didn't welcome women as coeds until the 1970s, with the complete merger of Harvard and Radcliffe not happening until 1999. Women couldn't join finals clubs in male-only institutions—they could only get access to the clubs as dates and partymates. When the university presented clubs with a challenge— welcome women or lose official recognition—the clubs voted to stay single-sex and went private. But in the late '90s and early 2000s two women's clubs emerged and were socially recognized by the existing men's clubs, enjoying shared social activities and matching punch calendars.

When I got punched for both women's clubs, I hopped with giddiness around my room with Adaora, who'd been punched too. I was aware of the controversial history of the clubs and had mixed feelings about them, but never one to let a red flag stop me, I charged ahead. Even in the year 2004, the very existence of the male clubs could make women at Harvard feel like second-class citizens. Being a member of an original club was an experience—a privilege—I could never have, simply because I was born female. I hated it.

And yet, I reasoned this was the sausage being made of assimilating to the Ivy League. At least I could use the privilege to help diversify the type of girls the club went after. It's what Black men did, after all.

Oddly enough, when a Black boy got into a club, you quietly cheered for him, knowing he'd symbolically overcome centuries of systemic racism to defy the odds. You also secretly knew that if you were cool with him, you'd reap some of the small benefits, with invitations to parties and less trouble at the door. Patriarchy required some creative workarounds.

At the least, if girls made it into the clubs, they wouldn't need to be trophy girlfriends or dates of male club members to get access to the social scene. They wouldn't endure the humiliation of having a door closed in their face on a Friday by some member who sat in the same classes with them during the day. They'd be social equals—at least in theory—to the guys in their classes. But the truth was, property ownership was power on campus. When I was punching the women's clubs, they still didn't own buildings on campus, and once they acquired property it paled in comparison to the size and wealth of the mansions the Harvard finals club boys played in.

Despite the contradictions, I vowed to stay true to myself while being introduced to the scene, to see if I'd make it to the end of the series of group social gatherings and private dates where we were spoiled with food, drink, and fun. I ended up getting into my finals club of choice, right along with Adaora; the club members happily whisking us away in the night then serenading us to welcome us into a club of love. That welcome took place in the basement of a boy's finals club.

But all those months of partying across campus, fulfilling extra-curricular commitments, and staying out later than I normally did caused my grades to slip. I slept through morning classes with my section, unable to get out of bed, trying to play catch-up on board member duties for ABHW, my number one priority.

ABHW gave me what I cherished my whole life—sisterhood with other Black women. And it made me feel less alone navigating a world where the intersections of my race, gender, and sexuality seemed to matter more and more. As a Black woman in this world, I sometimes felt as if I were on the bottom of the social totem pole in every way. But missing classes turned into missing homework, which turned into a D and an email from my professor that I'd been dreading.

Dear Natasha,

I wanted to touch base with you about your grade in Science A-47 Cosmic Connections as we head into the final weeks of the semester. You are currently at risk for a failing grade in the course.

It was like watching a car crash in slow motion, and all I could do was brace for impact. Getting a D at the college meant automatic academic probation. I imagined my classmates walking to get their diplomas without me while I sat home in Syracuse, at the yellow house on Garfield, the failed poster child of the city, trying to earn my way back to school.

But I brought the D on myself. Despite a very solid freshman year, I'd still had a negative internal script in my head about what was possible for me in this place. I wanted to prove myself academi-cally, and to do that I majored in the hardest nonscience major pos-sible, an application-only honors concentration in social studies.

Far from the fifth-grade study of maps and geography that the name conjured, social studies concentrators were billed as true social scientists—interdisciplinary scholars who could navigate complex political, economic, and social issues and analyze classic theorists like John Stuart Mill, Jürgen Habermas, Karl Marx, and Michel Foucault.

It was social studies where I'd first encounter Simone de Beauvoir's "The Second Sex," and the Combahee River Collective, finally getting a vocabulary to describe why I'd always felt so uneasy about the "no women pastors" rule at church back home or why the finals club system still bothered me even though I'd gotten in.

Social studies' interdisciplinary approach gave me a chance to take an African American studies course with a famed Black photographer, Deborah Willis, where I learned for the first time about Sarah Baartman, the South African woman who was exhibited around the world for her large buttocks. It reminded me of the hip-hop video vixens I'd watched in music videos all my life, and I wrote a paper about them for class. Here I was learning how to translate my experiences into the language of this world—the way academics talked.

The big hurdle of my social studies major was the thesis requirement—a twenty- to thirty-thousand-word research paper and intellectual examination of a topic of our choosing, which we would defend in front of oral examiners. Writing a thesis supposedly separated hardcore academic students from the regular ones. I reasoned that surely this would earn me respect, proving the college hadn't wasted a spot on me. I never thought to ask *why* I was still trying to prove this after getting in.

I did well in courses for my concentration, like Protest Literature and Social Studies 10, but in quantitative classes like EC 10 and Science A-47, I was another casualty of stereotype threat—my fear of confirming to the worst stereotypes about Black people, women, and people who came from "regular" families overtaking any sense of my actual abilities.

At times I self-sabotaged, not really giving it my best in case my best wasn't good enough. Other times I didn't realize I could ask for help until too late. I didn't know how to advocate for myself or game the system, like my friends who dropped classes they were struggling in early. I thought you were supposed to stick it out. I was flirting with failure, daring the universe to show me I didn't belong there, and creating a self-fulfilling prophecy.

What's worse was that I'd been ready to apply to a summer study-abroad course in the Dominican Republic. The five-week course about biodiversity in the Caribbean represented my personal goal of studying abroad in a Spanish-speaking country to practice my mother's native tongue. It would be a way to meet a core science requirement while getting to know a different side of the Latino experience.

I stared at my computer screen, trying to figure out how I'd navigate academic probation and find the money to cover the trip that Mamí said she could not afford to—and would not—pay for.

After connecting with my academic adviser to go through the formalities of the probation period, I finally was ready to reply to Mamí's email. I was not going to concede or even admit that defeat was possible. I opted for deflection and minimizing the situation.

Re: Subject: Your Mamí

yeah, i already dropped out of the play to have more study time. my tutor said as long as i pull my grades up this semester i'll be fine and get taken off.

thanks
natasha

Deep down I knew the truth, though. I had to do way more than pull my grades up. I had to pull *myself* up.

———

"Como te puede ayudarte?"
"Pase buen tarde corazón, que quieres?"

I'd landed in the Dominican Republic to applause, surprised when the airplane touched down on the ground that I was really there. This was the first international trip I'd ever taken in Latin America, outside of Puerto Rico. With my adviser's help, I'd made a persuasive case that the science course in the Caribbean would allow me time to get my head together about my academic future while making up for my grade. I also managed to get more than half of the trip's cost covered by school scholarships and took out loans for the rest.

As we drove into Santo Domingo, the capital, I looked through the windows of the big square white van I sat in with my classmates, chatting with my roommate Kayla. Kayla was a California pageant queen, majoring in biology, who was of Korean descent, and we hit it off right away, bonding over our love for Calle 13, Nutella, and being two of a few minorities on the trip.

Our first stop was at a local food stand before our drive over to the Hotel Gazcue, a family-run hotel near the University of Santo Domingo, where we'd be based all summer. As we chatted back and forth, I looked up at the sign with handwritten food options listed and made my order.

"*Arroz y habichuelas, por favor. Y una empanada tambien,*" I told the cashier, who got to prepping it right away.

I felt eyes land on me like daggers. Apparently I'd ordered my rice and beans with a pronunciation so natural, it caught the attention of my assistant teacher, a fair-skinned Dominican native with dark black hair named Sebastian, whom we'd just met at the airport for the first time.

"How did you know how to say the words so well?" he probed with surprise, his brows raised under his wire-rimmed glasses. "Your accent is like a native."

I'd been here before. It was in this moment I could try to explain that I was Puerto Rican—or rather that my mother was, but my African American father didn't speak Spanish, and my mother didn't want me to get confused by learning Spanish and English at the same time, so she prioritized English, so I could understand it with my ear, and the few words I could speak came out native-sounding . . .

But it all sounded too complicated, or like an excuse—and excuses were weak. I didn't know how to simply explain that Spanish was in my heart but didn't live on my tongue.

"I'm Puerto Rican—well, my mom is—and I understand Spanish, but I'm not fluent," I replied.

"Wow," Sebastian said. "That explains it. Just keep practicing. You sound like a natural."

As we got back in the van and drove along the road toward Gazcue, I took in the view of DR. Driving past the busyness of the capital, with people on bikes, in cars, selling fruits, batteries, and other random goods on the side of the road, I couldn't help but notice something I'd heard before but still hadn't mentally prepared for—there were Black people everywhere.

Dominican people. Not African Americans from the South. And not just brown or tan, the typical descriptions of Latinos who have a little splash of melanin in their skin, but Black—period. Their mix of facial features and hair textures made it undeniable that while these residents spoke Spanish fluently, the people they descended from had unquestionably come from Africa.

Right away, I became aware of myself and my body. I looked at my brown hands and traced the shape of my nose with my hand. In the States, I sometimes found myself explaining to skeptical questioners how it was that *I* was Latina. And yet here, Black Latinos were everywhere. Of course there were Dominicans who came in all shades and colors, with a couple of them who looked as white as my college professor, and others who were mestizo. But the sheer number of Black people was notable. Now I understood why certain people in the States I told I was Latina assumed I was Dominican.

We got into our daily routine of heading to the University of Santo Domingo for class and then trekking to places like the National Botanical Gardens, into the field for exploration, taking photos of plants and bugs and all sorts of trees.

We stopped at the grocery store regularly for lunch, and I piled my tray with *arroz blanco, habichuelas,* and *pollo a la plancha.* At the cash register the employee, a woman the same color as me with pressed hair, casually greeted me and proceeded to ask in Spanish how I was paying.

I was learning what it felt like to blend in among Latinos for the first time.

I tried to minimize talking so as not to expose myself at first, loving the feeling of being a chameleon. But if the conversation went deeper, I had to admit my limitations—that I wasn't fluent. *"Lo siento, entiendo español pero hablo mas ingles,"* I'd explain apologetically.

Cashiers and vendors would be taken aback for a second as they reset and looked at me with fresh eyes, seeing the gringa that I really was.

Here it was not my race that disqualified me from Latinidad. It was a novel feeling. But with race off the table, in a place where more people looked like me than didn't, what was left . . . was culture.

It became more apparent as the weeks went on that I may have looked Dominican, but I was American. Here in the DR I'd actually felt the most American I'd ever felt in my life, as my eyes took in a new country.

In my travels, I was seeing two DRs emerging. There was one side that was a tropical paradise, complete with wealth and luxury. When we went to Punta Cana for a weekend, there were sprawling all-inclusive resorts, with gorgeous beaches and the deepest blue waters. Kayla and I danced at a beachside bar where we drank Presidentes, and listened to pop hits instead of the reggaeton and dembow we heard in the streets.

Another weekend we went to a mansion rented just for our study-abroad group, with meals prepared daily and an infinity pool dropping over the edge of the mountain we were nestled in.

And yet there were parts of the country that had crumbling roads, homes, and infrastructure like nothing I'd seen before. Coming from a working-class family in an economically divided city like Syracuse, this was my first look at poverty abroad. In El Mogote,

Kayla had met sharecropping families living on two dollars a day, who had to hand over half of their gross product to landlords who provided the bare minimum.

Just as in the United States, it was a reminder that there were always haves and have-nots. As an American, I'd grown up always hearing about our country first, as if the world orbited around us. Now I was seeing with my own eyes how much I'd missed.

The Dominican Republic had a natural beauty like nothing I'd seen in the States. The fruit we bought at stands was fresher than anything I'd had at a grocery store, with mangoes and pineapples so ripe they gushed sweet juice. During one of our camping trips near Valle Nuevo, where we studied pine forests, plants, and other flora, our feet covered in mud from fresh rain, I reluctantly ate goat for the first time and felt guilty about how tasty it was. I drank fresh passionfruit juice and munched on soft, buttery *pan* each morning at the Gazcue.

One day, as we inched our way through the sweaty hot forest on our usual daily excursion, Professor Smith made the pronouncement, "We're going to the border, near Dajabón next, gang! Grab your binoculars and hop into the van."

When I signed up for the course in the Dominican Republic, I never imagined I'd be crossing any border to touch Haiti. For much of my life, I was ignorant of the fact that Haiti and the Dominican Republic even shared the same land: Hispaniola.

Hispaniola has a complicated history, and depending on who tells it, the heroes and villains of the island's story change. In 1492 Christopher Columbus claimed he "discovered" the island, but this land already had inhabitants—indigenous people known as the Taino.

Just as in Puerto Rico, the Spanish colonizers contributed to the decimation of the Taino population on Hispaniola by enslaving them, killing them, and infecting them with foreign diseases. To make up for the resulting loss of human labor in their gold mines and sugar plantations, the Spanish brought in enslaved Africans.

There were Black people who had come from the Spanish Empire and were already Christianized, known as *ladinos*. Enslaved Black people who came directly from Africa were known as *bozales*. Later, on the west side of the island, the French started to settle what we know as modern-day Haiti, creating a Creole-speaking country called Saint-Domingue. The name *Haiti* derived from "Hayti," used by the indigenous Taino people to describe the "land of high mountains."

Both French and Spanish colonizers used the labor of enslaved Black people who toiled to produce sugar and coffee, to amass wealth and resources. However, it was Haiti's side that was the wealthiest and hosted the largest and densest population of Black people of approximately a half million Africans. Nearly 90 percent of Haiti's population were enslaved Black people, compared to 5 percent free Black people and 5 percent white, mostly French people.

Meanwhile, in Santo Domingo, the population was much less dense. The first slave revolt on the island happened in 1521 in Santo Domingo in the Dominican Republic, on a sugar plantation owned by Diego Columbus, Christopher Columbus' son, a precursor of the revolution to come. After nearly three hundred years of slavery, in 1791, on the Haitian side, enslaved Africans gathered in a special vodou ceremony in the forest, before taking up arms and revolting, killing whoever stood in their way to freedom.

On January 1, 1804, Haiti made history and became the first independent Black nation in the West. Their constitution made their priorities known:

Article 2: Slavery is abolished forever.

Not far down the list read another revolutionary concept:

Article 14: Because all distinctions of color among children must necessarily stop, all Haitians will henceforth only be known generically as Black.

Not only did Haiti fight for its own freedom, but it welcomed African Americans to its country, offering automatic citizenship to any Black American or Black person, period, who wanted to emigrate. And emigrate they did. An estimated twenty-five hundred Black Americans came to Haiti from cities like Philadelphia, Baltimore, and other urban areas. Haiti even intercepted passing slave ships, freeing Black people and upholding a "free soil" policy that refused to send anyone back to bondage.

But not only did the French refuse to acknowledge Haiti, they demanded that Haiti pay 150 million francs—equal to about $21 billion today—to compensate for lost slave labor and property. Choosing between facing another bloody war to defend their independence or paying up, President Jean-Pierre Boyer agreed. Haiti could not get on its feet under the weight of the crippling indemnity, which at one point took 80 percent of the country's wealth to pay the debt.

The United States was terrified of what the Haitian Revolution represented. What would happen if *their* enslaved Black people got word that the cruel institution had been toppled, not far away from their borders? French masters were already fleeing with their slaves to the Louisiana Territory in the U.S., with rumors of Haiti's rebellion coming with them.

It was Thomas Jefferson who vowed to ignore Haiti—implementing a policy of nonrecognition of Haiti by the U.S. right after the revolution that lasted for decades, until it proved too costly.

Despite having a lucrative trade relationship with Haiti, our American forefathers knew if their plantation slave economy crumbled, they'd be toast.

In 1821, on the other side of the island, Santo Domingo, also known as "Spanish Haiti," declared independence from the Spanish crown. The following year, Haiti would take over Santo Domingo, banning slavery, and bring the entire island under one government.

For twenty-two years, Haiti and the Dominican Republic may have been one on paper, but eventually divisions of all kinds from political to cultural to religious emerged that could no longer hold the two countries together. Haitian president Jean-Pierre Boyer lost support across the entire island, and Dominicans expressed concern over the struggling economy and political leadership. But even the so-called line between Haiti and DR wasn't a perfectly clear one. Under unification, the two sides intermingled, built communities, and shared space.

A unified Haiti and the Dominican state would ultimately be short-lived when Dominicans seceded in 1844. But it would not be the end of violent battles between the two nations. Haitian soldiers attempted to take DR back multiple times, the enmity between the two countries increasing.

Dominicans would go back under Spanish rule in 1861. Not until 1865 would the Dominican Republic declare itself independent again from Spain.

It was against this winding historical backdrop—the above summary just the tip of the iceberg of complexity—that I entered our tour near Dajabón completely naive about just how Black and intertwined we were in all Americas.

My classmates and I casually climbed a mountain, walking into a museum space that had been etched into the rocks, as our tour guide, a light-skinned Dominican man with a strong accent, explained to us in English a tragedy I'd never heard of before. "In 1937, a Dominican dictator named Rafael Trujillo called for the mass killing of Haitians living in the Dominican Republic," the guide said.

Raphael Trujillo (also known as "El Jefe") ran the Dominican Republic for more than thirty years, from 1930 to 1961. A former U.S. National Guardsman, he learned military tactics from the U.S. Marines during the near decade in which our military occupied the Dominican Republic.

It turns out it was the U.S. that implemented strict border policies, disrupting what were generally cooperative relations and multiethnic communities of Dominican and Haitian workers along the border. During the occupation, many Afro-Dominicans saw their spiritual and cultural practices—like drumming—banned by U.S. soldiers. Despite their always affirming and celebrating their African heritage, a campaign had begun to tamp down on it.

Ironically, Trujillo's own maternal grandmother was Haitian, and according to Michele Wucker's essay "The River Massacre: The Real and Imagined Borders of Hispaniola," Trujillo even used makeup to conceal the melanin in his skin.

Despite having visited Haiti multiple times—the only Dominican president to do so at that point—Trujillo reacted to these border conflicts with violent force, ordering the execution of Haitians.

"We have already begun to remedy the situation," Trujillo was quoted as saying on October 2, 1937, while visiting Dajabón, a town that bordered Haiti and DR. "Three hundred Haitians are now dead in [the town of] Bánica. This remedy will continue."

It was called the Parsley Massacre, or *"kout kouto"* in Creole, which translates to "the stabbing." There is an oft-repeated story (considered an urban myth by some) that Trujillo's soldiers pulled workers aside and forced them to say the word *parsley* in Spanish, a word whose pronunciation would reveal whether a person was truly Haitian, and those unfortunate souls would be killed in an act of ethnic cleansing. But scholars have highlighted that the killings were indiscriminate and included Dominican victims, such as the *rayanos*, who lived, worked, and had been born on the DR side of the border.*

My eyes watered as I took in a group of black-and-white photographs mounted on the walls of the museum. There were bodies piled up on the ground, arms and legs splayed in every direction, the life slashed away from them, blood running in the river. I read the tiny captions that explained the massacre before me, which explained:

---

* Lorgia García-Peña, *The Borders of Dominicanidad: Race, Nation, and Archives of Contradiction* (Durham, NC: Duke University Press, 2016).

Trujillo told Dominican soldiers to use machetes to chop them in pieces.

Trujillo okayed the cutting of children and babies as well as women and men.

An estimated fifteen to twenty thousand people were killed at his order.

I was astonished. All my life, I'd been told the Dominican Republic was the "Blackest" Latino country, and I felt at home seeing so many Black people on this trip. But now I saw there were political forces—including outside colonial powers—that stoked divisions between two peoples who shared the same land.

With my American eyes, I saw "Black" as one large family. But here, each nation had developed its own identity and retelling of history. Scholars have also argued that whiter creole intellectual elites were invested in defining Dominicans as Hispanic first—and in stark opposition to their Haitian island neighbors.

It reminded me of the ways I'd heard some Puerto Ricans discriminate against Dominicans on *la isla*. "The Dominicans in PR? They're just like the Mexicans here in the U.S.," a fellow Puerto Rican told me, a hint of judgment in his voice, trying to explain the racial profiling and mistreatment of Dominican immigrants, particularly darker-skinned ones, who swam across water and traveled in canoes to get to the U.S. colony.

And yet in the eyes of some Americans, Black meant Black and immigrant meant immigrant—so any Dominican, Haitian, or Puerto Rican who crossed U.S. borders was automatically an "other."

The mood was somber in our group as the tour guide finished his lecture on the Parsley Massacre and returned to discussing the park at large. I found myself zoning out. I couldn't shake off the sadness of learning how race and ethnicity could be weaponized in battles over citizenship. It would be foreboding of decades of unrest to come between the two countries long after my trip ended.

Four weeks after returning home from the course, I got the news that I'd received an A in the class, and it would count as a full semester's credit. I was officially off academic probation, putting me back in Mamí and Daddy's good graces, and on my way to junior year. I wasn't the only one whose life had been changed by the trip—my roommate Kayla shot me an email saying she was so moved by our time, she was now working on building a school for Dominican and Haitian kids back in El Mogote.

I promised one day I'd return to Hispaniola to see it for myself but I never returned. Just four years later, Haiti would be hit with a magnitude-seven earthquake, killing an estimated 220,000 people and costing over $8 billion in damage.

Sitting in my dorm room, I hung a medium-sized canvas painting I'd bought from a vendor near Los Haitises: a Black woman's face in silhouette, her hair wrapped, against a sea-blue swirl of paints. Was she Dominican or Haitian? It didn't matter to me. I just wanted to be reminded that just an ocean away, my feet had touched soil seeped with revolution and the sweat of freedom-dreamers that would never die.

9

Black Majesty

B ack in New York, I stood at the gate of Central Park near
Fifth Avenue and Sixty-Ninth Street among thousands of
people trying to get into SummerStage, the annual free concert
series held in Manhattan's biggest park. The sun beamed on my
skin and I wiped sweat from my forehead, shaking out my arms
and my nerves to stay cool.

"Gabriela, Gabriela, over here!" My friend Gabriela had agreed
to come with me to serve as my translator for an interview with
reggaeton artist La Sista. I had found La Sista's manager on her
website and asked for an interview. He told me to swing by the
annual SummerStage Festival in the park and interview her backstage, but now I was sandwiched between thousands of people to
get to her.

I was meeting La Sista because I'd come back from the Do-
minican Republic for my junior year of college with a vengeance.
After twenty-one years of living in what felt like mostly ignorance
about the richness of Black history in the Caribbean, I had to
make up for lost time. The first thing I did returning home from
DR was sign up for an Af-Am studies class called "The Other
African Americans," with acclaimed sociologist J. Lorand Matory.
The class explored the experiences of other ethnic groups such as
Black Indians, Cape Verdeans, and even the Black bourgeoisie.
But most importantly, we would study Afro-Latinos.

In all the Black history I'd learned, the story of the Afro-
Latino had been obscured, even within African American history. Our public schools were so U.S.-centric that most students

weren't taught much about international relations. I didn't know Black Cubans had immigrated to Tampa, Florida, so far back that they'd lived alongside African Americans in communities like Ybor City, as was recounted in the memoir of Afro-Cuban writer Evelio Grillo. Or that Fidel Castro courted African American leaders during the civil rights movement, hoping to create allies and transplants. Or that numerous Afro-Latinos had gone to HBCUs for college during the civil rights movement, or served in the segregated U.S. military with "Negro" battalions. Afro-Puerto Rican Sylvia del Villard experienced such bad racism in segregated Tennessee when she was attending Fisk University that she returned to the island to finish her education, and then worked to carry the mantle of elevating African influence in the culture.

I didn't even have a passport until I was nineteen, let alone the ability to explain the intricacies of other countries' histories. Even the fact that we said "America" and assumed it to be the United States, as if there were no other countries in the Americas, reflected a state of mind that held it wasn't a priority to know the world beyond our borders deeply.

When we reached the point in Professor Matory's course about Afro-Latinos, I went through the reading material with fury. We read Victor C. Simpson's *Afro-Puerto Ricans in the Short Story: An Anthology* and Angela Jorge's *The Black Puerto Rican Woman in Contemporary American Society*, discussing the contradictory and illuminating experience of being racialized in the U.S. mainland and in Puerto Rico.

I encountered the work of Jorge Duany, who analyzed the phenomenon of hypodescent, a.k.a. the "one-drop" rule, which often subjected mixed people to rules of segregation in the U.S. depending on their degree of Black blood. Supposedly in Latin America different rules applied, allowing people's race category to be more fluid and not just "Black" and "white." This alleged difference came from what was again, supposedly, a more racially mixed society, without strict segregation like the continental U.S., or more interracial proximity in social interactions during slavery, even in the midst of the brutality.

Duany described dozens of categories used to classify Puerto Ricans by their facial features, skin color, and other physical characteristics. He showed that due to a history of slavery and colonialization, these categories could be used to distance oneself from Blackness and African ancestry, intentionally or unintentionally. But even Duany noted that in certain instances, a binary of Black vs. white that marked Blackness as bad would still make itself known in Latin American society.

These works were scholarly proof that so many of the stories I'd heard growing up about "all Latinos being a little Black" or, for Puerto Ricans specifically, the "three races" of African, Taino, and Spaniard that made us all one people, weren't as historically accurate or simple as I thought.

We were not all mixed together; our experiences did in fact vary by our skin color and racial phenotype. These Afro-Latino scholars critiqued terms like *racial democracy* and *colorblind society* that made sense to me, as I considered how racism was often downplayed in the Latino community.

Without a Spanish surname or ability to speak Spanish fluently, perhaps I was less vulnerable to seeing myself as anything but Black. Or had my father been a Black Puerto Rican or both my parents Afro-Latino, perhaps I would've seen myself as not being Black like *those* morenos.

After all, even some Afro-Latinos thought themselves culturally superior to African Americans, hoping to distance themselves from *"esos negros"* when they arrived in this country, a phenomenon perfectly demonstrated in "Negrito" by the Puerto Rican poet Tato Laviera:

el negrito
vino a nueva york
vio milagros
en sus ojos

su tía le pidió
un abrazo y le dijo:
"no te juntes con
los prietos, negrito"

The little Black boy
Comes to New York
Sees miracles
In his eyes
His aunt gives him
A hug and tells him
"Don't play with
The Blacks, my little Black boy"

Laviera's poem captures the cutting contradictions of diasporic delusions: an aunt who sees the Blackness in her nephew enough to use a term of endearment based on his race, but doesn't want him to associate with Blacks—African Americans specifically—the stigma of Black Americanness outweighing solidarity. Afro-Latinos who thought this way were victims of a campaign of propaganda, a stereotyping of generational African Americans that many immigrants of all backgrounds encountered upon hitting U.S. soil.

Perhaps here is when my sense of American *Negra* identity started to form. I had been racialized from birth—called Negra or Morena by Latinos who described me by my color first in this country and abroad, while also experiencing Blackness apart from the Latino community's conception of it, rooted in my African American roots. That apart-ness had given me a unique positioning between two worlds.

The more Afro-Latino scholars I encountered who had been born in Latin America and the Caribbean and were proud of and unconfused about their Blackness from childhood, the more I wanted to understand their experiences of Blackness in *their* worlds. Under no illusion about how racism, both systemic and personal, worked to deny rights to Black people—they had lived this truth themselves;

many allying with African Americans in every way, from personal to political—they had made contributions to Black America too.

I decided to use my research paper in Professor Matory's class to delve into the duality of all kinds of Black Latino experiences. In addition to reggaeton artists, I would interview fellow Black Latinos at school, and document their similar struggles with negotiating identity in different places.

Gabriela, my friend from Freshman Black Table who had a Dominican mother and Bahamian father, was one of them. We sat across from each other in the dining hall while I interviewed her about her experience.

"What do you call yourself? How do you identify?" I asked.

"I am, first and foremost, Hispanic—I'm Dominican. I didn't grow up with my father and don't know anything about his culture," she replied, explaining that her mother was a few shades lighter than her but still brown and most definitely had African heritage.

I understood. Gabriela was the version of me I would've been if I'd grown up just among Mamí and all the other Puerto Ricans she knew.

"When I was little I watched as my mom told my sister, 'Joanna, you can go out and play in the sun, but Gabriela, stay inside cause I don't want you to get any darker.'"

I was shocked. I couldn't imagine the pain of being told that by the mother who birthed you.

"I was the darkest one in my family, so I was like la negra, la morena. My mother would place a clothespin on my nose in an effort to 'refina la nariz.' She told me not to worry because one day I could get my nose fixed."

At this point, my heart broke. Mamí had never, not once, told me there was anything about my face that needed to be changed or altered. In fact, when I told her I wanted a nose job as a kid, she shuddered, telling me I didn't need it and that I was beautiful just as I was. Only now could I appreciate the depth of the love Mamí demonstrated to me as her child, even though we had different features. She might not have always understood my Black experience, but she never disparaged it.

Hearing Gabriela's story made me realize how much race could be downplayed for a sense of unity in Latino communities. In the case of Afro-Latinos, it felt more important than ever to uncover the dirty laundry that sat unaired. The assault to our sense of self happened on such an intimate level that it was easier to sweep it under the rug, to not challenge it, to keep the peace with our loved ones.

I was ready to get to the heart of the matter. I decided that not only would my final paper for this class be about Afro-Latinos but my entire senior thesis would be. I wanted to better understand how we got here, but most importantly, where I could find like-minded people who were challenging the status quo.

I found myself at SummerStage to interview La Sista because I'd developed a happy obsession with her music. I had not been invested in reggaeton—a genre inspired by hip-hop and dancehall from Jamaica that emerged in Panama through canal workers and traveled to Puerto Rico—in a thoughtful way; I danced to it and shook my hips at parties, but I didn't think of it as a tool for social change or know that it had once been denigrated as "ghetto" music that police fined people for playing in public.

Most of the American kids I knew didn't associate reggaeton with Black people. To them it was "Latino," which per usual was a separate category. As I perused the web in my dorm room, I stumbled upon a music video thumbnail of a young Black woman, with locs, wearing a long green skirt, red headwrap, red shirt, and African-style beads. Her name was La Sista, and she was Puerto Rican. The song was called "Anacaona" from her new album, *Majestad Negroide*, or "Black Majesty."

I googled the album cover and saw La Sista against a backdrop by Puerto Rican artist Celso Gonzales, which featured the *vejigante* masks Mamí would decorate the house with when I was a child. Made from coconuts, these masks are worn by *vejigantes*, clown-like characters featured at parades who scare away evil spirits.

I was struck by La Sista's image. She was a *reggaetonera*, not background material. She didn't fit the stereotype of the half-naked skinny or busty girls in music videos, who were mostly light-skinned or mestiza Latinas. La Sista was sun-kissed brown, full-bodied, far from dainty, and I'd never ever seen anything like her in reggaeton.

I went down a rabbit hole of her music videos and saw mixed reviews about her work. Puerto Rican journalist Raquel Z. Rivera, who ran a blog called *Reggaetonica*, praised La Sista's "charisma. And skill. And charm." Another blogger, Gazoo, ripped her as a rip-off of Tego Calderon and called her an "ugly Negra," mocking her African aesthetic and clothes and saying she looked like a witch. The racist comments made me angry. This was the ugliness revealed when someone openly embraced their Afro-Latino identity, and it was positioned to be "outside" of the mainstream culture.

I needed to connect with Raquel Rivera to meet with a Latina who got the same excitement and promise I saw in La Sista. When I emailed her, she replied right away. It turned out that she was also an adjunct professor at Columbia University and writing an anthology about reggaeton. She handed over all the academic research she had available about reggaeton and encouraged me to go to the Center for Puerto Rican Studies (Centro) at Hunter College in New York City for more resources.

I boarded a bus and headed down to New York. Walking into Centro, I was completely blown away. There were rows upon rows of books about Puerto Rican life and history, with writings from Puerto Rican authors of all backgrounds. I just wondered why, if Puerto Rico was technically part of the United States, so much of this history had gone untaught to me at school. I saw the power of having physical institutions representing your community.

There I would learn about the 1868 Grito de Lares, the first major revolt against the Spanish Empire by Puerto Ricans, who were tired of paying heavy taxes to their colonizer while watching their economy tank. Despite careful planning, an information leak led them to start the revolt prematurely in Lares, Puerto Rico, and the rebellion's leaders encouraged enslaved people to take up arms. Spain intercepted a ship carrying weapons for the rebels from the Dominican Republic, leaving them in a bad spot once official Puerto Rican troops came in to quell the rebellion. About 475 rebels were sentenced to death, but the cry for independence never fully went away.

It was spring of my junior year, and I would have less than a year to finish the project in time for graduation. I was more invested in completing this than in anything I had ever done in college. But before I could find a way to get to La Sista, life would throw me a curveball, and it wouldn't be an academic one.

———

I had been sitting in the sterile white room of the campus health services center for too long, waiting for the results of my blood work. I knew I had to be flexible during walk-in visits, but based on my calculations, something was up.

"I hate having my blood drawn," I'd sheepishly told the doctor earlier when he told me to sit tight for a nurse to come take blood.

"Do I have to?"

"Yes, it's just to run some tests," he replied. "Just a safety precaution."

I had gone to the health services center on campus because I had hurt my leg while running.

Smack!

I heard the plastic band pulled against my brown arm.

Thump, thump, thump

I felt the nurse's fingers patting to see where she could find a vein. The sensation of my blood gathering and swelling in one spot made me nauseated.

"Make a fist," she instructed.

I squeezed as if my life depended on it.

It's true I didn't know where all the black-and-blue bruises on

my body had come from. I'd been so obsessed with everything happening on campus, my goals, preparing my thesis, fulfilling dreams,
I hadn't had a single moment to think to follow up.

As my eyes traced the otoscope for the hundredth time, a group
of three doctors walked into the room. Only one had come to see
me before. It seemed I was being ambushed, and now I was more
afraid.

"Hello, Ms. Alford," said the main doctor, a white man with dark
brown hair and a clipboard in his hand.

"Hello," I said, mustering up a smile so as not to seem guilty.
Did they know I hadn't been taking care of myself? I barely slept. I
barely ate. I'd lost ten pounds.

"We don't know what you're doing, or what's been going on, but
you need to go to the hospital right away."

I froze on the crinkly white table paper.

"Your blood platelet levels are so low that if you were to trip, fall,
or bang yourself into anything right now, you would bleed to death.
This is truly serious, Ms. Alford."

I looked down at my feet. I had only come here for a follow-up.
My mind did various calculations to try to figure out what this would
mean. What had made my platelets so low?

I shook my head and gathered my things. I was heading to the
hospital.

At the hospital I was tested endlessly and sent out with a referral
to a place I'd never expected to go at twenty years old: the Dana
Farber Cancer Institute. I was told to see Dr. Donald Jamison, the
center's leading blood doctor. Dr. Jamison reminded me of Santa
Claus, a white man with a full white beard and mustache.

"You have ITP," Dr. Jamison told me, a week after campus doctors had first sent me to the hospital. "Idiopathic thrombocytopenic
purpura."

"What does that mean?" I asked, numb from shock.

"The *idio-* in *idiopathic* means we don't know," he explained gently. "But some researchers have theorized it may be caused by stress or trauma or infection in the body when you were younger. *Thrombocytopenic* refers to the sharp decrease in your blood platelet levels. And *purpura* references all the bruises on your body."

I listened as Dr. Jamison explained that ITP was a chronic blood disorder, where my immune system had turned on my body, attacking my healthy platelets. I had noticeable dark bruises, and while it was rare, I risked fatally hemorrhaging because my blood couldn't clot. Treatment options were limited, although drug infusions and steroid treatments often worked to stabilize patients, and there was no known cure. Dr. Jamison was hesitant to do heavy interventions at the moment, but he would give me a steroid called prednisone to see how that helped stabilize my system.

"We'll figure this out, dear. One day at a time," Dr. Jamison told me gingerly. I was terrified but felt safe and went back to campus in a daze to take the medication I was prescribed.

In the weeks that followed, the drug would have terrible side effects. Depression and weight gain sent me into a double spiral as I saw my puffy new face every time I looked in the mirror. My body felt foreign, as if an alien presence had taken over to steer the ship and I was dragged along for the ride.

But as Dr. Jamison predicted, the steroids gave my platelets a boost, and soon I could do the one thing I really cared about: get back to work on my thesis.

———

Now all I had to do was get through the massive crowd at SummerStage to connect with La Sista.

With patience and a little bit of hustle, Gabriela and I navigated the crowds, running and pausing, running and pausing, trying not to step on the backs of ankles. Finally we made it to the VIP area.

There she was: La Sista, with her signature head wrap, long skirt, and a white T-shirt with orange beads around her neck. Her brown skin was smooth like mine. She was only two years older than me, at twenty-three.

"Hola hermana!" she said with a big smile, surrounded by a group of family and friends. She said something to them in Spanish, and they all exited the room.

I had only fifteen minutes with her, so I quickly pulled out my recorder. I saw the battery bar drop to one and wanted to scream. Apparently, it had *not* charged like I hoped.

Luckily, Gabriela was on top of it—she had brought a backup recorder—and we dove in.

La Sista began with her life story, explaining how she started singing reggaeton at fourteen in her hometown of Loiza. It was the part of the island Mamí had always told me had a lot of Black people.

"The town has a very Afroantillano culture," La Sista explained. Afroantillano, or Afro-Antillean, refers to the Antilles chain of islands, also known as the West Indies—Cuba, Jamaica, Puerto Rico, Haiti, and the Dominican Republic. When La Sista expressed a desire to do reggaeton, she was dissuaded by her brother. "Reggaeton is for the boys," she remembered him saying.

La Sista explained that reggaeton's boy's-club sexism gave her strength to perfect her craft. When I listened to her rap about issues like being a strong woman, and channeling African orishas like Yemaya, I saw her Black diasporic feminism as a site of resistance, an antidote to racism, colorism, and sexism.

La Sista said that she felt more discriminated against because of her weight and not fitting the traditional model of what a Latina woman should look like.

"I look different in every sense," she answered, motioning at her body. "Maybe it is because I came with my culture, like bomba, and I represent folkloric heritage."

After a few more questions, we wrapped the interview and I thanked her for her time.

"Anytime," she told me in Spanish. "Whatever you need, I'm here."

That night I wrote in my "Dead End Journal," a space where my professor suggested that we sort through frustrations about navigating the thesis project. I realized something was bothering me. I needed to follow up with Gabriela to ask her a question: When interpreting the dialogue between me and La Sista, why had she used the term *mujer de color* instead of just calling La Sista negra? I was certain she'd be comfortable with the term, considering she wore locs and African-inspired attire. I shot Gabriela a quick email.

She wrote back almost immediately:

> *I definitely remember being very hesitant to say "mujer negra" during the interview and found myself having to replace this with the more neutral phrase, "mujer de color."*
>
> *A lot of this has to do with a pretty sad truth and reality of Hispanic-Caribbean culture: there's a lot of hesitancy to associate with African ancestry. I personally identify strongly with this part of my ancestry. However, I recognize that not all other Black Hispanics do the same thing.*
>
> *Thus, avoiding the phrase, "mujer negra" seemed like a respectful thing to do. The word "negra" in Spanish is very strong. It's the kind of word that you only use with people you know intimately, but at the same time it could be used as an insult as well. It's simply not the kind of word you use freely amongst strangers.*

I was taken aback at first. Why would simply calling someone "negro" or "negra" be an insult, if they were in fact Black? Was it not just a description? I tried to think of a parallel in African American culture that I could relate to. As far back as I could remember, Black people had just been called Black.

While it was true that we, as a people, were generally considered "Black" now, there was a time when we were referred to as Negroes and, before that, as "colored." The term *Black* had to be claimed, reclaimed, and normalized so that it didn't feel like a weapon. Ushered in by a new generation of young people in the 1960s who refused to be ashamed of their race, culture, and the phenotypical characteristics that society so often told them to be ashamed of—4C Afro hair, broad noses, thick lips, and darker skin—"Black" was a way of saying "I am, and I dare you to take issue with it."

I saw the hesitancy to use the word *negra* as an unfortunate consequence of racism in Latin America—having to distance oneself from Blackness, to emphasize mixedness and dilution. It made sense now that there had always been so many other terms to describe someone as Black-adjacent in Latino culture without actually calling them Black—*trigueño, morena, mulatto.* Now I better understand that these forms of oppression were across *all* the Americas, just in different flavors.

It was in this moment, looking at Gabriela's response, that the word *negra* began to take on a special meaning for me. I was awakening to its power. Its defiance.

I hit play on La Sista's album again on my laptop while I typed away at my thesis.

People could call me morena all they liked, with my medium-brown skin and curly hair, but I didn't want any special softening of my Blackness, or to ever be praised for being less negra.

Negra was enough for me. Surely there had to be others who felt the same way.

———

I looked around the waiting room, staring at the ceiling tiles and practicing my deep breathing. I'd been busy enjoying the summer, working on my thesis, and interning at an educational nonprofit, but now I was back in the hospital to face my bad blood, hoping for a miracle.

While things had been steady most of the summer, shortly after my interview with La Sista, I got an alarming email from Dr. Jamison, saying that my latest blood tests weren't good.

Natasha:

Your platelet count today has fallen further.

Dr. Jamison laid out how my blood platelet count was dropping fast each week. The lower the number, the harder it would be for my blood to clot.

202,000
188,000
129,000
89,000

We could not let it go any lower.

"I think it is very likely that the downward trend will continue," Dr. Jamison continued. "It is now very unlikely that the continued use of steroids will result in a sustained remission of your ITP. Please come to see me so that we can discuss what the next steps should be."

I was stunned. When I was called in to get my usual pricks of blood and then sit with Dr. Jamison, he laid out the options before me.

"You can either get your spleen removed, which many patients have done, or try an infusion called rituximab. We use it sometimes for chemotherapy patients. It is very effective, but I can't predict what the side effects on your body will be down the line, as you are so young."

The thought of surgery was scary, but whatever it took, I was willing to try. When I called Mamí, though, she was less than enthusiastic. "*Dios mío*, you are not letting those doctors take your spleen out!" she said sternly, pointing out the uncertain success rate of the procedure. "Abuela knows very good natural remedies from Puerto Rico for blood issues," she explained. "I'm going to mail you some *maltaglobina*, which you should take every day."

I deep-sighed. This was so typical of her, the distrust for institutions. But I understood it. By the time I was seven I'd already memorized Mamí's tale of how Abuelo Felix died. When Mamí was a child, Abuelo had stopped in a bad New York winter storm when a buddy asked for help with his car stalled on the side of the road. When Abuelo was cranking up the jack to get under the wheel, it fell on his foot, leaving a deep cut.

As the flesh turned green, Abuelo opted to let it heal on its own—or not—and continued drinking his way through the days, shooting up drugs where he could. Eventually one of those friends of his would return the favor, carrying him into an emergency room in Manhattan. But the hospital left him sitting in the waiting room for hours as the untreated gangrene in his foot worsened. By the time doctors saw him, it was too late.

Abuelo's story of being neglected in the hospital illustrated Mamí's distrust of hospitals; I'd grown up hearing plenty of skepticism about medical institutions for years. Daddy always talked about the Tuskegee study, when from 1932 to 1976 the U.S. Public Health Service recruited six hundred African American men in Tuskegee, Alabama, to participate in a study about their "bad blood," which referred to problems such as syphilis and anemia. But the "study" never medicated them, instead letting them die.

Not until much later in life would I learn that at the same time, just south of Alabama and across the water, Puerto Ricans were also being experimented on without their knowledge. In the wake of contraception being outlawed in the United States, fertility doctor Gregory Pincus and scientist John Rock got funding from contraceptive advocate, eugenicist, and Planned Parenthood founder Margaret Sanger to experiment on Puerto Rican women. Their projected goal was to create birth control, but their so-called feminist ambitions employed a racist methodology that saw Puerto Rican women as lab tools.

Beginning in 1956, in the town of Rio Piedras, poor women were recruited to take part in trials to take a pill that would prevent pregnancy. Approximately two hundred women would sign up, without knowing that they were part of a clinical trial. Researchers led by Pincus and Rock gave no indication of what health risks were involved in taking the pills, then known as Enovid. These pills had much higher doses of hormones than what's used in birth control pills today, and the researchers involved had no idea how that would affect the participants.

Nearly one-third of Puerto Rican women had already previously been sterilized against their will, with many going into doctors to deliver children and coming out with their tubes tied. The motivation was population control for a community high in poverty. For some women who signed up to take this supposedly magical Enovid pill, their goal was to avoid the same fate. But instead they suffered the worst side effects and were given no relief for them. During the course of the trial, three Puerto Rican women died, and researchers never performed autopsies on their bodies.

Skepticism that outside medical intervention would make things better was perfectly logical to the people I'd come from.

"You know they just want to cut you open as soon as they get a chance to!" Mamí argued. "Your body will never be the same after that."

I was attending the best children's cancer and blood hospitals in the country, and she wanted me to try island medicine, as if I were treating the common cold. "You can't put Vick's on this, Mamí! I have a blood disease. This is serious," I replied, exasperated.

When I hung up, I told Dr. Jamison. I would do his Rituxan infusions. It would mean going into the hospital weekly while I continued to work on my thesis, but I was determined to get it done.

Then I foolishly told Mamí about my intentions to get down to Puerto Rico to try to interview another reggaetonera for my thesis. I got one of her usual letters. Mamí wasn't having it.

Subject: [empty]

*You are not to go to Puerto Rico the last 2 weeks of summer
because your father and I want you to rest, and we are taking you
to a specialist for a second opinion, and that is final.*

   *You can do your research in another city or in Syracuse.
Abuela said that her sisters all work and no one is free to do
anything for anyone. Right now she is stuck in the country. She
is coming to Syracuse cause she is blind and bleeding in one eye,
and has a lump again. The hospitals let people just lay in the
corridors (if emergency) unless you are rich. It is not like being
in the United States. You will have to figure out another way to
do the research.*

   *You are young, you are getting sick and your father and I want to
make sure nothing happens to you while we are alive and can help
you. I want you to ask Dr. Jamison to check you for Lupus.*

   *Your father and I are very worried about you. We love you and
want the best for you, but it is time to slow down, or you will end up
hurt badly.*

*This week I get paid and you will have 75 in your checking, so if
you need more let me know. Did you know a James Johnson? Let me
know. Love Mamí and daddy.*

The following week, I thought about Mamí's message to slow
down as I lay back in the chair. I went through my usual routine:
Took a deep breath. Chattered about the weather. And squeezed my
eyes tight as the nurse tried to find my vein.

Smack! I heard the plastic band tighten around my forearm. My
blood gathered in the swelling spot where she would poke to find a
vein. I tried hard to stay calm. To squeeze my fist so she would find
it. IVs were even worse than blood draws. And IVs in the hand were
the worst thing I could think of.

The GOLDEN girls surrounded me as I lay in the infusion chair. They'd taken time out of their classes to meet me at the center for my first rounds of treatment. "You got this, Tasha," Adaora said warmly.

They made small talk and jokes to make me laugh. Mamí and Daddy had to work and couldn't make it to Boston. In the end, all I had was my girls. I breathed out as the skinny IV plastic came in and the blood came out into the long tube. I felt the cool of the Rituxan antibody medicine infusing into my veins. I'd come too far to stop here.

———

A few months after my infusion, Dr. Jamison had called me into his office with news. "Your platelets look great, dear. You are officially no longer a chronic ITP patient."

I wanted to cry with joy, but instead I booked a trip to San Juan to finish the final interview I needed to do for my thesis project. It was the first time I'd been back to Puerto Rico since I was nine years old.

Reggaeton artist La Hill's song "Paso a Paso" was one of my favorites during my reggaeton research. La Hill's voice was gritty, like a female DMX, and she rode the beat effortlessly.

> pa' los machistas con un grado de egoista
> que en las producciones no quiere que canten damitas
> mejor que tu me sale el style y la rima
> a dios gracias por darme este color aunque tu misma presees
> que el tuyo es el mejor oye redneck cuidado con el sol no vaya
> a aser que te pongas negra como yo

> *and for the machos with a degree in egoism*
> *who don't want women to sing in albums*
> *my rhymes and style are much better than yours*

to God, thank you for giving me this color
even though you presume
that yours is better,
hey redneck be careful with the sun
that it doesn't make you as black as me

La Hill was proudly Black, talented, and unafraid to call out sexism in her industry. This was an example of the kind of womanist ideology I wanted to argue existed in reggaeton music for my thesis.

Somehow, with my broken Spanish, I had reached her on My-Space.com, coordinating an interview where we'd meet up in the hotel lobby of La Concha in San Juan to talk.

We would have to wait for her to get off work, because she had a nine-to-five. Apparently reggaeton didn't pay all the bills.

It was dark at La Concha, but I walked in, following the directions she'd given, and there she was, sitting by the pool on a chair.

We hugged, and she signaled that we could sit.

We decided that I would ask the questions that I'd prepared in English, and she would respond in Spanish. It was an odd yet serene exchange for me, a sort of reversal of what I'd experienced my entire life, where they spoke Spanish and I replied in English. And yet I was home in Puerto Rico.

La Hill spoke in soaring monologues, her raspy voice still melodic, almost as if she were rapping. "For us women it is very difficult. When I started in this business there were several men that offered to have sex with me. I said, 'Whoa.' A DJ said to me, 'In order for you to get initiated or get started you have to sleep with me.' So there isn't machismo, but ego. . . . But for me, it does not interfere. I don't get involved. I don't sleep with the men. I keep walking by." I consider myself from the lowest class, the ghetto. I have felt like that [the lowest], but I have used it to succeed and used it for reggaeton."

I was grateful that she brought up class because it allowed me to understand a connection that was important—the ways that class and the darkness of one's skin intersect to determine one's destiny on the island. People often use class or someone's "poorness" as a proxy for race.

"What are your experiences with racism?" I asked, holding my tape recorder close.

She sighed. "One day I went to a network program similar to ones on MTV in Miami. When I was walking down the hall, I heard a woman say, 'UGH, negra.' I heard that, and you know I felt sad, but then I said to myself, *This negra, God made her. And I love my color.*"

La Hill went on talking, with very few interruptions from me, as I tried to process in real time everything she was saying. Her Spanish was much more rapid and hard to decipher in real time than I expected, and I regretted not bringing a translator. After we wrapped, I immediately ran back to the condo, uploaded the audio, and emailed it to Mamí, asking her to help me translate instead.

Before I left Puerto Rico, I stopped by a small tattoo shop in a strip mall in San Juan. I wanted a souvenir, a reminder of my first trip back.

"This, this is what I want," I said, showing the man a picture I'd printed off the internet. "You can put it right on my right hip." It was a Taino cave painting of the island's national animal, a coqui.

I grimaced as the needle went in and out, surprised that a tattoo so small could still hurt so much. Now Puerto Rico would be with me wherever I went.

———

By the time I landed in Cambridge, it was time to get to work. I had interviews with both of my case studies, La Sista and La Hill, and I could finally form the words I needed to articulate an answer to the driving question of my work: Was Black feminist consciousness being expressed in reggaeton?

I titled my thesis "Towards a New Morena Consciousness." Veronica and Adaora blessed me with help, copyediting, and reading chapters before I turned it in.

I printed the pages in the copy room of Dunster and then boarded the shuttle to the quad, running with fury to reach the Social Studies 10 office to turn it in before the deadline. I'd done it. What had seemed an impossible academic feat was not impossible after all.

Two weeks later, I received feedback on my paper. It turned out my two graders had starkly different views. One, a specialist in pop culture studies and identity, whose work I was familiar with, gave it high marks. But as I turned to the second reader's remarks, it became clear she did not like it. In fact, it seemed she hated it. That reader, a graduate student, said there were weaknesses in my methodology.

So a third reader had been brought in as the tie-breaker; she too was a graduate student, and she gave me worse marks than the second. I looked at her comment on the paper: "Sounds like you're just a fan of reggaeton, who wanted to write a thesis about music you like." That couldn't be further from the truth. This was music that had the power to inspire negras everywhere—a diasporic connection worth plugging into.

I feared the thesis grades would put my overall honors status in jeopardy. As soon as I processed the news, I hurriedly rushed back to my room and googled my graders, looking for details about who they were. The two low graders were getting PhDs. One was African American and a resident tutor, and the other Nigerian. I felt an irrational pang of betrayal.

The thesis wasn't perfect. It had flaws. But how could neither of them, Black women who surely knew how hard it was to walk this road, find one positive thing to say about my work? They had no idea of the hurdles I'd overcome to be here. It seemed that after trying my best to learn this language, the language of academia, and speak the way these university people spoke, it wasn't enough.

I wish I could say I took it on the chin, licked my wounds, and counted my blessings for having successfully completed the program I'd set out to prove I could complete. But I did not. I needed something that attested to this struggle being worth it. So I wrote an email complaining to the head of the social studies concentration,

Dr. Klaus, who promised to look into it for me, although I ultimately let any challenging of my grade go. What real power or proof did I have that I deserved better?

Although I managed to get cum laude honors for my major, that didn't translate to honors from the university—an important fact I didn't know when I'd signed up for the grueling program. "What a waste of time," I thought, wishing I'd pursued an easier major so I could've spent my senior year partying and not stuck in the library. Though Raquel Rivera, the generous Puerto Rican journalist from New York City, had offered to help me publish parts of my work, I was so disheartened by the experience that I didn't follow through or press for guidance on making it happen.

I couldn't help thinking about my research paper from Professor Matory's class, which now seemed prophetic: "Dual Invisibility: Afro-Latino Experiences at Harvard and Beyond."

Inside these Ivy walls, it didn't seem like the story of the Afro-Latino was seen as serious business—at least the way I'd written it, I figured.

If only I had looked to the lessons of La Sista's own words in that moment, I might have seen the salve for my aching ego:

> Tu no puedes ver
> Lo que puedo ver yo . . .
> Dame le merecumbé
> Contigo yo me cure

> *You cannot see what I can . . .*
> *Give me merecumbé,*
> *With you, I will heal myself*

No degree or grade or outside validation could be a proxy for self-worth. Beside some walls, especially these Ivy ones, you could be left waiting forever for others to see what you could. To see your Black majesty. Still, that spring, when senior photo time came around, inspired by the women I'd met in Puerto Rico, the women I'd met through history in my Af-Am courses, I decided to break a rule I'd followed all my young life. Instead of the long, pressed, straightened hairstyle I had been trained to wear in professional settings, I went with a slightly different look: my Black graduation gown, pearl earrings, and a nice, big, natural curly Afro.

10

Sell Out

The tension in the room oozed out of the doors. I sat at a boardroom conference table in the Charles Hotel, the lights low, as seven other sweaty seniors in blazers and button-up shirts looked around intensely.

"So, what is justice? Let's hear it," asked a polo-wearing brown-haired investment associate who'd only graduated a few years before us.

I was in a group interview for the largest institutional hedge fund in the world. Just a month ago, I couldn't have told you what a hedge fund was. But now I was in my own version of Shark Tank with other soon-to-be graduates. We were pitching ourselves for another kind of golden ticket—a six-figure job offer right out of college at an infamous, unconventional investment firm known for its culture of "radical honesty" and meritocracy.

I never would've thought of myself as being here with these people. I'd spent four years trying to position myself to be "somebody" upon leaving college—launching a magazine at the Harvard College Women's Center, where I now worked alongside feminists and LGBTQ+ activists—far from the circle my old fundamentalist Baptist pastors would've likely approved of. I'd gone to New Orleans after Hurricane Katrina to build houses with Habitat for Humanity, and even made it on a new campus comedy TV show, which was our version of Jon Stewart's *Daily Show*. But with each little résumé boost acquired, I still wasn't quite sure who I was or where to go next.

Harvard had a reputation for attracting big consulting and

financial firms to campus who were thirsty for Ivy League grads in their entry-level ranks. Recruiting felt like a well-established factory, and we were pushed through the process with machinelike precision. Firms hosted fancy events on campus, wooing undergrads with free Brie cheese and meals to sell them on their company's benefits.

SPECIAL EVENT!

An Invitation from McKinsey & Company
Interested in CONSULTING? Come through!

Our inboxes were flooded multiple times daily with opportunities to work for consulting firms, investment banks, and hedge funds that doled out big salary offers to a lucky bunch of twentysomethings, training them and, in return, demanding sixty-to-eighty-hour weeks to boost profit margins over the next several years. It fit Harvard's careerist culture—it was a place where some people plotted their job moves from the moment they stepped on campus.

The limited entry-level career tracks meant that students who had spent all four years cultivating different interests in history, anthropology, fashion, social justice, even African American studies, would still get caught up in the corporate recruitment machine, forsaking their real interests for a shot at a good income and stability. "Out of Harvard, and Into Finance," read a 2011 *New York Times* article. According to the article, in 2008, the year I graduated, 28 percent of us went into finance. This was during the Great Recession, when college kids of all backgrounds were going out with their diplomas into a depressed labor market.

With the exception of those born privileged, or super brave, who could take low-to-no paying internships and entry-level jobs, many of us needed to have an assured professional path queued up for graduation, and were getting our first shot in life to move ourselves and even our families into a new tax bracket.

Mamí had been pushing for me to take a year off school to deal with my ITP. To graduate a year later without shame felt like a luxury someone other than me could have. So I found myself at an interview for a hedge fund—having landed a job this early in my senior year would mean there was one less thing to worry about on the path to graduation. If I could score an offer, my life would be almost set, even if my health hung in the balance.

I wouldn't have seen myself as hedge fund material if it weren't for Mary, a fellow finals club member who had also faced health issues in her college years and understood the unreliability of a body that betrays you. She was a blond girl from the Midwest; on paper we couldn't seem more different. But Mary was one of the most genuine people I'd ever met—a person I could always be the most relaxed version of myself with. After I disclosed my illness to her, she wrote me at the start of the school year with hematologist recommendations and a note:

> I gave Bridgewater (the company i worked for) your name as they begin full-time recruiting. I don't know what direction you are thinking of going in after graduation, but I'd love to talk with you about this place, my experience, and why I think you would be a huge asset to them and also why I think you'd like it there.

I was both flattered and intimidated. I didn't fit the profile. I had only done internships in public service and education, mentoring kids in the Harvard Summer Academy or working at a foster care nonprofit in New York City. Where did my study of politics, intersectionality, history, and Afro-Latinidad fit in there? But she had in mind a management associate role, intended to cultivate future bosses of the company, sort of an internal consultant who would implement the company's unique nonhierarchical culture and principles of organizational leadership.

I could see myself being a boss one day, albeit in public service or government. And a lack of any corporate experience on my résumé felt like a weakness—a flaw that screamed that I possibly couldn't make it in "those" circles. Maybe there was something to learn. I thanked Mary for passing my name along and thinking of me, promising to attend an information session. What did I have to lose? I probably wouldn't get a job offer anyway.

Since Harvard was full of student overachievers—from Olympians to published authors—my mindset was, if you weren't already excellent at something in college, it probably wasn't worth trying. It hadn't even occurred to me that things I naturally enjoyed like launching the gender studies magazine at the Women's Center, or interviewing subjects during my thesis or anchoring that comedy news show, could be considered journalism. Tragically, at twenty-one, I just felt it was too late to pursue that professionally. Plus Veronica was the journalist in our group, and she was damn good. She was destined to have bylines.

The only other track that felt equally safe and attractive was a program called Teach for America. TFA, founded by a Princeton alum, just so happened to be the next-biggest recruiter outside of Wall Street firms on campus. The elite two-year program recruited top college grads to become educators in underserved classrooms that desperately needed teachers. TFA had been both praised and maligned: it was fertile ground for young leaders, but it put teachers into needy classrooms only to see them leave for law school and greater ambitions, their résumé padded with leadership skills and public service. To critics, the model seemed well intentioned, but they insisted the inconsistency and short-term commitment hurt students.

"We are creating the leaders of tomorrow!" a high-energy sandy blond recruiter named Brad explained during the info session I attended in the Dunster House event room. The table was covered with free snacks, cheese, and desserts. "Beyond your two years, Teach for America will teach you skills that can be translated anywhere. But the true goal is impact. It's measurable and it's real, what our teachers accomplish in the classroom."

The TFA recruiter sold a different vision than what critics said—that it created a pipeline for college grads who would've never taught otherwise, and many chose to stay in education long-term.

Even Mamí had been pressing me to consider teaching again. "M'ija, you would make a great teacher! So many of our kids don't see examples like you in the classroom. You get summers off too. Think about it."

I felt conflicted here too. I'd spent my entire education trying to get out of a broken school system, where the majority of working-class kids and kids of color seemed set up to fail. Mamí had been a public school teacher for two decades at this point. The pay sucked, and the hours were unrelenting, save the few summer months teachers got off to restore their sanity. Why, after fighting so hard to get to college—this college—would I sign up to go back to that? To be a cog in a wheel of a broken system? I was afraid of people saying, "You went to Harvard to become a teacher?" It was yet another reflection of how much we undervalue the teaching profession in our society, and as a twentysomething, I got the message loud and clear.

Although my heart pumped with excitement at that TFA info session, inspired by the idea of leading a classroom and making a difference, I never finished my application once things started to advance with Bridgewater. I had a very shiny interruption.

———

The hedge fund's top executives, including COOs and CIOs, sat casually mixed in with us student interviewees at the conference table, peppering us with questions and challenging us in front of each other. This was the second round of the process. I'd done this debate format before, but the group was much smaller and the setting more intimate, with just three people in one of our career counselor office rooms. To get ready for it, I'd practiced with Mary, some other applicants, and my best friend Tommy, another Black student leader who wanted to cross into the corporate world. But here at the Charles, the group was larger, the intensity higher, and the candidates ping-ponged answers across the room, words zipping by like cars on the freeway, barely listening to each other before getting a word in.

I'd have a thought and pause, unsure if it was worth saying. Then someone would say what I was thinking. Time was running out—the interview was scheduled for only forty minutes—so I saw an opening and jumped in, making a minor point that piggybacked off another. A Southeast Asian guy with short, dark hair slightly agreed with me but offered another point. The ping-pong continued. I jumped in once more to make a point phrased as a question. And just like that, the clock was up. Interview over.

The dread in my stomach settled. I'd failed.

Not only was I the only Black Latina in the room, but I'd managed to avoid speaking up or taking center stage. I shrank, fearing my voice wasn't substantive enough. Sweat trickled on my forehead, making my hair frizz. I might as well have packed my bags and gone home, but I still had two more one-on-one interviews with hedge fund executives to finish.

Just finish with some dignity. So they know you took it seriously.

I walked into a small hotel room in the corridor. A petite white woman with dark-brown hair and thin-rimmed glasses was sitting in a chair. She stood up to shake my hand, looking at me intently. "Hello, I'm Sloan Givens."

"Hello, I'm Natasha. Thank you so much for making time to meet," I said with a smile.

"So, tell me about yourself, Natasha."

It was simple. I gave Sloan my entire life story. From Syracuse to college. Stories of overcoming fear at oratory competitions and fighting to get resources for Black women on campus. She nodded along as if she understood the unspoken as well.

"Why do you want to work at Bridgewater as a management associate?" she asked me.

"Honestly, the things you value as a firm—truth, honesty, calling it like it is—that's how I live my everyday life. I'm not afraid to speak up or challenge authority when needed. And I want to learn what it takes to lead and build great organizations."

Sloan nodded along.

"You're looking for the next generation of managers. People who can lead from day one. My work as president of the Association of Black Harvard Women has taught me how to motivate people to reach a goal, with inspiration and not just authority. This job is all about cultivating leaders who can impart Bridgewater's culture. I know a lot about creating positive culture because I've done it here. As women, we've often been seen as underdogs, but it's been my mission to raise our profile on campus because we have something to offer too."

We shook hands.

"Great to meet you, Natasha," Sloan said with the same smile and even tone. I had no idea whether I'd done well or not. After my final one-on-one interview with Polo Shirt Guy, I left and strolled back along the Charles River toward the houses.

Back in my room at Dunster, I fell into my black-metal-frame twin bed, unbuttoning my blazer, kicking off my shoes, and wiping away quiet tears. Shame sat in my belly. I'd had an opportunity to get a good job, had the backing of multiple people within the company, and I still blew it because after all these years, I was afraid to sound stupid in front of people I didn't know. It seemed no matter what I did to prepare, I couldn't shake this fear of looking foolish.

I called Tommy, who'd also completed his interview with Bridgewater.

"I bombed, Tommy. Like I froze and barely said the things I could've said in the moment. I am so embarrassed—straight-up humiliated."

"Ugh, I'm so sorry, Tasha, I hate to hear that," he said softly. "Listen, don't be so hard on yourself. You did the best you can do, and that's all that matters. You are brilliant and talented. What's for you will be for you."

"Thank you, Tommy," I said gratefully. Tommy always knew the right thing to say. The sooner I forgot about this whole thing, the better I'd feel.

Two weeks later I was sitting in my bed in Dunster House, staring out the window at the annoyingly loud construction of brand-new graduate apartments across the street, when the phone rang.

"Hey Natasha, it's Cara," said the fiery petite Bridgewater recruiter I'd been corresponding with over the past month. I sat up straight in my black metal twin bed.

"Hi Cara! It's great to hear from you," I said, somewhat surprised that she was calling.

"I just wanted to let you know it's been a pleasure to get to know you throughout this entire process. . . . To get to the point, would you want to work at Bridgewater? Because we'd love to have you."

I couldn't believe what I was hearing. They picked me? I felt like a fourteen-year-old all over again, onstage at that oratorical competition where I'd forgotten my speech. How was my perception of how I was doing, how I had performed, so far off from how other people saw me? It seemed my selective memory was a mean girl, showing me only the worst things about my performance. Whatever I thought they were looking for, perhaps I was wrong.

"Oh WOW! This is amazing news—thank you, Cara!!" I replied, gushing.

Only eleven other Harvard seniors had been offered jobs at the hedge fund that year—and the only other Black person was my friend Miles, the jazz saxophonist and brilliant mathematician I'd met at BSA. He was headed to the investment side of the company. We lucky admits would have a starting salary of at least six figures—$100,000— way more than the average twenty-one-year-old was expecting to make right after college in 2008. It was more than Mamí and Daddy ever made in their lifetime, separately or combined. It was many zeros beyond what Abuela Sonia had made at the bacon factory, or what Grandpa Lee had to slog to at Crucible Steel each day. It was pretty much a no-brainer—I was accepting the job offer.

I'd won the lottery securing a job this early in my senior year at a time when people were still applying, and now I could focus on finishing my Afro-Latina reggaeton thesis and figure out my ITP treatment plan. Miles and I had gotten the ultimate golden ticket, and as small as the Black community was, word spread fast in our circles. Most of my peers were celebrating with me, giving me that extra nod of approval for getting into the fabled firm, including Tommy, who'd congratulated me with joy once he heard the good news. But a couple days later I got a call as I sat at my dorm desk, typing away on my thesis.

"Hey . . . ," Tommy said, sounding forlorn.

"Hey Tommy, what's up? Are you okay, what's wrong? You sound down."

"I didn't get the job at Bridgewater. . . . I literally can't believe this. How could they not give it to me?"

"Oh my God . . . I'm sorry, Tommy. Damn, that sucks. That's their loss for real. You would've been *so* great."

I was trying to muster as much positivity as I could. That familiar feeling of guilt crept in through the conversation.

"It just doesn't make sense how you got it, and I didn't. . . . You said you struggled in your interview. Maybe it was because you were a girl or something. I mean, only a few people got offers this year."

It felt like getting smacked in the face. "Really, Tommy? How could you say that to me? You're supposed to be my best friend— and you think I don't deserve the job? How could you even *fix* your mouth to say that to me?" I huffed.

"Look, look, I'm sorry, I didn't mean it that way, I just . . . I shouldn't have said that. I was just trying to make sense of it all. It's fine."

The damage had been done, though. Just like that, the cloud of joy I was floating on over my job offer at Bridgewater dissipated. I tried to forgive Tommy; I knew it was disappointment that led him to say that to me. But his words were planted in my mind. Was my being a woman, a Black woman in particular, why they gave me the job? Tommy was brilliant. I also couldn't fathom why he'd been passed up. I almost wished he'd gotten the job instead of me, so this wouldn't be between us.

I was still sorting through my mixed feelings when, weeks later, I got a Facebook message:

> Tasha, reality is reality. Working for a hedge fund or other similar institutions is detrimental to the hood on numerous levels. i can't hope to dissuade you from such a path since you've probably already signed on (have you?) A hedge fund functions to concentrate and increase the wealth of the already wealthy. this is antithetical to economic justice. the more the wealthy have the less the poor have on a very basic, seesaw kind of level. if you did work in a field such as the one you're entering i feel that your talents would be much better used giving financial advice/managing the investments of people from poor/working class backgrounds.
>
> Those management and leadership skills you talked about can be developed in myriad other settings. you know what is honestly the best training you can get for that? teaching
>
> i say all this to say that, in the words of one of my idols—angela davis—"Revolution is a serious thing, the most serious thing about a revolutionary's life. when one commits oneself to the struggle, it must be for a lifetime . . ."
>
> Ade

Adebayo, or Ade, as we called him, was a recent Harvard grad I idolized for being a social justice changemaker, who'd just completed a teaching residency in the rural South. He laid out his thoughts methodically and passionately, like a prosecutor before the judge. I was being confronted and called to the carpet by someone who looked like me for selling out and working for "the man." I felt guilty as charged. I responded to him with thanks and a promise that I was doing what was best for me, and would be sure to give back later.

But I was just one person. Hundreds of Ivy League kids went off to corporations each year. Why did I have to be the one held to a higher standard?

Nobody ever wanted to be a sellout, but because I was choosing to take an opportunity in finance and live a better lifestyle financially, I was now betraying the ancestors? From Tyler Perry movies to rom-coms, the educated, rich, successful Black person seemed to always be the jerk. It didn't mean I had to be.

Students like me who came from working-class backgrounds, were trying to make it into the same networks and jobs that many of the most socially conscious among us denounced. At the heart of Ade's concern was that I was betraying my own gifts for the immediate dopamine hit of financial security, and I had an added responsibility not to do so because I was Black.

But I wanted to make my family proud by not relying on them and being able to take care of myself. *That* was success where I came from. This *was* a good leadership opportunity—a rare chance to have a management role so early in my career. I'd pick up skills that would translate to the real world, where I would eventually go back and serve my people—once I got rich, of course. I would figure that out later. But for now, I was going to enjoy my free ride.

During graduation, I sat in Memorial Church and reflected on how the journey to this college had changed me. I was a *sancocho* of contradictions. I had not become the card-carrying liberal Pastor Jake had warned me about years ago, but I was more accepting of other people and ways of life than I had been when I left Syracuse. I wanted a more just world and the elimination of racism, sexism, and poverty, but I did not understand how I was supposed to make a difference coming from a working-class family if I didn't use my new education and privilege to move up in that world.

I watched as President Drew Faust, Harvard's first woman

president in its 370-plus-year history, took the high podium to offer a word of advice during baccalaureate service.

"Life is long. There is always time for plan B. But don't begin with it," President Faust insisted.

"I think of this as my parking space theory of career choice, and I have been sharing it with students for decades: Don't park twenty blocks from your destination because you think you'll never find a space. Go where you *want* to be and then circle back to where you *have* to be."

I questioned: Was where I was headed where I actually wanted to be or where I thought I had to be? I wasn't 100 percent sure, but there was only one way to find out.

———

One year after college graduation, I was in the bathroom stall. Visiting the stalls in the afternoons was how I passed the time after sitting in back-to-back meetings.

I'd already learned a few things about the benefits of working at a hedge fund thus far. It was a nice feeling buying everyone the Christmas presents they wanted: for Daddy, his own CD maker; for Mamí, tickets to her first Broadway show, *In the Heights,* by a Puerto Rican guy named Lin-Manuel Miranda—the only kind of Broadway show I could see us being interested in, since it promised salsa dancing, reggaeton, and hip-hop. "Wow Tasha, thank you! You didn't have to do that," Mamí exclaimed in shock as she opened the present, and I sipped on *coquito* in the background, satisfied. I had my own place, a huge one-bedroom condo in Stamford, Connecticut, a nearly new used car I'd bought for myself, and on my twenty-third birthday I rented a limo for my friends and I to go to the club, with full bottle service. So why was I hiding in the bathroom?

I went back to my desk and reopened an old email from Mamí before my next meeting.

Subject: Mamí
May 5, 2008

Boonky, I like the apartment advice from Bridgewater, Norwalk
sounds like the cheapest, closest to work, and you get more for
your money. I read the "Onboarding" stuff and "social activities"
calendar they sent you. As far as the parties for the new
employees that does not impress me because corporate america
has always been about getting drunk, making money, etc.

My advice is to go in and do your job, keep your private
business private, not drink at their functions (keep it clean, soda,
1 glass of wine), and be on your way to your home life. It can be
dangerous to get caught into their world. There is nothing wrong
with enjoying certain benefits of a job, but the drinking does not
have to be done.

Work, save your money and go for what you want to do in life.
If it is to be a lawyer, or work in an area that makes a difference
in young people. Something that gives you a purpose in life. How
can you make a difference and leave a legacy for those who are
not empowered. Even though I complain about teaching the youth
today, I would never trade it for an office job.

That is great that the company does a lot of socializing, but
always keep in the back of your head what your daddy always
taught you, because he is still going through it trying to make ends
meet in a world that is unfair because of your gender or your skin.

This may sound like I am being negative, but I am not, just like
we say always watch your back in the corporate world (you know
what I mean). I will download the rental guide and check out some
places. your package arrives on Wednesday.

love Mamí

Mamí told me before I even left to start my first day of work to
keep my eyes open toward a job with a greater calling. She knew

nothing about *"ese mundo"*—that world of finance—but she did have a hunch that I wouldn't fit in.

In the beginning, I thought she was being Debbie Downer, the overprotective Latina mom who still, no matter how many times I described to her what I was heading off to do, could not repeat it back to me. When you are navigating spheres that your parents haven't navigated before, seeing and doing things they've never seen or done, it can be easy to dismiss them. But now I saw that Mamí was a sage who knew the future. And I didn't know how to build a bridge from where I was to where I needed to be.

Things had started out promising at the firm. On my first day of work, I drove into a parking lot full of Maseratis, BMWs, Range Rovers, and Benzes, and knew I'd entered a different realm. The company was located in an isolated forest enclave in Westport, Connecticut, a world unto itself, with a beautiful sprawling campus that felt more like a wellness retreat than work. The walls were mostly glass, a nod to the company's deep commitment to a radical culture of transparency.

I'd been assigned to what was the most coveted team on the management side—the core management team led by the hedge fund's famed billionaire founder, Ray Dalio. It was my job, along with three other MAs, to support Ray's senior managers at the firm. We would serve as "leveragers," essentially chief-of-staff-like consultants, who observed their management of departments and worked to make it better.

Ray had also recently drafted a management guidebook of sorts called *Principles*, a collection of his rules and approach to keeping Bridgewater's culture the unique culture it was. This meant meritocracy over hierarchy—a meager recent college grad like myself could challenge a manager who'd been there for years if their idea didn't make sense. Transparency over decision-making was so prized that tape recorders were installed in nearly every conference room so conversations could be recorded. While some outsiders blasted the culture as "cultlike," Ray insisted that it was the outside world that had it wrong. He believed that the problem with most companies was the tyranny of hierarchy that suppressed great ideas, let egos run wild, and buried problems that people were too afraid to escalate.

At first I drank the Kool-Aid like it came from a family reunion plastic jug. It sounded that good to me. After years of being told I had too much mouth and constantly getting in trouble for challenging authority and calling it like it was, I found this culture to be a dream come true. In the first months, MAs were tasked with sitting in meetings and just learning culture.

"You guys don't know shit. You're dumb shits," was a common refrain. "But it's okay to be a dumb shit if you know it. The point is to learn and observe as much as you can." It felt like a mini business school, one where MAs went to Bridgewater case studies and even got to "probe" (our word for interrogate) real staff members over real business problems, although I left some probing sessions feeling uneasy.

I managed to make good friends and enjoy myself socially at the firm. My finals club experience had prepared me for it. One Halloween-night event, I dressed as Rihanna and danced to her song "Umbrella" while people circled around and clapped like I was RihRih herself. I was the only Latina girl, let alone Black girl, in my management associate class. Ironically, that would not be the only factor that made me an outlier.

"Everyone be sure to log in for your Myers-Briggs test!" a peppy HR rep told us in our first weeks at the firm as we sat at our laptops. According to Ray's principles, knowing ourselves as managers was as important as knowing the people we'd be building culture with, and so we each were assigned a Myers-Briggs personality test, which categorized us into sixteen different personality types, mine being ENFP: Extraverted Intuitive Feeling Perceiving.

After taking the test, it turned out I was the only person in my entire class who tested with an F ("Feeling") instead of a T ("Thinking") preference. I stared down at the printed report as it explained that F people preferred people-centered, values-based decision-making over logical, objective analysis. Great. Now I really stood out.

But it was once I was paired with my senior manager that I got the ultimate reality check about the hedge fund job. Although I was on the core management team, my manager had been sent to revamp the one department I couldn't have cared less about: IT. That's right, information technology.

This was the department that handled keeping the company's website running. Procurement. Handing out laptops. And ensuring there was internet security around very important trade secrets. Basically, the most boring department I could've joined, considering my background.

My work consisted of long, intense meetings. Data tracking. Helping probe people. Observing. "Supporting" my manager. The more I did it, the more it all felt intangible. With the exception of the special core team meetings I got to attend, where I had a front-row seat for Ray's thoughts on building company culture, now *I* couldn't explain to anyone back home what I did: the hedge fund had its own rules.

All this was happening as the larger world was changing around me. Barack Obama had been elected the first Black president in U.S. history, shifting the axis of the entire earth toward new political possibilities, yet in my department there was barely conversation about it the next day. Headlines were covering what was being called a growing movement to change America's public schools, but here I was in a cushy isolated finance building. Friends were launching blogs and using technology where digital articles were going viral and mattered as much as what was printed in newspapers, a total paradigm shift. I had no outlet for my true voice at a hedge fund. It turns out I had parked in the first spot I saw, and now I had a long way to walk to my ideal destination.

I'd tried to build a life in Connecticut that would allow me to stay put. I belonged to an AME Black Baptist church and helped lead the young adult ministry. I was studying Spanish via Rosetta

Stone during my commute, and for the GMAT on weekends. But I still wanted more—something that couldn't be bought. Mamí's words from her old email to me hung in the air: I had to break out of my golden handcuffs.

"So why haven't any of you done this week's assignment?" Ray's voice boomed throughout the conference room later that week, as every management associate and senior manager on the core team sat quiet as a church mouse. The majority of MAs had fallen off on their case studies and homework, something that became apparent in the boardroom.

"We need to probe to the root of this issue. So let's go down the line." One by one he called on each MA to explain to the group why they hadn't finished. As he got closer to me, my heartbeat picked up. I'd been toying with the idea of leaving the hedge fund but didn't know how to break free. The moment called for something bold. Something fearless. Something only a young and dumb person would do.

"And you? Why didn't you complete the homework?"

"I've actually been trying to figure out if this role is for me," I told the entire room as they looked on quietly. "It might not be a fit."

Ray looked at me briefly. "Sounds like something you should work through," he said sincerely without a hint of sarcasm, before going on to probe the next person.

It was a huge gamble. I could've been fired on the spot. But instead what it served as was the ultimate kick in the ass to find my next job. By announcing it to the room, I had essentially set a deadline to leave for myself. No one was going to beg me to stay in this cushy job, where we sat around talking philosophically all day about management. Miles, my Harvard classmate, had long gone from the firm, and the Kool-Aid that kept me so intoxicated initially had started to wear off.

It was time to move on. But to where?

Over the next few months, it took discipline, ordering fewer clothes and Domino's Pizza and redirecting each paycheck toward paying off my car, spending every night combing job sites. Teach for America's deadline had long passed, so I couldn't circle back on that, but maybe education was an area I still could pursue. Then I found it.

"Tash, you should check out this site called Idealist.com," Adaora chatted to me one day after our usual postwork Google hangout unwinding. She had moved back to her hometown of the Bronx and was working at a nonprofit, a perfect fit for her résumé and profile. But even she yearned for uncharted territory, and we'd daydream out loud to each other about really doing something novel with these college degrees.

"Thanks, girl, I'll give it a try. I just know I gotta get out of here soon, now that they know I want to leave. The worst thing would be getting fired from a place I don't wanna be at anymore."

The search would be easier than expected. After filtering jobs based on location and interests, one opening popped up at a brand-new charter middle school in Washington Heights, the same neighborhood I'd seen depicted in that Broadway play. The school offered a unique proposition—it would scrimp on unnecessary expenses to pay teachers a whopping salary of $125,000 annually. They would hire only the best of the best, and give these children—mostly Dominican American—a real shot at equity.

The available job was that of a Leadership Fellow—a versatile role that would pay far less than $125,000 but instead offer $35,000 for an energetic go-getter who would do everything possible to help run the school its first year, from packing lunches to managing communications with parents. This would mean a $65,000 pay cut for me but I didn't care.

Instead of hiding in the bathroom at lunch, I started working on my application. When I applied and got an interview, I laid my entire heart on the line. The principal, who happened to be a Teach for America alum, wanted to know why I was willing to walk away from such a high-paying job to sort papers, answer phones, change ink in the copy machine and get my hands dirty, literally and figuratively.

"I didn't come this far to stay comfortable," I told him, sitting outside on a metal bench near the trailers where the school was based, since they had no building. "The kids in Washington Heights and at this school look just like me," I continued, explaining that I was moved by the premise of equity, both as a Black Latina and as the daughter of an educator.

I waited on pins and needles every day. The principal told me the job was very competitive, but he would circle back as soon as he could. I sent thank-you notes to as many people as possible and prayed to God for some favor in the process. As I listened to Mamí describe some of the realities of worsening poverty she saw back in our hometown, I second-guessed if I was making the right decision.

Two weeks later, I got the offer and, almost a year after my start date, put in official notice at the hedge fund and packed my U-Haul to head to New York City.

Back home in Syracuse, the news had spread about my move, thanks to an article by Sean Kirst, one of the local *Post Standard* journalists who'd documented my public speaking journey from high school.

"Nottingham Grad Forfeits Cash for a Calling," his story headline read.

To my surprise, when I scrolled down to read comments, a relatively new feature of newspaper articles, the majority of them were nasty.

"Why was she making that much money to begin with?! For a major in SOCIAL STUDIES?" one commenter wrote.

"Big deal!" typed another.

In that moment I had an epiphany. I was no longer the underdog-city-school-poster-kid to root for—I was now considered to be an elite, a person of privilege by virtue of my education regardless of nothing materially changing for my family. Whatever difference I wanted to make in society, I should do without expectation of applause or anyone's approval. Now I was back in the real world and it was time to serve.

Miss Education "

In Washington Heights, I met myself. Living in Harlem and commuting to work uptown every day, I answered phones, changed ink on copy machines, played crossing guard for kids at the dangerous intersection where the group of trailers that comprised the school sat, and did whatever it took to help the little school in the big city run.

The students at Washington Heights Charter were observant, thoughtful, caring and funny fifth graders. After an entire year of working with finance and business people in the woods of Connecticut, I was learning just how magical it was to be surrounded by children all day long. Their questions and their innocence—and sometimes their lack of innocence—made me hyperaware of the example I was providing them.

The benefit of working in Washington Heights was that I was hearing the most Spanish I'd heard since leaving Mamí's home. With the mostly Dominican students and parents I served, I again was reminded of my connection to the Afro-Latin diaspora, seeing it now through the lens of mostly second- and third-generation kids who'd grown up as Americanized New Yorkers. Some of them spoke Spanglish or with various levels of Spanish fluency. Many listened to hip-hop (with a few frequently dropping the N-word much to my vexation). Had I grown up here, in Wash Heights, I would've visually blended right in too.

African American students were the minority in this predominately Latino school, which I found fascinating. (There were no white students whatsoever.) While I didn't witness major racial

incidents between the two groups, I nevertheless was able to identify on some level with the generational African American students'
unspoken outsider status.

My year as a leadership fellow flew by, and soon I'd be met with
another major decision: Would I be ready to head up my own classroom?

First I applied to a traditional graduate program to become a
teacher. But after submitting my application, I got disappointing
news: in order to be a K–12 social studies teacher, I'd need to enroll
in multiple extension courses—seven, to be exact—to meet the program requirements.

The prerequisites felt so ridiculous, outdated, and out of touch. I
came from a working-class family—one that required financial aid
to attend college—and here I was being told that I had to pay out of
pocket to go *back* to school to enter a profession that wasn't going to
pay me much. There had to be a better, easier way.

And so I went all the way back to where it started. I shot an email
to the Teach for America recruiter I'd met two years earlier and told
him that I was ready to apply.

———

I thought I was being pranked. I stared at the principal in shock and
tried to keep my composure.

"I know, it's unexpected, but you will be just fine. You're in great
hands, trust me!" he said, a smile flashing across his face. I stared
at his receding sandy brown hairline as he fumbled with papers on
the desks.

I had only been a middle school English teacher at DC City Charter, located in Washington, DC, where I now lived, for two weeks,
and the man who had hired me—who'd sold me on this grand vision
for changing students' lives in the neighborhood where I worked—
was now jumping ship and quitting. Two. Weeks. Into. The. School.
Year. At a time when we needed a leader the most.

The next few months were exactly the trial by fire I'd predicted it was going to be. Nothing prepares you for the grind of getting up at 5:00 a.m. every day, Monday to Friday, and being *the* adult to almost a hundred children at different stages of their educational development. Teaching middle school isn't for punks. There's a reason people give so much respect to middle school teachers, and that's because you're a teacher, parent, social worker, negotiator, and peacekeeper all in one.

I decorated my bulletin boards, handcrafting signs for different HBCUs and colleges—Morehouse, Spelman, Howard, Stanford, and, of course, Harvard. I wanted my kids to be eager and inspired by the legacies of Black colleges and universities, the same way I was in middle school, while knowing that they were also valuable enough to have an array of options, especially with Howard University right down the street.

I crowdfunded for brand-new books on Facebook from all my college friends and some of my former colleagues, and set up an inspiring library for my students that featured Black protagonists, illustrators, and authors. I called Mamí daily, this being the first time in our lives that we shared a project in common—something I could seek out her guidance on and absorb her wisdom as a veteran teacher.

Unlike at Washington Heights Charter back in New York, nearly all of my students at DC City Charter were Black, specifically African American. There would be only five Latino students and not a single white one. I really was in Chocolate City now.

During the next two years, I would become the teacher I had been in denial about wanting to become all my life. It turns out Mamí was right: I had a knack for the job. Going into education was like flipping on a light switch in my head and heart. My students were my world, and they gave me a reason to get up at 5:00 a.m. every single day. DC City Charter had once been a Catholic school, which converted to a charter school to stay afloat financially. I arrived shortly after the transition; the school was a mix of kids whose parents once paid tuition, and students whose parents couldn't afford to send them to private schools and hoped for a different educational journey.

As a teacher who looked like my students, I felt a special responsibility to give them the best education possible. It was a drive that would sometimes become a pressure too heavy to bear.

The weight of educating an eighth grader who read at only a first-grade level was crushing. Each day I'd try to cultivate specialized lessons for him, while also protecting his pride when including him in large group projects. Whether he would show up to class or not was a toss-up, and when he did, I could count on taunting or bullying from other male students that would lead to full on blow-ups.

I was twenty-three years old, just a few years older than my students would soon be after high school. Despite the advice of an older Black woman educator at my Teach for America summer boot camp to not take anything personally, I took it to heart when I saw any student get off track. Couldn't they understand what they were up against as students who were Black and of color, in a world that often assumed their failure? But thankfully I had a lifeline in Mr. Collins, our math teacher, a DC native who'd been teaching for a decade.

"What's up, Padawan? How's it going?" Mr. Collins said, stepping into my classroom one day that fall, his almost waist-length black locs swinging behind him as he planted himself down at one of my round tables. A Star Wars fanatic, Mr. Collins called me Padawan, reminding me that I was both an apprentice and, potentially, a future Jedi. As the only Black male lead classroom teacher in the school who'd been there since the school's inception, Mr. Collins knew how to let childish behavior roll away like water off a penguin's back, walking the tightrope between calling out misbehavior and making jokes that diffused situations quickly. Not all his methods resembled the methods I was taught in my teaching manuals, but they worked, and Collins was well respected by students.

Following his lead, I pushed the books to the side and began to tap into my instincts. How had I wanted to be treated as a young person when I was their age? What made me respect adults most? Competency, consistency, and offering something interesting in class. I vowed to make my class the most interesting and created custom lessons.

"Go home, Padawan. You can't be stayin' late like this every night. You're gonna burn out before the semester is even over," Collins told me one night as he found me poring over my lessons for the week. It was seven in the evening, and I had to be up early the next day to do it all over again.

I packed up my things and headed home to Northeast DC, where I rented a house with two other Black women educators from Teach for America, Amanda and Joan. We'd each moved to DC in the middle of a gentrification wave, and the capital had already begun the process of going from Chocolate City to Black Coffee with Cream City years before. House by house, you could see neighborhoods transitioning.

There were white girls and guys jogging and walking dogs in neighborhoods that apparently had never seen white people before on their streets. We'd walk into carry-outs that served delicious fried chicken wings, french fries, and homemade iced tea and lemonade mixes, only to be told that they would soon be replaced by chain stores. Every now and then a student would unenroll from the school, their parents announcing a move to the cheaper, more affordable outskirts of the city.

Despite the changes, pockets of the city remained untouched. I lived in Northeast DC, right on the border of Hyattsville, Maryland, where Black homeowners abounded, and we rented from one. DC wasn't my hometown, but I loved it for its Blackness—and especially its American Blackness. You could see the generations that had made the city's culture and were fighting not to be erased.

When I started, I was the only Black woman or Latina teacher in the middle school. I called every parent I could reach to let them know who I was. For the occasional parent who was Spanish-speaking, I used what little Spanish I could to establish a level of comfort for them.

In person, a look of surprise mixed with relief would cross their faces as they tried to assess just how I knew the language. Still I felt inadequate. The pang of not being fluent haunted me. I knew I could've helped these families way more if I spoke Spanish. I knew they were often nodding through meetings that made no sense, asking their own children to translate for them. Mamí had become a bilingual education teacher for this very reason.

There was one little boy in particular who would get in trouble in other classes frequently, but I knew he was mercilessly bullied for his accent and weight, which was at the root of his trying to fit in. I wish I had had the language to communicate his needs with nuance.

As their English teacher, I paired every student lesson with real-world connections. I leaned into the Socratic method and deep discussions. I took them to the White House and to field trips around DC, where we planted gardens. When Trayvon Martin's killer went to trial, we held a mock trial of our own, which enabled them to simultaneously sharpen their critical-thinking skills by having to argue both sides of the case and process their feelings. The exercise taught them to see the power of their words and how they could shape outcomes both inside the justice system and in their everyday lives.

I was a good teacher to most onlookers, but in my first year I felt like a fraud. People had studied teaching for years, and even with the natural talent my supervisors said I had, there was no substitute for experience. Skipping steps to be head of a classroom came with intense pressure, and I didn't always know what I was doing. Standardized testing was always hanging over our heads like dark clouds, pulling for our attention and blocking the joy of the school—one test could bring you up, while another could crush your and the students' spirits.

As the year progressed, I got better at teaching and settled into DC as my home. I soon found a Black church with other young professionals to attend, thanks to a connect from Anthony, one of my Syracuse Baptist Church friends who'd also moved to DC. The local church down the street from DC City Charter served hot breakfast and soul food every day, and I'd pop in often to get my lunch of fried chicken, collard greens, and sweet potatoes on days when I could fend off the itis. I prayed many mornings to God to help me make it through an assignment where the stakes felt higher than ever.

In DC, I also attended my first Howard University homecoming weekend, thanks to Amanda's brother being an alum there. It gave me hard-core PWI regret and plenty of fantasizing about what could've been if I'd gone to the Mecca. Every HBCU alum I met talked about their college days as though it had been the best time in their life and spoke of their closest classmates as if they were family.

We'd do brunches and happy hours across the city, clubbing at places like the Park at 14th and Lux. This was the era of Roscoe Dash and Waka Flocka Flame, full of swag surfing and long dance music sets. Nearly every cab ride I'd encounter an Ethiopian driver who swore I was Habesha and needed to know what I was, an expected interrogation which I now smiled at each time.

Despite the tumult of the first year of teaching, with the uncertainty of leadership at school (we were on our third principal by spring) and the weight of trying to learn as I taught, I felt myself becoming the leader Teach for America promised I could be. I made hundreds of decisions each day, feeling empowered both within and outside of my own classroom to do so, and I saw my students growing in character and wisdom, not just academics.

As usual, Mamí came with a right-on-time message.

Subject: Mamí
July 20, 2011, 9:23pm

H'ija, You are a great teacher. The pay is not good now, but it balances out as you get more credentials, they pay more. Teachers deserve much more pay. I just bought 25 boxes of crayons at 19 cents each. Shop around before buying for the kids. Save receipts for tax credit. Too bad they can't combine hedge fund pay with teacher pay. We could have the most up to date classes.

*Teaching is never boring, everyday there is a challenge, and when
the kids finally get what you are teaching it is the best reward. Get
organized in your own way and all will run smooth. Next year do not
work summer, and enjoy each moment, take yoga, read books, meet
with friends, visit museums, take 1 course, and just enjoy. Summer
school is not so bad as long as you are settled in one city. I think once
you get settled in one place, you will feel like aah, this is the place.*

*It is 2011, women have careers, buy homes, get involved in events,
and can be picky about a mate. We (me) went from home, to college,
and to our mate, and that was it. You can not change the world, but
with God in front of you, you can do wonders for the children. Middle
school is hard, but that is your strength. You can handle them.*

Love,
Mami

———

At the start of my second year, just as I felt myself coming into my
own, I received another bombshell. Mr. Collins had been handed a
letter of "non-return" from the new administration right as we were
preparing for a family information night—a decision that seemed ridiculous, considering he was one of the few teachers the students actually listened to. There was no explanation given for his firing, and as
a nonunion teacher, he didn't need to receive one. In a country where
fewer than 2 percent of teachers are Black men, this was a huge loss
for our students. The remaining teachers on our middle school team
were leaving for other schools, along with our only social worker, *and*
we were getting yet another new principal. I was on my own again.

The lack of consistency made me furious. And resentful. And
scared. Why, just as I was getting my footing, would I have my legs
cut from under me? And more importantly, how would my students
respond to what would essentially be a brand-new middle school?

The drastic turnover was incredibly emblematic of what mostly students of color from under-resourced neighborhoods had to face in schools, particularly in charter schools, where teachers were not unionized and could be fired or leave at will. The policy was ideal to get rid of bad teachers—but Mr. Collins wasn't a bad teacher. As I cried hot tears of frustration, Amanda tried to encourage me. By default I'd become a lead middle school teacher at twenty-four years old. I didn't feel ready, but I knew that, just as in those first two weeks of school, I had no choice but to move forward.

And move forward I did. Wasting no time, I walked into the second year, not fumbling around for validation of what to do but instead seeing our setbacks as an opportunity to set a new tone. I wouldn't make the same rookie mistakes I'd made before, such as leaving students idle to figure out what to do while I set up. I narrated in the classroom with praise for students as they did the right thing and quickly addressed misbehavior as soon as it happened.

Other teachers eventually followed my lead, and we became a true team. It seemed all would end well.

Yet my Day One vices would catch up to me. They did every time.

"Ms. Alford, I heard there was some concern about the message I'd sent?"

I sat on the phone, contemplating how to respond to this school administrator on the other end, knowing my opinion would get me in trouble, but feeling like the truth needed to be stated.

"Yes, I just don't think it's fair to ask parents to spend money they may not have on clothing for one day," I finally said. Administration had recently introduced a new uniform policy for eighth-grade graduation, a requirement I knew some students would have trouble meeting. "This could be prohibitive for parents, and it just doesn't seem thought—"

"Ms. Alford. The decision was made, and I as an administrator have every right to—"

"I know, I'm just saying—"

"Ms. Alford, are you arguing with me? This is COMPLETELY

unacceptable, and you will be getting a follow-up about this. Is that clear?"

I was shocked. I didn't realize I'd pissed the administrator off that badly.

"Um . . . okay, yes, I understand."

She hung up the phone. I hated the politics of education. I resented how outside administrators would issue top-down edicts, like this eighth-grade-graduation-uniform rule. It seemed to me that some schools could be so invested in the respectability politics of appearance and uniforms that they occasionally missed living out their values.

Adult work drama was a distraction from what mattered—the kids, of course. To me, the inability to question the rules was a relic of the status quo past.

My beloved dean, Mr. Brice, a Southern born-and-bred educator, who was a few years older than me but was full of gravitas with a genteel aura, pulled me aside the next day to share the impact of my phone call with the admin.

"Ms. Alford, you know it pains me to say this . . . but you've been disinvited from the eighth-grade graduation."

I stood stunned.

"You know this is some BS, right, Brice?" I responded.

"I know, I know. . . . You are literally the eighth-graders' favorite teacher, it makes no sense," he said, shaking his head.

I was being put in my place. Reminded of my spot in the hierarchy. This was not the hedge fund and Bridgewater culture didn't work in this world. What hurt most was that the reprimand came from people who looked like me. People who could've just pulled me aside and coached or redirected me with love but instead chose iron-fisted tactics.

True to my Alford blood, I showed up to graduation anyway to see my kids, my students well aware that drama had been brewing. When I walked into the room, I couldn't relax for fear of being removed, the discomfort in my gut rising as I realized none of it had been worth distracting from my kids that day. Thankfully it didn't happen, but sure enough, Dean Brice would later be demoted for defending me and not making me leave the ceremony.

I felt awful. In my youthful bullishness, I was still learning that advocacy didn't always mean charging full speed ahead or being the loudest voice in the room, even if you were telling the truth. There was a long game to play when it came to navigating organizational politics. Power always mattered.

Back home in Syracuse, I was sent constant reminders I was just one step removed from the working-class community I'd come from. My cousin Yamarys, now nineteen, was out of high school and pregnant with her first child. Violence in my hometown still persisted, with bad news of shootings making its way back to me through texts and news articles that Mamí would share. Each Friday, I got my meager teaching salary and charged more on credit cards, seeing I was just one paycheck away from needing to pack it all up and head back home to live with my parents.

As my Teach for America commitment winded down, I started to think about what was next. Most days I didn't feel like a Harvard grad—my life hadn't magically become wealthier, or as privileged as that of many of the friends I went to school with. I had privilege, for sure—but I was still trying to move up. To feel whatever power it was that I supposedly had to make the life I wanted—to make a difference in the world that mattered.

I took the eighth-grade graduation incident as a sign that I wasn't cut out for the politics of being a schoolteacher, nor did teachers have enough power to make systemic change. With the influence of my Ivy peers still looming large, I applied to business school on a whim, hoping it would lead to a higher level of financial and professional security.

I was of course rejected, my naïveté apparent as I applied only to the top two schools in the country at the time—Harvard and Stanford—with an old GRE score and only a couple months of application prep. But I'd also enthusiastically applied to a policy and educational leadership graduate program at Stanford and gotten in.

I'd long been attracted to policy work, despite feeling like I couldn't afford to do it. Perhaps policy work could give me that sense of large-scale impact I was looking for—that I wasn't just treading water or patching holes in a sinking ship of broken educational systems.

"You could be principal of this school one day," Dean Brice told me as I was grading papers one Friday afternoon during our professional development.

I looked around at the laminated college signs I'd posted on the walls of my classroom. I knew that Black teachers were in short supply. Our very program had been accused of helping to push some of the older Black educators out, a claim TFA had long denied. I didn't want to leave my kids behind. I actually felt sick at the uncertainty of where they'd go next. But I thought of all the inspirational messages I'd given my scholars, telling them that they should aim for whatever they could imagine.

I had to ask myself if I'd truly given myself that same opportunity. While it was true that I was a good teacher, did that mean it was *the entirety* of my dream? Or was it a dream passed on to me and fulfilled out of a sense of duty? I found this path while trying to break the golden handcuffs, and I did—but had I ever really given thought to what I wanted to do or was uniquely gifted to do?

On a student field trip to the Newseum, DC's famous journalism and media museum, I jokingly hopped in front of a TV green screen exhibit sponsored by CNN. There I read a teleprompter script and got to play news reporter, imagining "what if." I took a photo and texted "A future in this? Lol" to Adaora, who now worked as a page at NBC Universal, taking a leap of faith from her nonprofit work and finding success. "Loved it! A future for sure," she replied with a smile emoji.

I had finally walked a mile in Mamí's shoes and experienced what I'd always suspected: teachers got the lip service of being told they were doing God's work, but our society truly didn't honor or appreciate them. From the modest pay to the ways certain people in fancy DC circles' eyes glazed over once I told them I was a teacher (and not a lobbyist or staffer on the Hill), I'd learned what it felt like to be looked past.

Teachers took on all the responsibility and had to take too much of the blame for many factors that were entirely beyond their control. The classroom was a calling for true harvesters, who were willing to go one student at a time, one lesson at a time, investing in America's future.

"Ms. Alford," my student said one day as the school year winded down. "You're going to leave like the rest of the teachers, right? Can you please stay?"

What hurt the most was that my student was right. I'd come into a school in need of teachers—of leaders—and yet I felt I couldn't stay another year. Maybe I was a different type of sellout. I was easily disillusioned by the system. Even if I did my part, too many other parts seemed broken. So many veteran teachers—especially Black ones—had taken heat for their long tenures in failing schools across the country and not being "reform minded." But they stayed. Maybe in the end all that matters is who stays.

———

There's a saying that life will keep presenting the same lesson again and again until you learn what you are supposed to.

After TFA ended, in true Gemini fashion, I skipped out on policy school at the last minute after I was recruited to an education political lobbying firm out in California. I jumped at the chance to live on the West Coast and make a living with a front-row seat to policymaking, rather than taking out massive student loans to learn it. I'd been warned that education reformers got a bad rap, but never one to back down from a challenge, I figured I'd get to see for myself what worked and what didn't in the effort to improve American public education.

I learned quickly that "education reform policy" really meant politics. America was divided over how to teach children in the broken system it had created. Race, class, and political party all converged to create a special kind of nasty. I watched uncomfortably as news headlines dragged the policy firm where I'd been hired, a place of so-called reformers with high-minded ideals who claimed to be Democrats while taking big money from conservative funders.

"Reform" was branded as elite white folks who were out of touch on public education, but I saw with my own eyes that there were a lot of Black parents and teachers in the charter school and education reform community too. Could they be blamed for taking whatever life raft was offered to them for their children instead of waiting years for systemic change—that arguably would never come? It became apparent that there were good charters and bad charters serving the estimated 5 percent of American school kids who attended, but I struggled to determine which of these policies promoted by reformers were actually good for students and the public school system overall.

The experience was raising more questions within me than answers. And just like that, I was ready to leave again.

There was also another reality crystallizing for me. Out in California, three time zones away from home, I longed for Mamí's *arroz con gandules*, and hearing salsa and reggaeton on Sunday mornings. Working day in and day out in the office, I was missing the warmth of *familia*, hanging with Daddy, gathering at Titi Nina's house, hearing Abuela and my cousins chatting over the already-loud TV while *tostones* fried on the stove and laughter filled the air.

I missed seeing blue one-starred flags everywhere and being able to grab a fresh empanada on the street or listen to spoken word at the Nuyorican Poets Café in Manhattan. While there were some Black folks in Northern Cali, I missed my people back East. For the first time in my adult life, I really, truly longed for home.

"M'ija, you move way too much," Mamí told me over the phone. "This is really starting to be a lot. You gotta settle down at some point."

"I know, Mamí, but I'm figuring it out," I pleaded. "Millennials are just different—we don't have to stay in one job for twenty years like your generation did."

But deep down, I knew Mamí was right: my next move had to be the right one.

I was going to give business school one last shot. But this time I would apply to MLT—Management Leaders for Tomorrow, a well-respected program designed for Black/Latino and Native American kids who didn't know the inside baseball of the business school admissions process and would receive specialized training.

Once I got into MLT, I spent my weeks studying for the GMAT and writing essays with the few other admits in the Sacramento area, determined to remove the sting of my previous rejection and earn my acceptance. Everything seemed aligned.

Until I got an assignment at work that blew up my plans.

"Can you interview the CEO for her book tour at the next staff meeting?" my coworker Ashley asked me.

It was a no-brainer. The company's education reform CEO was nationally renowned and her book tour was certain to get media attention. Anytime our CEO was present, staff meetings became a big deal at our office. Would I be nervous? Sure. But I was going to channel my inner Oprah and get it done.

And I did. Getting lost in my curiosity and the story we were unpacking, the interview ended and I soon heard applause.

"Nice job," the CEO said to me.

My coworkers flanked me with praise and told me I had come across as confident; the conversation seemed natural and effortless, like I'd been interviewing people my whole life.

I was transported back to my teenage self, standing onstage after talking about the Constitution, and to myself in the classroom, seeing my students' lights go on in their heads as a lesson I delivered clicked.

Sometimes the person you're supposed to be has been the person you were all along—a person obscured by the noise of shoulds and can'ts, hidden behind fears that you can't afford to fail in pursuit of the greater vision. I began to ask myself: With all the wandering and moving in my twenties, what had I really been looking for? How had the pressure of going to my college incentivized playing it safe, whether it was being financially secure or certain to get a pat on the back for being a "do-gooder"?

The new epiphany had even started to make its way into my business school practice essays, and my MLT coach, Kendra, called it out. "It sounds like you want to go into media more than you want to go to business school, no?" I stubbornly denied it to her, insisting I could make both dreams work together, but Kendra was forcing me to be real with myself.

I WAS ALSO STARTING TO SEE PEOPLE, AND PARTICULARLY BLACK women who I'd gone to school with, appearing on television and making a name for themselves in media. Adaora had moved up quickly in her page program in cable news and was now a full-fledged producer for CNBC—and a successful one at that. Abby Phillip, one of my ABHW friends, was at the *Washington Post*, breaking news, getting major stories, and even starting to appear on television. When I reached out about the transition I was considering, she was nothing but supportive. In fact, the more people I told about what I was considering, the more "I can totally see you doing that" responses I got.

But I also got some loud doubters. "I just don't get why you'd quit your job to do . . . journalism?" said one of my coworkers smugly. "If you do this, you will have to start at the bottom and go to some random town in the middle of nowhere making zero money," warned an older career mentor who once worked in the business. "Do not pay for journalism school! It would be a total waste of money in this day and age," said another mentor, but with a single caveat: "Only if they give you a full ride."

The affirmation and the doubt both activated something within me. And so I decided to give myself a chance. To return to that eighteen-year-old girl who'd left Syracuse and wrote in her college essay: "I'd like to become a broadcast journalist."

I quietly applied to two journalism programs—Syracuse's Newhouse School, with a hope of returning home, and Northwestern's Medill School of Journalism—following the advice of a fellow MLT'er from Chicago. I realized that dedicating myself to J-school would mean leaving the certainty of the glory of getting into business school *right* as I was perfectly positioned to get in, but that was the risk life was asking me to take. I would forfeit a more certain and respected path for the potentially greater reward of the unknown.

As luck would have it, I ended up getting into both J-schools—but it was an angel in Northwestern's financial aid office, a Black woman—who knew I was scared to leave my full-time job for this dream—who found a way to get me a full-tuition scholarship beyond the school's generous initial offer.

"I *know* you are going to have a fantastic career," the woman said with knowing and gentle affirmation, as tears of gratitude flowed down my face from my couch in Sacramento.

And with that, I was packing up my bags and selling my apartment furniture for one more cross-country move, this time, to Evanston, Illinois, another cold city with grand promises.

12

Second City

When I arrived in Chicago in the summer of 2014, I had one mission: get a job in television. I would not jump ship and deviate from this plan. I had road-tripped twenty-six hours from California to make it to the majestic town known as the Second City to begin a master's program at Northwestern's Medill School of Journalism. The city of Oprah. It seemed that after five long years of trying to figure out who I was, from the hedge fund to the classroom to another corporate office, knowing who I'd wanted to be all along came with a special kind of urgency.

I had one short year to learn a new craft, establish myself as a serious talent, and find a TV news station willing to hire me out of school. I was twenty-seven years old, older than most of the other students in J-school. While it seemed many of my friends were starting to get married, settle down, and build a life for themselves, I'd blown it all up to chase a dream that could very well not work out.

While I sat in orientation the first week of school at Medill, I looked hard around the room. Just as at Harvard, there were a sprinkle of Black students in my cohort. Remarkably, though, many of the professors were Black, and I counted down the days when the curriculum might bring me into their classrooms. But first, the school had a message for us.

"A lot of people might say the journalism industry is dying," a thick-mustached man told us from the stage of the auditorium we'd been huddled into for our welcome. "And in many ways, it is."

Damn, I thought. Although I'd received a full-tuition scholarship, I'd taken out student loans to cover my housing and living expenses. I would need to start paying these immediately upon graduation.

The speaker went on to explain how in a world of massive newsroom layoffs and growing disruptions from social media, more people than ever were calling themselves journalists, and more journalists than ever were tasked with doing more and more with fewer and fewer resources. These days, it seemed that not only was a journalism degree unnecessary, but some questioned its value altogether.

It would be our mandate to go into this program, not just specializing in whatever we thought we'd come to J-school for but also coming out as multimedia journalists who could do everything. Not only would the industry demand it of us; the fast-changing world would benefit from our ability to shoot, produce, edit, and, most importantly, report stories.

At Medill, the speaker said, we would learn how to report and write news first, before touching anything in our field of specialization like video or shooting, which would come toward the end of our year there. This was not music to my ears. I wanted to get in front of a camera as soon as possible. I'd fought for a scholarship, and I needed to prove I'd been a good investment.

Although the school insisted that we take no outside jobs or internships while we got the fundamentals of reporting down, I devised my own plan. I would borrow equipment, shoot and develop my own TV reel, utilizing the school's network to get feedback on it, and start submitting for jobs as soon as possible. Chicago would be my classroom, and I'd seek out the stories, both for class credit and my own learning.

Chicago, with its towering buildings in the Magnificent Mile, wide boulevards, vast blue lake, and warm, tree-lined residential streets, was beautiful to me. I fell in love with it instantly.

All I'd known of the city was *Love Jones* and the Bulls, and the fact that everyone who seemed to come from there was incredibly proud of it. This place had given birth to many gifted people, from

Lorraine Hansberry to Shonda Rhimes, Common, Bernie Mac, Chaka Khan, Lupe Fiasco, Jennifer Hudson, and Kanye West. The city was rich with arts, culture, music, and history. It felt more manageable, lighter, and even cleaner than New York City in its architecture and atmosphere.

And in Black Chicago, I felt right at home. Black folks who'd settled here were my cousins in the Great Migration, heading from the South to the Midwest, veering slightly left instead of right to the Northeast. Chicago felt reverential to the Black American experience. Rooted. This was a place for people with deep ties to family. I liked it. In many ways, it felt familiar.

What was also familiar was its segregation. Black Chicago and White Chicago seemed two worlds under one sun. There was the South Side for Black people and Wicker Park and Lincoln Park for whites, Bodi for Black people and whatever bars or pubs white folks hung out at.

My entry to Chicago would come from the young Black professional party scene, a scene that like DC's, was tight-knit. The ambitious, and fun lawyers, consultants, entrepreneurs, and business school students who occupied these spaces felt very counter to the negative news that the media often fixated on in their reporting about Chicago.

I was quickly adopted by my fellow young, ambitious Black millennials and attended everything from house music parties to fashion shows to food festivals every week, savoring Lou Malnati's deep-dish pizza and loving the city's lounges. It became my world outside Northwestern, a respite from the classroom, and unlike in college, I was old enough to know how to pull off dancing until 3:00 a.m. and then hightailing it to class. I was living it up more than I'd lived in all the years before combined.

Though I was welcomed, there were still a couple moments of intrigue and awkwardness when my Puerto Rican heritage came up. Chicago, like Syracuse, seemed a lot more Black and white in its sortings around race.

"So do you speak Spanish?" asked my new acquaintance Jayden, a six-foot-five former basketball player who grew up in a Black suburb of Chicago and graduated from Morehouse. After delving into our respective family histories over a drink one day, the conversation was starting to take a predictable turn.

"Well, my mom spoke it to me and I understand most of it, but I'm just used to replying in English, so I'm not fluent . . . ," I started to explain.

"Oohhhh, so you're a Sorta Rican!" he said, cackling.

"Noooo, definitely NOT true!" I protested.

As Jayden went on explaining why I should've known Spanish, I quietly wondered why people had such limited imaginations about what it meant to be Puerto Rican and Latino in general. Did they not know Puerto Ricans had been in the United States for a minute now? That there were so many aspects of our cultural experience, from food to dance to the way we kept our homes, that went beyond one language?

This conversation was precisely why I'd experimented with not telling people my background very early in introductory conversations. I didn't want to have to loathe someone so soon after meeting them.

Back in the mock newsroom at school, I reported and wrote stories on tight deadlines, publishing a student-run website daily. We had to get real sources and interviews, and deal with the real problems journalists faced: people who wouldn't call back, having to be in two places at once, and running out of time. At Medill, there was an infamous policy known as the Medill F. If you had one single comma, letter, or fact out of place, it didn't matter if the rest of the assignment was perfect: you got an F. That was the standard of journalism we sought. To publish stories right the first time. To never put information out unless we could stand behind what we wrote.

"If your mother tells you she loves you, check it out," my newsroom fundamentals professor told us regularly, to which we all moaned with laughter.

Graduate school tested my mental limits as I learned about media law and ethics, or the ways in which one small mistake in a story could ruin a journalism career forever. It seemed almost like a career for masochists—people content with walking a tightrope every day of their life, on deadlines that hung over them like guillotines, only to just make it by the skin of their teeth each time, and then start the clock all over and do it again the next day.

And I loved it.

The adrenaline rush of reporting suited my personality and instincts. I was a person who lived minute to minute anyway, barely able to plan ahead. I needed deadlines. And for once, school felt practical, the craft of journalism so tangible. Unlike at my college, with its liberal arts education centered on theory and scholarly inquiry, I felt a real sense of satisfaction when I saw a story publish. Journalism was entrepreneurial, blue-collar in its origins, and allowed me to manifest a single question or idea into a physical product. I reveled in learning both sides of a story, preferring to be a translator of other people's experiences, rather than being locked into one opinion or label. Perhaps it had been growing up between multiple worlds that made me this way. Maybe I'd never been meant to be an academic, but instead, out there chasing stories.

At night, as I worked on assignments, I looked out of the window of my apartment overlooking the Millennium Park bronze statues, thankful that I hadn't listened to people who told me journalism school was pointless. I'd found what suited my natural abilities and was getting the space to sort through what kind of storyteller I wanted to be.

And yet I still had a longing for the comforts of home, the kind I could get only with a plate of rice, beans, and tostones. Mamí had told me to look up Puerto Rican culture in Chicago, and so I sought an enclave with its own flavor that I could take solace in.

After ten-hour days of class, writing, editing, and reporting, I hopped in a cab and sneaked away to a neighborhood called Humboldt Park. Chicago had the second-highest population of Puerto

Ricans in the country, after New York City. Puerto Ricans had begun to migrate to the city in droves in the 1970s, which saw the formation of influential political movements like the Young Lords Party and other activist groups who fought for independence from the United States.

In a section of Humboldt Park was Paseo Boricua, where I found Puerto Rican restaurants on every corner, salsa dance studios, and cultural destinations like the National Museum of Puerto Rican Arts and Culture. Puerto Rican flags, symbols, and sculptures decorated the barrio, making it feel magical to pass through. Much as on my visit to the Centro library at Hunter College years before, I saw that Puerto Ricans had not only moved to Chicago but also established institutions that honored our history and culture.

"Arroz y gandules con tostones y pollo frito, por favor," I said to the old man behind the counter at a Puerto Rican restaurant I'd found. He smiled at me and took the order, asking if I wanted anything to drink with it, then passing me a warm loaf of bread as I waited.

I appreciated that he didn't press me about how I knew the little Spanish I knew, making me a spectacle. He just treated me normally. I switched back over to English, explaining *"Necesito practicar mas, lo siento."*

"No, mi amor, hablas tan bueno!" he replied, his black eyes dancing above his gray mustache. He was tan like Mamí and reminded me of my tío Jose.

The old man was so kind to me that I came back to eat at the restaurant every few weeks, and sometimes every week during the coldest, harshest months in Chicago, when I missed Mamí most.

———

"Look, I'll be honest with you. Being an on-camera talent in a top market is *really* hard to do right out of school. Most people don't get a job in places like Chicago," a professor told me as I sat in her office, trying to keep a pleasant face. I had scheduled office hours to ask for an assessment of my reel. She'd given practical feedback but was now laying out the big picture for me.

"You have to be one of two things to get a good on-air job so early," she said: "really well connected in the business, or exceptionally gorgeous."

It was fine, I told myself. I knew exactly what I wanted and was going to keep aiming for the impossible. I'd find warm receptions from plenty of professors—like Craig Duff, a video storytelling savant with the patience of a saint, who taught me how to shoot and edit news packages with care, or Caryn Ward, whose signature silver bob always bounced as she lectured enthusiastically about reporting.

I was also finally getting to meet the abundance of Black professors and administrators—like Ava Greenwell, Michael Deas, Stephan Garnett, and Charles Whittaker—whom I couldn't wait to work with in the newsroom.

The professor I'd work most closely with was Deborah Douglas, a Medill alumna herself, who'd been my newsroom fundamentals instructor. Deb, as we called her (she wanted no honorifics and said we should think of her as a newsroom editor) had long black locs, wore signature pointy-rimmed glasses, and always had a good story on deck. She was a straight shooter, and I loved it; I could get better faster, because she never let up on my mistakes.

"Remove all these 'that's from the story. Don't need them," she'd command.

"The lede, Natasha. Rewrite this, please," she'd instruct me.

Deborah perfectly balanced feedback with positive affirmation and asked questions of her students to understand their needs. She pushed me out of my comfort zone, assigning me to cover the Republican primary for governor in Illinois, even though I was slightly intimidated. Every opportunity for growth she pushed me towards, proved necessary.

"You are Puerto Rican, right?" Deb asked me once.

"Yes . . . ," I said, bracing.

"We need a student to participate in the upcoming Latino USA Quiz the Media event, where a team of Latino students from three journalism schools will ask questions of leading journalists, the prize going to the best questions. It's last minute, but a great opportunity," she said in her bubbly, excited fashion. "You know John Quiñones, right? The journalist from *What Would You Do?*"

I recalled Quiñones's face easily. He was the ABC News journalist who would pop up on people in surprise scenarios where hidden cameras had been recording to unpack their responses to everything from xenophobia to verbal abuse—almost like Ashton Kutcher's *Punk'd*, with some socially redeeming value. Quiñones himself, a Mexican American with deep roots in Texas, had humble beginnings—his father was a janitor, just like Daddy. He spoke Spanish all of his early childhood, until he went to school and had to learn English. He was one of the few Mexican men of color on mainstream English broadcast news.

I jumped at the chance to meet Quiñones, although representing the Latino community at Medill felt a little awkward because I knew only a handful of Latinos at the school. Did I deserve to take that spot?

"Sure, for you, Deb, yes."

"You will be in fantastic company, have a lot of fun, and get a chance to shine in all your Latina glory!"

Deb was always affirming, but in this moment I saw her intentionally affirming me as a Black Latina.

At the event Quiñones sat on a panel with other media folks like Mexican American journalist Maria Hinojosa, who to my surprise looked like a carbon copy of Abuela, our faces strikingly similar. As I looked around the room, as I anticipated, I saw I was the only Black Latina.

"Why don't we, as journalists or the media, spend more time profiling the success of Latino communities in business, government, and other professions?" asked one student, who pointed out that most mainstream issues covering Latino communities were focused on immigration and crime.

"Because we're not calling the shots. We're not assigning the stories," Quiñones responded frankly.

"I am!" Maria Hinojosa chimed in, to audience chuckles. "The narrative around Latinos is being determined by people who have no relationships to the topic sometimes, even though you may be living amongst them." She went on to explain that's why she chose to work in independent media, creating her own brand to tell Latino stories.

It made sense. There were Black versions of what she spoke of— Black websites dedicated to Black issues.

At the end, the winners of the event were announced. My team lost—but I didn't care, because I was there to meet John. I beelined to him immediately afterward with my notepad and gave him my thirty-second pitch: I was a graduate student, a little later in my career journey, trying to find my way—would he mind if I sent my reel and we kept in touch?

"Absolutely, Natasha. Message me, and I promise I'll get back to you."

And he did.

After inviting me to tour ABC News in NYC a few weeks later, he gave me the best reaction I could've asked for. "This reel is excellent. Exceptional for coming straight out of school. You can land a job. I'll ask around and let you know what I can find out about opportunities." John promised to put in a good word for me at ABC's Syracuse affiliate, and I left the office that day floating with excitement, thanking God for the alley-oop.

Without me knowing, John gave a call to the news director there. While John was doing that—like a metaphor for my life—Jackie Robinson, the first Black female news anchor in Syracuse, introduced me to Jennifer Sanders, a vibrant and affable Black reporter-anchor at Syracuse's ABC station. Their efforts together got me a meeting with the news director. This is what it meant to look out for each other.

Although media was competitive, and invisible race quotas existed, making it feel like too many people of color couldn't occupy prominent spots at the same time, there was an understanding among journalist communities of color that opening doors for new talent was necessary.

"I don't have any spots for you, and you know it's unusual to come to a market as big as this one right out of school," the Syracuse news director told me the day I trekked to Syracuse to sit in his office, adding that he was impressed with my reel. Damn, I thought. That professor was right. No one else from my class had landed a TV gig in their search. Maybe I was being unrealistic. "I do, however, know a news director in Rochester who just had a slot open up. Let me call her and see if she'll meet with you."

As badly as I wanted to fulfill my fantasy of going back to Syracuse to report the news, Rochester seemed like a perfect next-best option. It was actually a bigger market, ranked seventy-sixth compared to Syracuse's eighty-fifth. TV news markets were almost like the NFL draft—the best and most ambitious journalists wanted to eventually end up in top-ten markets like New York City, Chicago, or Los Angeles. But to even be considered, many journalists would have to serve their time in some small town seemingly in the middle of nowhere, ranked at market number one hundred or ninety-five, then work their way up or get "traded" up. Getting into a number seventy-six TV market meant that I was off to a great start. I was ready to put my draft hat on and get onto the field.

It took no more than a few days for my phone to ring. When I picked up, I heard the voice of a breathless yet polite woman who got straight to the most important questions: "Hi! It's Dianne from News7. Heard good things about your work. Do you know how to write and turn around news stories under deadline pressure? Do you know this city well enough to develop contacts? If you got the job, how soon could you start?"

I answered yes to everything, and just like that, she was flying me in for an in-person interview. Little did Dianne know, I'd hatched a plan: I would arrive a day earlier than the interview, shoot and edit a news story myself, and then show it to her during the interview.

Despite the airline losing my tripod equipment and having to scramble to find a rental, all went well. My trip had been perfectly timed with Rochester's local LGBTQ festival, and I would film a news package centered on an attendee who was attending her first event as a newly transitioned trans woman.

Dianne and I were both in for a shock the day I arrived at the station for my interview. When she walked down the hall to greet me, my eyes squinted as I took in her brown skin and Black hair. It was rare to see a Black news director in TV at that time. I was immediately impressed to see a Black woman calling the shots.

I was entering a career where the lack of diversity in news was a major problem. It made me feel that much more certain that I wanted a coveted spot reporting the news. I felt that a responsibility came with the title, and now, having worked in classrooms with children, I knew how real was the need for people with a platform to say something worthwhile.

There has always been a lack of brown faces in American newsrooms. The majority of us were still enslaved when papers ran their presses and abolitionists were making their case to end the cruel institution. The press was segregated, leading both Black and Hispanic communities to form their own papers, and eventually their own radio stations and media brands, which unsurprisingly focused a lot on civil rights.

For the Afro-Latino in the U.S., it meant being pulled between two worlds per usual, and by default being left out or overlooked in one or the other. Afro-Cuban author and intellectual Bernardo Ruiz Suárez tried to overcome these representation barriers by writing a Spanish-language column in 1922 in the Black newspaper *The New York Age*, according to Dr. Reena Goldthree. Even Marcus Garvey, the leader of the UNIA (Universal Negro Improvement Association), had a powerful global newspaper called *Negro World*, with Spanish- and French-language sections. It makes you wonder how many important conversations Black people across the diaspora haven't had directly with each other due to language barriers.

Journalists like Ida B. Wells worked around the media industry's racial barriers too. Wells was my hero because we shared a lot of similarities. A former teacher who refused to get up from her segregated train car seat, Wells wasn't afraid to expose the lynching of Black people in America. She called her investigative exposé *Southern Horrors* and was such a threat with her truth-telling that racists bombed the printing presses of her newsroom.

The segregation of America's news and lack of diversity was not just a problem for optics' sake, though. In 1967, after numerous urban riots, President Lyndon Johnson ordered the Kerner Commission to investigate the root causes of the unrest. The report the commission released in 1968 blamed the press for promoting two separate and unequal societies. "The journalistic profession has been shockingly backward in seeking out, hiring and promoting Negros," wrote the report's authors. "The press has too long basked in a white world looking out of it, if at all, with white men's eyes and white perspective."

The Kerner report issued multiple recommendations for change; its directives for the press included covering Black communities and people in all aspects of news, assigning reporters to beats that focused on race issues and promoted familiarity with Black and Hispanic communities alike, and, most importantly, recruiting more Black and nonwhite people into the journalism profession.

As is the pattern, once the pressure of the report subsided, so did the commitment to enact change. News stations stopped their diversity efforts (which usually included hiring one or maybe two Black reporters, but never more than that) and provided even fewer opportunities for Black journalists to advance or move into management positions.

This is why organizations like the NABJ (National Association of Black Journalists) and NAHJ (National Association of Hispanic Journalists) were created—to help journalists of color stick together to save their careers, and even their lives. I'd gone to the NABJ's convention, and it felt like family, opening me up to an entire network of Black journalists who took care of each other, providing interview tips, workshops, and connections to jobs. I'd heard of the NAHJ, and although I intended to join, I knew being in a predominantly Black space would be easier to navigate, with fewer questions to answer about why I was there, so I went with the path of least resistance and signed up to be a member of NABJ.

I was already familiar with the racial politics I'd be up against as a journalist in upstate New York. Rochester was a segregated city, often with very different experiences, depending on your race and ethnicity. Headlines blasted the high concentrations of poverty in the city for Black and Latino children of all races; as a member of both communities, I promised to highlight what life was like for those who were struggling, and to explain the *why* with nuance, the same way I saw Soledad O'Brien do on CNN with her acclaimed documentaries *Black in America* and *Latino in America*.

Dianne, the Rochester news director, reviewed my reel and unofficially hired me on the spot. I quietly pledged I would do everything in my power to make her proud of me; when you're working for another Black person in a predominantly white space, you know that everything you do reflects on them. A Black person who succeeded in the workplace could open doors for another to be brought in. A Black person who failed would be justification for not letting in any others. Sitting in her office that day, I saw my entire future before me.

13

Prodigal Daughter

As a newly hired general assignment reporter, my face and voice were set to appear in thousands of television homes across the region. I arrived in Rochester ready to take on my first television reporting job.

I hit the ground running at News7 after getting a warm welcome from the lead anchors and my news director. As I walked into the newsroom, the place felt warm but old, with decor and wood panels that hadn't been updated since the late 1970s. Each morning, I'd come into a meeting, pitch story ideas with my fellow reporters, and go out into the world to try to drum up some interviews and b-roll before the 4:00 p.m. show began.

From the moment I woke up, the stopwatch was on, as I counted down the minutes until I went live on TV. While not as slow as some cities in smaller markets, Rochester wasn't teeming with nonstop news like in DC or Chicago. Most days you were covering car accidents or business openings or city-led initiatives. On the weekends, you could usually count on there being a shooting or some sad crime story.

Although my news director was Black, the rest of the staff was white, and I figured out quickly that I was filling the unofficial minority slot at the station. I was the only Black Latina TV reporter, replacing the station's sole African American reporter, Stephanie Green, who'd left for greener pastures.

"Hey Stephanie! Are you going to live in studio or head out to the field?" one reporter (who happened to be blond and white) asked me one day as I passed her in the newsroom.

"My name isn't Stephanie," I said with my signature deadpan stare, my straightened and pressed hair falling over my blazer.

"Oh, oh my God! I'm so sorry, totally honest mistake."

I looked around at everyone who'd heard the interaction. They cringed at the silence, and I could see my news director's eyes grow big as she visibly noticed my discomfort. She was right: I was annoyed. I never confused this blond for the other blond who anchored the news—how in the world could she confuse me for another Black girl who was about five shades browner than me?

Torn as to whether it was a microaggression or an honest mistake, I offered up a weak smile and went on to my pitch meeting for the day.

Right away I became aware of the need to *not* be seen as a journalist who was obsessed with race. As with affirmative action, which had been thrown in the faces of underrepresented students throughout the country, race consciousness could be weaponized against you as a journalist. Viewers talked back to you on social media, and judging by the comments on any stories we did centering Black people, some of our audience was hostile to the discussion.

Once, while covering a school board meeting in a neighboring suburb—an area not far from the one I'd tried to go for that sleepover over two decades prior—I encountered a squad of worked up parents, angry over a proposed bussing program that would bring in nine city students to their district.

I observed as each parent in this predominantly white school went up to the microphone and passionately made their case about the unfairness of city students benefiting from the extra tax dollars they'd spent to attend this school district.

"Are you actually going to report this story fairly?" a tall older white man said to me as I prepared to do a live shot. I didn't like the way he felt comfortable confronting me, or his assumption that there was a possibility I could not report the story fairly.

"Of course, why wouldn't I?" I said with a smile. "I'm just here to share what's happening and let people speak for themselves." The man then made quick small talk before exiting, ultimately deciding that he didn't want to be interviewed.

Although racism against Black people had been documented in both individual instances and larger policy decisions, some white folks saw the act of even bringing up or pointing out race as racism itself. And onlookers saw reporting about the impact of systemic racism as an excuse to air what they perceived as the moral failings of the Black and Hispanic communities.

Evaluating local news, I wasn't surprised. We, the media, wittingly or unwittingly played into the worst stereotypes of these marginalized communities. As the saying goes, "If it bleeds, it leads," and whenever tragedy—like a shooting or other violence—happened in a community, we were first on the scene to report it. I saw how police accounts of incidents always made it onto our shows immediately; contacts were firmly established between police and reporters, and our deadlines were so tight that we rarely questioned law enforcement's account or had time to investigate it before running to go on air. So much of what we focused on with communities of color was their struggles and pain.

As the only Black Latina TV reporter at the station, I was the only person they'd see reporting their stories on that channel who looked like them, and I wanted them to trust me despite the strained relationships between our newsroom and the community. I wanted to be sure I got their stories right.

A few months into my new job, I got a tip from a man who claimed that Rochester police officers had beaten him during an arrest because he was Black. I heard the panic in his deep voice, and my own wanted to shake as I tried to remain calm. I recentered my body at my desk and said gently into the phone, "Could you please give me the details, sir?" I sat in an open floor plan, and I was conscious of others around me hearing the conversation, so I stepped outside to finish taking the call. I took notes and agreed to meet the man in his neighborhood, so he could walk me step-by-step through what had happened.

I drove out with the photographer on duty and we filmed an entire in-depth interview, the man reenacting his interactions with police, showing how they'd allegedly twisted his arm and punched him. He poured his heart out about the ways he'd been dismissed at every turn in trying to get justice.

Back at the office, I stayed late to finish the story. By the time I left, I felt like a zombie; I was beat. I had carried that man's story the entire day; I could feel him. His pain was inside me. Later that night, I tossed and turned for hours until the sun rose.

I arrived at work eager to review the piece. At my desk, I turned on my monitor but couldn't find the story. Where was it? I started clicking around through my files. I knew that I'd saved it. Or had I? I clicked around some more. I felt sick to my stomach.

"Dianne, I'm looking for my police beating story footage in the system, and I'm not seeing it," I said to my news director in a panic.

"Oh, if you didn't already save it separately, the editors clean out the system every Friday."

It was Tuesday. The story was gone.

"I didn't know that. . . . No one told me that," I said, trying to hold my emotions together.

As I stared at the screen, thinking how I could convince the man there was no conspiracy to protect the police, but that I didn't know the rules of video storage management, Dianne interjected. "This doesn't look great, I know. Just apologize and tell him we will reshoot the interview."

I braced myself for that phone call. As I tried to explain that this was all because I was new to the newsroom, he rightfully didn't trust me and refused to reshoot the interview. But to make matters worse, he threatened to release his recordings of our phone conversations on social media.

My heart dropped at the thought that my casual chatter with him could be released. I'd be fired before I even hit year one on the job. I remembered the first lesson of real journalism: someone is always recording your conversations. Realizing his actions were beyond my control, I could only apologize and send up a prayer that he wouldn't sabotage my career. "I'm so sorry," was all I could say. "I'm sorry."

Years after, in 2020, as I watched the Rochester Police Department make national news for the death of Daniel Prude, who died naked in the snow with a spit hood over his head as officers restrained him, I would hear that man's voice.

As I grew as a reporter, I was still getting doors slammed in my face left and right. Most of my job was apologetically negotiating interviews with people who'd just lost loved ones. It was beginning to take a toll on me emotionally, watching the cold aftermath of death scenes over and over again. But one day, on a slow weekend shift, I was sent way out into the boondocks to cover a fatal hit-and-run accident, and things took a different turn.

After driving for what seemed like hours, me and my videographer, Tracey, who happened to be the only other woman videographer I'd ever seen at the station, pulled up to a large wooden house situated on a grassy knoll.

Before I could even open the door, I saw them: huge Confederate flags splayed across the front windows.

"Um, do you see that?" I said to Tracey, visions of me being chased away or coming face-to-face with a Ku Klux Klan member filling my head.

"Yup. You better go knock on that door. I'm not going up there," she said with a chuckle. There was not enough white guilt in the world to make Tracey do a single iota more than what was required in her job title. And she was right—I was the reporter, and she was the photog. It was my job to get the story.

After waiting a beat to gather my courage, I sucked it up and exited the car, then walked up the steps to knock on the door. A white man with a scruffy beard opened it.

"Yes?"

"Hi, I'm Natasha Alford from News7, and I am so sorry to hear of the loss of your loved one. I apologize for even bothering you at a time like this . . ."

"Okay."

I was shocked. He hadn't shut the door on me or cussed me out or called me the N-word. Instead he agreed to do an interview about his loved one.

I walked back to the van where Tracy sat. "Grab the cameras! He wants to talk."

For the next hour I spoke with the family, obtaining memories of their loved one and watching their kids play in the backyard in the aftermath of tragedy.

I thanked the people for their time and was grateful that in the name of the story, I'd pushed forward and connected on a human level.

I thought that if I returned home to Rochester, the place where I'd spent my early childhood, attended my first day of school, made my first snow angels, and swam at the YMCA, reporting would be much easier. But the truth was, the city felt different from when I was a child. Most old friends had moved away, no one really knew me locally, and while certain parts of the city thrived with businesses, universities, and investments in art and culture, the poverty persisted. Houses crumbled, and empty business locations stacked up. The city's concentration of poverty for Black and non-Black Latinos came second only to Syracuse's.

As with most things in my life, I put on my brave public face as I reported, smiling and channeling the confidence of the oratory stage, even if I felt deeply confused. Those oratory skills got me through my first live shot ever, during a school lockdown in the middle of a rainy day. After mustering up as much poise and calm as I could on the scene, I walked in with the newsroom looking at me as if I was Steph Curry and had just hit a three-pointer from half-court in game 7.

"You were SO good!" my news director exclaimed.

"That was your first live shot?!" another coworker proclaimed.

"Great job, Alford!" a senior male anchor said, passing by me.

It felt like I was sent to do every live shot I could possibly do. More and more I was sent to do the serious stories. After just a few months of working a hard weekend shift and then the day shift, I got the best news a rookie reporter could ever get.

"We'd like to move you to the evening shift," Dianne told me, pulling me into her office. "And I'd like you to be fill-in anchor this weekend if you can."

People waited years for these opportunities, and I was getting them in the first six months of my first TV job. "Of course!" I exclaimed.

I'd even had the rare Black girl luck of wearing my hair naturally curly on-air, just to gauge reactions.

"Your hair is beautiful like that!" said a redheaded show anchor, passing by.

"Yes, I love that hair," said another (ironically redheaded) more senior female anchor. While the industry didn't encourage switching your hair look often, my hair change was well received. What more could I ask for?

———

The day felt off from the beginning. I'd checked into my shift reluctantly after asking for the day off and getting denied by my news director.

The night before, Daddy had called to tell me that he'd been diagnosed with prostate cancer. "It's gonna be okay, Ratty-roo," he said cheerfully, but I could still sense the fear in his voice. For the first time it really hit me that as an only child, all I had was my parents, and that sent me into a spiral. I wanted nothing more than to be home.

"We need you today, sorry, Natasha," Dianne said. "But the next day you can take off." Mental health days were not a thing in news.

I combed through my emails looking for story ideas, and that's when I saw it: a local college had issued a statement about a mobile phone app that had been causing a stir on campus. Yik Yak allowed students to post anonymously, and many were posting racist comments to other students. At the University of Rochester, Black students were complaining about threats to burn a cross outside the dorm where most of them stayed.

I set up a robust schedule of interviews to ensure a reporting of diverse perspectives—the Black Student Union on campus to talk about the impact, an official at another university explaining their issues, and stops to other schools who'd had problems with the app. I had to be extremely careful and detailed with this story because it was original and exclusive, not something we were rereporting from one of the leading news stations. I was also mindful that by centering race, I'd already be annoying a lot of viewers from the start.

I was working with a fellow rookie photog named Eric who had fresh energy and positivity that other photogs didn't always possess, and he was willing to drive all over the region to get the interviews I'd lined up. After some compelling conversations, I wrote my video package script and handed it to my news director for approval. Next, I sent it over to Eric to edit it all together, hustling over to my desk to get a jump on writing the web article. A producer and I would quickly glance over the final product, and then it would go into the show's lineup.

When it was showtime, I walked in the studio to introduce what I thought was an Emmy-worthy package, and then went over to my desk to pack up for the night. I got some verbal high-fives from my coworkers as I exited the studio, but suddenly I heard panic around me.

"Oh my God," I heard a producer say.

"What? What's going on?" I asked.

Apparently, when my photog had shot video for the package, he'd gotten screen recordings of real live comments on the Yik Yak app. But one of those teeny-tiny comments had the work "F*CK" in it, and it had just been broadcast to all our viewers clear as day on-screen.

My stomach knotted tighter than fresh cornrows against brow edges.

This had been the PERFECT package. Why, why, why hadn't I or any one of the many people who'd seen the package caught it? And why, why, why did my photog have to take screen grabs of the profanity, and edit it *into* the package?

I wanted to scream.

As annoyed as I was, my naïveté did not allow me to realize how big of an issue this was.

Although the producers were concerned, they promised to edit out the error so when the piece ran again in the morning, the profanity wouldn't appear—and we could breathe a collective sigh of relief about almost getting ourselves an FCC violation. It had begun to look like a "them" problem and not a "me" problem, so I hopped into my car and drove off to Syracuse, pushing the bad taste of work out of my mouth, eager to see Daddy.

But the next day, while I caught up with Daddy on the couch, I got a call that things had gone from bad to worse. Somehow the morning producers had run the *same* package with the profane error, and the wife of someone from corporate had seen it with their own eyes on the news.

The station's managers were livid. My news director asked me for a formal statement of what had happened.

Days later a verdict was handed down—I was suspended for a few days without pay, along with the photog who edited my piece. I was humiliated, embarrassed, angry, and confused. I had only the best of intentions to illuminate the struggle of marginalized college students who were subject to a different kind of white supremacy in the digital age. The one time I pushed the envelope with an original, exclusive story, daring to do something beyond reporting on shootings and deaths, we didn't have the systems in place to ensure proper quality control—and I hadn't demonstrated enough attention to detail to catch it.

I felt like I had failed; this was my responsibility. My community trusted me to tell this story. It didn't matter what an editor did. This was all my doing. I hadn't caught the mistake. It was my mistake.

My hurt only worsened when Dianne called me into her office postsuspension to tell me I was being moved from the night shift back to the weekend.

"I think Jessica is better prepared for the night shift," she said matter-of-factly. Jessica and I were friends, but we couldn't have been more different on paper—Jessica was a white Jewish girl and from a rural town. Now we were uncomfortably being put at odds with each other. "It will be better for you to return to the weekends."

My heart jumped out of my chest, and my body followed as I shot up out of the chair. "This isn't fair! It's like I'm being double punished when I already paid consequences!"

This was the same woman who'd hired me, cultivated me, and told me I was going to go far. Now she seemed to be taking it all away with a demotion. She was giving me the corporate line. I thought she believed in me. The hardness of my protective shell settled in. I decided to risk it all. "Just fire me then, please," I replied, my heart beating.

Dianne looked at me like I'd lost my damn mind (which I clearly had).

"I am *not* going back to the weekends. This is not my fault. I paid the consequences. And if you insist on demoting me, just fire me."

"You know this is insubordination," she replied, shaking her head.

I wasn't budging. I walked away, holding my tears in until I could get to the parking lot and into my car.

Despite my protest, and after more than a week of holding out and showing up for the night shift, I eventually did go back to the weekend shift and had to apologize to Dianne. There were meetings with my general manager and discussions of "moving forward," but I couldn't move past my own feelings. I'd gone from being a rising star to what felt like the black sheep of the newsroom.

The toll on my mental and physical health increased. Every day I had to show up and smile on television, but deep inside I felt more and more depressed and disconnected from the work. I was also worried about Daddy's cancer diagnosis, and I was going broke. Two prestigious university degrees hadn't taught me how to manage the pennies I was making, and I took odd jobs wherever I could, including at the local Black-owned radio station, WDKX, a unicorn in an increasingly corporate-owned radio industry. I mentored teen radio hosts, helping to produce their show and provide updates to the station. During a particularly rough week, I pawned my old iPhone and custom gold "Natasha" earrings that Mamí had bought me for my birthday in high school.

When I was on my last dollar before I needed to pay my rent, I approached the radio station's owner, Andre Langston, and he wrote me a check for two thousand dollars on the spot. "Just focus on the work; you'll earn it back," he told me. Even at this time in my life, when I was down on my luck and emotionally spent, it was once again the community, people in Rochester's Black community, who looked out for me in tough times, making me meals, inviting me to church, and letting me know they were proud when they saw me on their television screens. They brought me back to life.

Despite the support, I was terrified of making any mistakes, afraid that *this* time I would actually be fired. To make matters worse, when I went out into the field to report, I began to experience excruciating pain—a feeling like glass being ripped against my spine and shooting up my back—whenever I put my foot down. A visit to the doctor revealed that my foot had a tarsal coalition; two bones in the foot had fused together, causing it to land at an angle and throw off my entire gait. The muscle spasms and pain from standing could be fixed only by surgery, something I certainly didn't have time for.

Around that time, Freddie Gray, a twenty-five-year-old Black man from Baltimore, was shot by police, and national chaos took precedence over my own personal internal chaos. After the incident, my position as general-assignment reporter in a mainstream local news station felt more limited. It felt like I was being suffocated and handcuffed under the conditions around me in the newsroom.

Commentators flooded our coverage with hostile racist responses to protests by a new group that was taking increasing space on the mainstream stage: Black Lives Matter.

More than ever I was confronted with the duality of my training at Northwestern as a news reporter, which taught me to maintain a commitment to neutrality, and my reality of being Black and traumatized over Black death.

Then nine Black parishioners were killed during a Bible study by a twenty-one-year-old white supremacist in Charleston, South Carolina. I hustled to write a script to describe what took place in time for our 5:00 p.m. show.

Dianne looked over my words and then paused. "I'm not sure we can call the shooter a 'domestic terrorist,'" she said uncomfortably. I wanted to retort, "But isn't that what he is? Isn't shooting up a church with praying Black people who welcomed you with open arms a direct attack on our homeland?" Instead, I watched quietly as she crossed out "domestic terrorist" and wrote "mass shooter" instead.

It was becoming clear to me and my coworkers that I yearned for more, but it felt like I had a muzzle on my mouth in every way. The stories I wanted to do couldn't fit into ninety-second news bites. I wasn't the only one having this issue. And more and more I found myself scrolling on Facebook, where my classmates and people I didn't know debated this issue. We, the mainstream broadcast media, were often just amplifiers of stories posted on social media by citizens, rather than agenda setters. Race and gender aside, all of us were underpaid and overworked.

While my news director and general manager had spared me a firing over the Yik Yak story, it seemed I was sentenced to struggle in local news, and I no longer had the will to fight. Perhaps in my ambition to be the next Soledad O'Brien or Oprah Winfrey, I thought I had to walk the same exact career path they had. My school advisers had told me to go into local news and work my way up. But perhaps there was another way to tell our stories, and I just couldn't see what it was yet. Daddy's cancer, my health and struggling finances, and the persistent feeling that I was watering dead soil made it feel like I was drowning in quicksand.

I went to my station's management and on a wing and prayer asked if I could transfer home to the Syracuse affiliate. They said no. I told them then I needed to break my contract for personal reasons. They agreed under the condition that I pay a fee and understand that if I broke the contract, I would never work in any station under their news network again.

I submitted to the terms, torn about whether I was making the biggest mistake of my young career. I scheduled my foot surgery date for a couple weeks into my new sabbatical and planned to move back in with my parents once I recovered to face the unknown.

My last day in the newsroom ended so differently from the way it started. There was no goodbye party or lunch, no good-luck cards awaiting me at my desk. I finished my shift unnoticed, dropped a thank-you card for Dianne, hoping she'd still read it, and quietly slipped out the back door, bitter tears slipping down my cheeks, never looking up or looking back.

Seven years later, when I would eventually call her and apologize for letting her down, Dianne had nothing but grace for me. She saw me for the young woman I was, struggling to make my way while staying true. But in that moment way back when, I was certain we'd never speak again.

Mamí rode a bus to Rochester and was there to receive me after I got my foot surgery and faced the reality of being disabled in the short term of being unemployed. Everything required help, from going up the stairs of my second-floor apartment to going to the bathroom and trying to shower without wetting the healing stitches. The pain was excruciating.

Eventually Mamí would have to return to Syracuse, and I was left to pitifully hobble around my apartment, making calls, applying for jobs, and trying to edit together a reel for some freelance work. The pressure of having leaped without a net was so heavy that I realized I should book an appointment with a therapist before my health insurance ran out, or I just might not be okay.

I carefully crutched down the stairs, mindful that if I tipped over, no one would be there to pick me up. After about fifteen minutes, I finally made it down to the porch just as a maintenance truck pulled up and two men got out.

"Hey, miss, are you Natasha Alford, resident of apartment 2 at 146 Comfort Street?"

"Yes . . . ," I replied cautiously.

"Um . . . yes, miss, it says you haven't paid your electricity bill and you're thirty days past due," one man said, his eyes uncomfortably shifting as he looked at my crutches. "We're going to have to shut service off right now, unless you're able to pay by credit card."

Horrified, my face turned red at the indignity.

"Just one second please, give me a moment." I shifted my body away from him as I fumbled for my phone in my pocket.

"Mamí, can you please help me out? This is the last time, I promise. It's so they don't turn my lights off . . ."

I was twenty-nine years old. My age sank in as I listened to Mamí lecture about how she didn't have the money, and I couldn't keep doing this, and how could I quit a job without a plan?

For once I did not talk back. When the payment cleared, I hobbled to my car, hoping that somehow, someway, I could make it in time to see that doctor.

14

Becoming a Grio

"You have one month to get off my couch," Mamí told me as I lay down, my foot bandaged up on the edge of the love seat.

The warning felt cruel. I was unemployed, still hobbling around on crutches from foot surgery.

"Really, Mamí? How could you say that to me, *right now*?" I asked, putting on my best puppy-dog face.

"You're twenty-nine years old, Natasha. You have *two* degrees. When I was twenty-three, I was working and taking care of a whole family. You'll figure it out, but you need to get it together."

This was the hardest Mamí had ever been in my life, and Mamí was the sweetest person I knew. If *she* was saying I needed to get it together, then she was right.

The few weeks in Syracuse after leaving the Rochester news station had been comforting. Being around family restored my sense of origin after being away from home for so long and eased my anxiety about Daddy's cancer diagnosis.

Simple things like talking with Daddy while eating Green Hills fried chicken in front of the TV or turning through old photo albums together reminded me of how far I'd come since I was that eighteen-year-old girl leaving for Cambridge. But even restoration had a time limit, and Mamí was letting me know that "coming home" didn't mean relying on her help forever.

I'd applied to a journalism job at the local paper and some other opportunities but never heard back.

Mamí wanted me to move into my own space while I found a job, so I kicked into gear, talked my way into modest freelance

consulting work at the city school district's communications department, and rented a room from some Syracuse University kids who
needed a roomie. When I wasn't working, I spent long hours making
plenty of calls with mentors and advisers from all of my networks.

"You need to get to New York City." The advice came from the
talent manager of a fellow Harvard alum. Josanne, a first-generation
Caribbean woman from Brooklyn, was a self-made entrepreneur
with a track record of success in the TV news business and took a
straight-no-chaser but loving approach to giving me feedback on our
first call. "New York City is where everything is happening," she told
me in her signature New York accent when we met up for coffee in
Brooklyn, where I'd traveled on a bus to meet her for advice. "You're
still giving off local news, with the formal voice and speech and
the news anchor clothes. New media is the future. Loosen up and be
yourself—you have the 'it' factor."

Josanne's belief in me was just the validation I needed to keep
working my contact list, and soon I'd get a reply back from Todd
Johnson, a fellow Northwestern Medill alum whose photo I'd ironically passed each day back at school on the alumni wall. We'd met
at my very first NABJ Convention before starting grad school. Todd
managed the newsroom at theGrio.

TheGrio was a Black news website and the brainchild of David A.
Wilson, Barion Grant, and Dan Woolsey, three media entrepreneurs.
David and Dan initially partnered to film the documentary *Meeting
David Wilson*, a story about David meeting the white descendants
of the slave owners who'd owned his ancestors. After hosting a
special on NBC about the documentary, David pitched the idea of a
site called theGrio as a permanent online vertical under the NBC
umbrella.

The name was a play off the West African term *griot*, which
translates to "storyteller." Griots were the oral historians of their
time, living and breathing repositories of a community's information.
Sometimes they sang or played an instrument, but no matter what,
they were respected for their knowledge.

This new version of theGrio would be a place where Black stories would be discussed daily—the past, present, and future of Black America and the diaspora. Our legacy was not going to be a footnote or a sidebar; the talent would not be sidekicks in the news—we *were* the news. NBC greenlit the idea, purchasing the brand outright in 2010, and theGrio launched to much anticipation with a fully staffed team located at Rockefeller Center in Midtown Manhattan.

Black communities had traditionally had brands like *Ebony* and *Jet* magazines, created in 1945 and 1952 respectively, to cover our stories and public figures in ways that mainstream white news organizations wouldn't. The Black press had been central to the civil rights movement, and stayed on the front lines of the struggle for equal rights in America. Black readers were loyal and always had copies of their favorite Black magazines on their coffee tables, much as Daddy did in the living room. But theGrio represented a different era of Black media—one that was digital first and videocentric, for a generation that was way more likely to scroll their laptops or phones than pay for magazine subscriptions.

In its early years theGrio built a devoted and massive following, scoring exclusive interviews with Black athletes, celebrities, and politicians, serving as an important news source in the Obama era. It drew top talent like Joy Reid, who served as managing editor and was a career springboard for many Black journalists and creatives. It was highlighted by the *New York Times* as one of the brands whose early coverage of the Trayvon Martin case inspired mainstream news to take notice, propelling it into the national spotlight. In 2013, not long after telecommunications giant Comcast acquired NBC Universal, it was announced that NBCLatino.com was being shut down. TheGrio's founders took it as a sign that theGrio.com might face a similar fate, and made a proposal to buy back the brand to save it. Surprisingly, they were able to successfully reacquire the name and rights to the brand in 2014, going independent and full speed ahead on video and mobile efforts.

In my old newsroom, every story I wanted to pitch seemed to always come back to social issues and topics around identity, which seemed to be consuming more of the public's interest after the deaths of Trayvon Martin and Freddie Gray, and the Charleston church massacre. The stories I wanted to do were big in scope and didn't always fit the type that would run in a local daily newscast. The Yik Yak story, which nearly got me fired, would've been perfect for theGrio, and one little curse word in the digital realm wouldn't have done me in.

For me, theGrio represented freedom—a chance to really find the answers to burning questions about America's future and shift some of the narratives I'd seen so embedded in mainstream news coverage of Black communities. At Northwestern, I had followed the advice to "climb the ladder" the old-school way in local news. This time I was committed to doing it my way, finding a place that would let me tell the stories I cared about first and foremost.

One day as I typed away on the latest article from the school district's newsletter, far from the TV camera lights at the station in Rochester, an email popped up. "Natasha," wrote Todd Johnson, theGrio's then managing editor, in his note, "are you interested in doing video work for theGrio? We have a potential opening—perma-lance if you will—that we'd love to have you come in and interview for. . . . If you have other things in the works, I understand."

"Thank you for thinking of me! I'd be happy to learn more about the opportunity," I replied, trying to contain my giddiness. We spoke on the phone later, and I headed to New York City for an interview.

It was November 2015, and unseasonably warm. I didn't need a coat for my drive down to NYC. "This is a dream opportunity that could open doors, Daddy!" I said while packing the car. "Not only would I be working for a place where I can talk about Black folks and our issues, I don't have to try to convince somebody at the top that they matter. I got a real good shot at getting this job!"

"Aiight, well, we'll see what happens," Daddy said flatly. "Just take it one day at a time." I knew that he was being cautious, not wanting to see me disappointed.

Once in NYC, after a good night's sleep on my friend Tiff's couch, I headed downtown for my interview. I tried to hide the limp I still had from my foot surgery as I approached the sixteenth floor of the Center for Social Innovation, a modern-looking coworking space with comfy chairs and free coffee that theGrio had been operating out of since leaving NBC.

"Welcome to Grio!" said Dan Woolsey, who I now saw was a tall white guy with dark brown hair and a chill personality.

"Hey Natasha, welcome, welcome," said Todd with a handshake, his clean-shaven head and fair-skinned face matching exactly the photo I'd passed of him daily back at Northwestern. "You ready for this assignment?"

"I'm ready!" I said with a smile. "Where would you like me to set up?"

I'd been told the night before to come with three pitches of stories that I could shoot and edit into a one-minute video. Mindful that theGrio was a source of Black political news, I pitched a package about GOP presidential candidate Ben Carson going viral for saying during a CNN interview that the United States "would be Cuba if there were no FOX News."

True to my Northwestern training, I knew not to offer my opinion on Carson's comments, but to provide context for the audience about why they, and his candidacy, were stirring debate among voters.

Dan showed me into a tiny one-room office where they both worked and shot videos. I realized theGrio was much smaller than I imagined. This wasn't the grand newsroom in Rockefeller Center I thought it would be. I set up my camera on a tripod, wrote my script, and proceeded to edit on their laptop like my life depended on it, to give them a package as quickly as I could.

But when I went to hit export, Adobe Premiere hit a glitch. No matter what I—or even Dan—tried, it wouldn't export. My heartbeat shot out of my chest with nerves. I not only wanted this job, I *needed* this job.

"Don't worry about it," Dan said. "I see you've done the work. Let's just try another way later."

That night it hit me—I could take all of my project files and just upload them to the YouTube video editor. Like magic, it worked. Right away, I submitted the video to Todd and Dan, much to their liking. That hands-on quick thinking and problem-solving would end up being a lifesaver for me time and again in the chapter of my life that was to come.

Within days, I got a call back from theGrio: I was being offered a two-week "trial" to see how things went. I spent the next fourteen days being a nonstop problem solver, figuring out how to access Grio graphics for videos that had been sitting unused in a random file, shooting and editing videos for their current correspondent, and writing whatever articles were needed. One of my first interviews was of Erica Garner, the daughter of Eric Garner, who died from an illegal police chokehold.

After a brief extension of my trial, Dan, Todd, and Dave gave me the good news.

"Natasha, your work here has been phenomenal," Todd told me. "We'd like to offer you a job as deputy editor of the site. With 2016 being an election year, this could be a career-changing opportunity for you. Something you can really build on. I know you're a TV talent, but I hope you'll consider what this could do for you."

After months of feeling like a failure, after my first TV job didn't work out, I had a chance to start over. I could tell stories that mattered to my community directly and maybe educate others in the process. Faith had carried me far. But reality was also setting in. While I was excited for the opportunity, I was scared too—I hadn't come to NYC to work for a website. I wanted to be on television, on outlets like CNN, NBC, and CBS. How would being the deputy editor of a site so small help me get there?

"You'll do theGrio for a year or two, and that will open the door to move on to something bigger and better," my talent manager Josanne advised. Mentally I did the math of how I'd budget the $65,000 salary in NYC until I got to the bigger and better. "Let's start with getting the experience—stay focused, you can do this," she said.

———

I GOTTA GET OUT OF HERE. I THINK THIS WAS A MISTAKE.

I was texting Josanne on a rainy morning after just a couple months of being at theGrio. She calmed my nerves, as I stared around the nearly empty coworking space, trying to furiously type articles and keep up with a three-person job of shooting and producing my own videos. This was the real side of working for digital news media.

TheGrio's recent independence from NBC called for a season of financial austerity, with deep scaling back on staffing and resources as the brand looked to start its new chapter. In plain English, theGrio's grand beginnings were no more, and it was now a humble operation of six people, including an intern.

Within weeks, our already small staff of six got slashed in half with layoffs, and "deputy editor" became nothing more than a vanity title. Recent changes in Facebook's algorithm had sent many digital news publishing into a frenzy as traffic took a nosedive, and ours was in the tank. I'd jumped out of the frying pan of a small TV newsroom into the fire of working for a website hanging by a thread due to a barely-there advertising budget and no investments.

I was also learning that working for Black media sometimes felt like being a second-class citizen in the journalism world. Everywhere I went, I had the new problem of having to explain where I worked and who we served.

"You work *where*?" some fellow journalist or publicist or random stranger I had met would say.

"TheGrio," I'd respond, sending up a prayer to Black Jesus that I wouldn't have to endure the awkward back-and-forth.

"The *what*?"

"The GREE-O. It's a West African term for 'storyteller . . .'" I'd pause for their reaction. "It's a Black news website," I'd end up saying, trying to fill the silence in the air.

"OOOOOHH OKAY!"

Even Black folks would often get us confused with our competitor Black news website The Root.

"I saw your latest video on The Root, Natasha, congrats!" a well-meaning person would compliment me when I was out in NYC, mixing it up.

"I work for theGrio . . ."

"Oh sorry, I thought they were the same thing!"

It was bad enough that The Root kicked our butt each month in traffic numbers. I perpetually felt like I was working for the underdog.

As a news brand focused on Black stories, we also felt that we had to fight for a level of respect and acknowledgment from journalism at large. We were considered a "niche" brand, with a "niche" audience, despite Black America's overwhelming influence on culture and society at large.

But it was more than perception that was the problem. We were no *New York Times* or *Washington Post*, and it showed, from the small staff numbers that limited our original reporting to the lack of resources for us to amplify the reporting we actually did. Media brands made money through advertisers, and advertisers allotted hardly any of their budgets to Black-owned media brands. What incentive did they have, when they could always advertise with white-owned but Black-targeted brands to reach Black audiences?

The perception of Black media as being "less than" also meant having to fight to get the same level of access during interviews. On one red-carpet event I covered, I walked for what seemed like miles to get to theGrio's placard, only for it to be at the very end of the carpet.

"Over here, over here!" I'd yell as celebs and their publicists walked past.

One star, who was Black, had the kindness to stop for us—but by the time they came to interview, their publicist put the kibosh on my plans.

"They only have time for ONE question. Just one. You guys can all huddle and listen in," she told the remaining journalists. We squeezed together in our fancy clothes like sardines.

I pressed my microphone in to try to get a usable sound bite, not bothering to talk over all the voices.

The second-class treatment was highlighted by a dynamic fellow journalist, Keyaira Kelly, during her viral social media campaign #BlackPressMatters.

"In many cases, once a celebrity passes a certain status, they completely forget about those same Black media outlets who were among the first to cover them and their talents," Kelly wrote in her 2018 article for *HelloBeautiful*, "How Black Hollywood Is Failing the Black Press." "The lure of White validation is something we've all been conditioned to seek."

She was on to something. This didn't just apply to celebrities. As journalists, we found the lure of white validation applied to our work as well.

"You can do better than theGrio," a beloved news mentor, who was Black, told me once. "I don't understand this choice. You need to work somewhere where people will *actually* be reading your stories."

"But you don't understand," I retorted, ego slightly bruised. "People *are* reading my stories. Yes, we're small, but we have a loyal audience. Joy Reid started here. I just have to find a way to get on TV too."

"This production quality is terrible," said another Black news mentor, as they looked at my reel with our grainy Facebook Live videos and my one-woman-band interview shoots. "Get out of there now. Even if you have to start all over in local news."

But there was one mentor who insisted I stay the course. Nancy

Redd, a Harvard grad, *New York Times* bestselling author, and former Ms. Virginia whom I had met during a short-lived attempt to
qualify for Miss America, had a knack for cutting through the noise
of the media industry for me.

"Don't quit. Bloom where you're planted and be consistent," she
advised me firmly. "There's more potential for this brand than people may see—all that matters is that you know it."

———

I was running on a treadmill one night after work, about six months
into my tenure at theGrio, when suddenly every joint in my body
exploded with pain. My legs felt like hundred-pound weights as I
trudged along, trying to push through the discomfort, until after two
minutes I couldn't take it anymore.

Conceding defeat, I turned off the treadmill and limped my way
back to my apartment, trying to make sense of what had just happened.

Back in the tiny room I subletted, my credit still too bad to be
on any lease, I placed Icy Hot patches on my wrists and ankles and
collapsed onto bed, thinking relief would come in the morning.

But it didn't. When I awoke, my wrists ached with fire as I rotated
my hand in a circle. It was as if someone had inserted liquid cement
into my joints and they were frozen solid. Sadly, my first thought was
not that I should go to the doctor, but that I didn't *want* to.

"I don't have time for this right now," I muttered to myself, looking down at my uncooperative body.

I had my first big TV show junket coming up for a new STARZ
series, and due to recent layoffs at theGrio, I would have to officially
play the role of on-camera entertainment correspondent. I slapped
on some more Icy Hot patches and went about my business—or tried
to. My usual walk to work was excruciating. The pain in my joints
made them immovable, as if they'd been frozen solid.

Eventually, not being able to bend my wrists meant being unable
to type or do much of anything else for work.

"Hey, Todd, I'm so sorry but I need to take the rest of the day and run to the doctor, something is up with my wrists."

"Cool, take care of your health Natasha," Todd replied in his usual compassionate but authoritative way. "You can always pick this stuff up later."

One ride on the subway later, I was up in Spanish Harlem at Mount Sinai Hospital. As the nurse wrapped the plastic band around my arm to draw my blood, flashbacks of college and squeezing my eyes shut for needles suddenly came back to me. I always told myself that season of ITP was a blip on the radar of my life, an anomaly, like getting struck by lightning. Bad luck with my health had happened once, but it wouldn't hit me again.

Within days I got a voicemail while I was at work, telling me that my antinuclear antibody (ANA) test had come back positive and the doctors needed me to come in to rule out arthritis.

I scrunched my face. How could I be thirty years old with arthritis? And if it wasn't arthritis, then what was it?

After requesting yet another day off, I trudged back up to Mount Sinai and sat in a cold, sterile room while the doctor looked at my latest labs and asked me a series of questions.

He was a white man with a foreign accent, brown hair, and a poker face. After stepping out of the room for a bit, he came back and wasted no time getting to the matter at hand.

"I'm pretty sure you have lupus," he said curtly.

I sat up at attention. Lupus? This couldn't be real. The word was familiar, but the actual diagnosis was ambiguous to me. I knew it was a disease Toni Braxton talked about having. One of my Harvard classmates had had it, which caused her to lose her hair and go off the grid occasionally. But how could I get a life-changing diagnosis like lupus at thirty?

"But aren't I too young for something like that?" I responded, hoping it was all a mistake.

"You're never too young for anything," he told me with a blank stare.

I hated the doctor's smug, all-knowing tone, the fact that he chose to even risk the appearance of sarcasm at a time like this. But what I really hated was that he might be right.

I left the visit with my head spinning. The doctor had given me some pamphlets and follow-up appointments to attend, sending me off with a new lifelong companion. My diagnosis was systemic lupus erythematosus (SLE), an autoimmune condition in which my immune system mistakenly attacked my healthy cells and tissue, leading to the joint pain and inflammation that was making me unable to bend my wrists.

This barrage of pain was called a "flare," and it meant that the lupus was active in my body. There is no cure for lupus. Some versions of the disease affect the kidneys (lupus nephritis), and others affect the overall immune system (SLE, which is what I had). At its worst it attacks organs and cuts life expectancy. However, survival rates for the disease have improved over the years. What once was a near-death sentence can now be managed with daily medication, which keeps flares at bay.

But the illness also required a major lifestyle change: low stress, eating well, working out, and getting plenty of rest—all things I had yet to master. I was a journalist. I was focused on telling Black stories. I didn't have time for a slowdown. News was 24/7, and I had to be willing to jump on a story whenever it broke. Being in the field meant grabbing fast food or a slice of pizza on the go, stuffing it down during the ten minutes I had on break. And stress was the name of the game—whether it was working fast on deadline, dealing with evil online trolls, probing difficult people in power, or just the sheer inundation of bad news and, in my case, Black people's trauma, suffering, pain, and heartbreak.

It had only been a few hours since my lupus diagnosis, and I was already going through all the stages of grief—anger over what I'd been told, denial that this was a real thing versus some fluke on a blood test gone wrong, and bargaining with God about what lay ahead. *Why right now? Why would you let me get this close to everything I ever wanted and then give me this disease?*

After I called Mamí with the news, she told me all the things I didn't want to hear.

"I knew it! See, you work too much. You need to rest and take care of yourself, M'ija, you only get one body. You need to come home!"

I rolled my eyes for what seemed like the millionth time in our relationship.

"NO, Ma. I'm not coming home. I don't run home every time I have a problem. This is not helping me, by the way! Saying 'I told you so' isn't helping!"

But even if Mamí had told me what I wanted to hear—that she was sorry this was happening to me, that it wouldn't feel fair that my life had changed, but I would overcome this and still live my dreams—I would have a mountain of heartbreak that only I could climb on my own before I could gain a new perspective about what this diagnosis meant. Daddy for his part seemed mostly resigned about the whole thing. "Welp, you just gotta take care of yourself now. I had cancer before and pushed through. Can't play no games about your health at this age."

Soon after my diagnosis, I would learn that thirty was actually just the right age for a lupus diagnosis—90 percent of lupus patients are women, and the disease tends to strike just as women hit childbearing age. What's more, lupus is more common in African American and Hispanic women, who are three times more likely to be diagnosed than white women. There were more predictably devastating stats to follow.

Pamphlets said African Americans have more severe bouts with the disease and Hispanic people tend to develop the disease younger than the general population. Research showed that both African American and Hispanic patients tended to develop lupus nephritis earlier in the course of the disease than other groups. We also suffered from the depression and mental health issues that come from the devastation and loneliness of our diagnosis. As I read the stats I wondered whether the researchers who'd put together these studies counted Black Hispanic people as Black or Hispanic in their tallies.

Even in health, the way we categorized people could be confusing and lack nuance.

I had spent my whole life working twice as hard to prove myself, to the world and my own self. I'd managed to avoid becoming a statistic for both the communities I came from—but now I was among the sick.

To be among the sick was to be in need. To be chronically sick meant there was no end in sight.

I was most terrified of people finding out the news at work, let alone in the media industry. What if they thought I couldn't perform? As a Black woman, I didn't want anyone to pity me or think I couldn't do the things required of me to keep moving up and making it.

Through this diagnosis, I was coming face-to-face with just how much ableism I had internalized. It's so easy to feel sympathy for the sick when you are healthy, but that doesn't mean you'd want "their" struggle. Now there was no more imaginary boundary between myself and others with chronic illness. The diagnosis felt like a scarlet letter.

To make matters worse, I was single and already part of a stigmatized group—educated, successful Black women—that was told that they were the least likely to find a suitable, comparable partner or get married.

While New York City was probably the best place to be a single thirtysomething with big career ambitions, a fun place for the forever young, how would being sick with a chronic illness change that? It felt so . . . serious. Not to mention that Black women were perpetually preached to about the things we needed to *do* to have and keep partners. Who would want the responsibility of possibly caring for me?

I had a date planned that weekend and decided to charge ahead and dance my cares away. After spinning on the floor of a dimly lit underground salsa bar back up in Spanish Harlem, I hung out with my suitor uptown but suddenly experienced a bad flare and fell out with chest pains.

"I'm so sorry this is happening—I think I have to go to the hospital—this is so embarrassing!" I exclaimed, clutching my chest as he assured me it was okay.

Hours later we sat in the triage room of the hospital as I got a round of morphine pushed through the IV in my arm, swallowing the dreaded but familiar pills of prednisone. I stared at the clock, my heart pounding as I realized my press junket was that morning. As the sun started to rise and I got discharged, my date and I parted ways so I could get ready, but we both knew my health was too intense to unpack so early at that point in our meeting.

Back in my apartment, I curled my hair, put on my makeup, headed out the door. Lupus didn't exist to me.

That particular day, I was interviewing actress Tichina Arnold and the rest of the cast of *Survivor's Remorse*, a STARZ TV show that was getting a lot of buzz. As I ran to the subway and quickly Googled Tichina's latest news, trying to make up for lost time in the hospital, I saw a fact that would stop me in my tracks cold: she was a lupus advocate. Tichina's sister, Zenay, had suffered from the disease for years, and the two sisters had started a foundation called We Will Win to raise awareness and support finding a cure. I looked up at the sky yet again, a smile on my face.

You're funny, God. I see what you did there.

At the hotel room where I was interviewing Tichina, the perfectly lit room with cameras in both directions to catch me, the interviewer and her, the talent, I breathed in deeply and walked in with my questions prepared on a small notepad of paper. As I smiled and peppered her with inquiries about the next season of the show, pushing past the exhaustion in my body, I felt a surge of calm take over me watching her talk and laugh, none the wiser that I had just been in the hospital.

No one has to know, I thought. This was ideal. I had an invisible illness that no one had to know about. As long as I showed up and looked good, I could still do my job and reach my dream. I vowed to keep it a secret even as I approached Tichina for a quick photo at the end of the interview and internally wanted to scream for help—to ask her how to manage this life sentence I'd been handed.

"Come on over here, girl, that was great! So nice to meet you!" she told me, while I leaned in with a grin and posed. I looked down at my phone to see how the picture came out. "It's perfect," I exclaimed.

———

The junket had changed my perspective on theGrio. Maybe it wasn't the TV news job I'd come to NYC for, but now as an on-camera correspondent and deputy editor, I saw how entertainment has just as much impact on shaping Black culture and representation as news does. People often preached about wanting serious reporting, but celebrity and entertainment stories consistently got high traffic on the site. As I was wrestling with what this meant for me, a meteoric change would happen at theGrio—also known as Byron Allen.

Byron Allen was a comedian turned media mogul quietly building an independently owned empire called Entertainment Studios. Born to a teen mother in Detroit whose leap-of-faith move to Los Angeles gave him a front-row seat to Hollywood, Allen would make history as the youngest stand-up comedian on the *Johnny Carson Show* at just eighteen years old. Now he was making moves with Entertainment Studios, the company he had started at his kitchen table in 1993.

Little did I know, Allen had just become the new owner of theGrio, when the founders sold the company to him. We were going to have lunch with him at the Four Seasons on Fifty-Seventh Street and then tour the big, brand-new office we were moving into on Sixth Avenue to match Allen's outsize ambitions.

When I walked into the dimly lit private dining room in the restaurant, I saw Byron sitting at the end of the table in a suit, rocking his signature bald head and ageless face, surrounded by a handful of other professionally dressed people, the only Black man, fittingly sitting at the head of the table. After Byron had everyone go around and introduce themselves, me, David, Dan, and Todd introduced ourselves and listened to our new owner talk about his vision for a changing media landscape. I looked down at my jeans and leather jacket that was too hot for the occasion and realized that what I'd walked into was a way bigger deal than theGrio getting new management.

Not only were we moving out of our tiny coworking space in Chelsea, but I'd be getting new coworkers after months of nearly killing myself doing every job possible to keep the site running. Byron would fund our reinvention and expansion. TheGrio was getting a second chance and now we could rebuild the company at a time when digital media was transforming news and entertainment everywhere. I was staying put.

"We are going to be the best in the business. The Black *New York Times*," Byron told me and my new colleague, Gerren Keith Gaynor, a Morehouse and Columbia alum from Brooklyn with a warm smile and fierce writing chops, as we sat in the new, beautiful Sixth Avenue office just blocks from Rockefeller Center.

I looked around at the mostly empty office, with the small group of staff gathered around him like we were at Sunday-morning church, and wondered how we'd pull it off. Allen normally worked out of the Los Angeles office, where he had more staff and owned entire production studios that put out many of the TV court shows that ran on daytime TV programming.

After enduring decades of racial discrimination in business, having his sales executives told outright by prospective clients that they wouldn't do business with "that nigger," Byron had developed skin thicker than a rhino, and he was coming for anyone who blocked Black businesses from thriving.

Up until that point, Allen had seemed like an enigma—a CEO you saw only in magazines and on TV who signed our paychecks, the person I knew who had saved theGrio from complete ruin—but now he was standing in front of us, giving us an inspiring sermon on the purpose of our work.

"Black Americans get killed in the classrooms and boardrooms before they ever get killed in the streets. Our people are facing economic genocide right now. The way Madison Avenue tries to box out Black business is shameful—but we're holding their feet to the fire. Economic inclusion is *the* fourth and final chapter of the fight that Dr. King died fighting for. And your job, reporting and informing Black America about what is going on, is *key*."

I scribbled on my notepad without looking down, soaking in Byron's every word, while Gerren sat up straight next to me, equally enthralled.

"We're not playing to be pushed into the Negro Leagues. We're playing for the BIG leagues. We want to be the best, period. Digital is the future. And theGrio is part of that vision. You two—Natasha and Gerren—need to go live on that Facebook page every day, giving people the news, helping people understand it."

I liked how he thought. I was also surprised he remembered my name from our introductory lunch meeting.

And just like that, I had my marching orders. What had felt like starting from the bottom this past year now appeared to be the universe putting me in position to address a consistent issue I'd seen from my time at the hedge fund to teaching in DC—Black representation.

Not too long after that dinner, Allen made history again and bought the Weather Channel in 2018 for $300 million, and I watched as more and more people started to take him and theGrio seriously, although we still struggled with the expected challenges that came with ownership change and brand reinvention.

In many ways Byron reminded me of Daddy, with his soaring monologues and unapologetic Blackness. Just as dealing with Daddy for all those years had taught me how to think for myself and speak up in the presence of strong Black men, working for Byron Allen would teach me how to advocate for my needs, even if my voice quaked.

I was trembling but determined when I broke the rules of organizational hierarchy and messaged Byron directly after months of asking for a raise and not getting headway going through my managers. I was shocked when he messaged me back, and even more shocked when he agreed to speak about it.

"I'm a millennial, Byron," I explained after he demanded a lengthy contract in exchange. I'd put together a full PowerPoint, complete with traffic analytics of my video content to make the case that I deserved more. "We change jobs all the time. There's no way I can commit to being here for *years*, when I don't know what's ahead in the industry."

"Trust me, you're going to want to be here. *We* have big things ahead," he countered, his salesman skills in full force. "And I want to invest in people who are committed to the company for the long haul. Not just to take for themselves and leave."

Desperate for a raise—the costs of living in New York City had only started to climb along with my mounting medical bills—but also intrigued by the challenge, I agreed. I had a chip on my shoulder. The way some people discounted theGrio put fire in my belly. I wanted not only to prove them wrong but also to make the site a *destination* for talented journalists, not a pit stop. I wanted us to win industry awards but also to hand out our own too—showing that whether we were recognized or not, we knew the value we had within ourselves.

It's one thing to say that Black people deserve better media dedicated to our interests. It would be another thing to bet my career on it, and not be seduced by the conventional, traditional, mainstream media path. Rochester had taught me well that "the talent" were important, but disposable. The real power was in management and ownership.

"I may not stay the entire time, but I am committed to this vision of being competitive with and even better than any other mainstream outlet," I told him. "I know we have what it takes."

"All right, we'll see about that," Byron chuckled. "Let's get to work then."

———

"We need more writers, Byron," I reasoned one Thursday morning when I'd managed to get Byron on the phone from LA. "There are great freelancers who we need to make full-time with benefits before they get snatched up."

"I'm paying for this out of pocket. How much are we talking, Natasha? Speak to me numerically, always."

My heart pounding faster than ever, I stalled; I hadn't quite tallied the numbers yet, and had expected another manager to be on the call to back me up. "You've should've had this ready," Byron said.

It would be just one of many lessons I'd learn in the years to come: Be ready for my calls with Byron, and with people in general. Do the research. Plan for every outcome. I needed to be as business-minded as I was philosophical and passionate about the work. I remembered all those times I cried about missing out on business school—now working for a startup media company was giving me a priceless education.

Byron allowed me to express myself, speak honestly, and disagree without fear of retribution or ego getting in the way, harkening back to my Bridgewater days, and his mentorship gave me a front-row seat to some incredible moments for the brand.

I was there at the Supreme Court when Byron sued a corporate media giant for $20 billion, alleging racial discrimination for not agreeing to carry his TV channels or offer them in cable bundles. He eventually settled with the company and another cable TV provider, but still didn't let up, challenging advertisers to dedicate 5 percent of their budget to doing business with Black-owned media.

I felt like these high-level conversations about Black ownership needed to reach a wider audience, so I made it my mission to get Byron to agree to go on the nationally syndicated morning radio and online show *The Breakfast Club*, knowing that one of its hosts, Charlamagne tha God, had been interested in booking him, and that year it became one of the top-viewed interviews of all time.

The lessons I learned from watching one of the most powerful Black men in American media made theGrio no longer a pit stop for me but a meeting with destiny. I was witnessing the power to shape Black-community conversations at a grander scale, and I wanted to finish the job. "He who controls the media, controls the minds," rang loud in my head from all the way back in Mr. Freeland's class in seventh grade.

As I was finding my true voice as a storyteller at theGrio, it was also getting me to think more deeply about what it meant when I said I was Black.

"You're Afro-Latina, right?" said Kimberly Wilson, our then–social media director with a generous heart, a travelista who made friends everywhere she went. "I want you to moderate a Facebook Live for us about Afro-Latino identity for Hispanic Heritage Month. It'll be good. Just ask people about their experiences."

Not since my senior year of college had I tried deeply to study the subject of Afro-Latinidad. But now I was being presented with a chance to do it in the newest chapter of my life—as a journalist.

The panelists Kimberly had booked were all people I had never met but would soon become acquainted with: Claudio Cabrera, a Black Dominican journalist who then worked at the *New York Times*; Juliana Pache, a Dominican journalist and creator of the #BlackLatinxHistory hashtag; Janel Martinez, a Garifuna writer who'd started the blog *Ain't I Latina?*, and Crystal Shaniece Roman, founder of the Black Latina Movement, a grassroots theater and film company.

I was strangely nervous to meet them. I reviewed their names and bios ahead of time, practicing pronouncing them so I wouldn't get them wrong. But everyone couldn't have been nicer. All of them were young, Latino, and proudly Black too.

"Welcome, everybody. Hi! Great to have you," I said, as Kimberly held her cell phone up, streaming live to our nearly one million followers on Facebook. "One at a time. Everybody identify how you identify. How do you see yourself?"

Should I say I'm Latina too? I wondered. Would people assume I wasn't, with my last name?

I looked into the camera and said, "And for me . . . My mother is a Puerto Rican and my father is African American. I identify as Puerto Rican and Black and consider myself to be Afro-Latina as well."

My slippery semantics aside, I admit it still felt somewhat odd saying I was Afro-Latina, using a word that did not center my Blackness first—but I saw, looking around the room, that we all shared common questions and experiences, despite our differences.

Shaniece explained that she called herself a Black Latina because she was Black American and Puerto Rican, and felt it was the best term for her. Claudio insisted on calling himself Latino, his form of resistance to people who would try to erase him for his dark-brown skin. Janel said Afro-Latina was nothing more than an umbrella term for the community she was part of, but her true description was Negra and Garifuna, the name for Black Hondurans. This is what Mamí meant when she said that if I'd grown up in Nueva York, being a Black Latina would've been perfectly normal. But as I listened to the panel, I saw that didn't mean life would've been any easier.

"When they look at someone like myself, they automatically say, Oh, wow, you speak Spanish," Claudio recalled, remembering the night a cabdriver told him he looked like a "regular Black" guy, and was surprised he dressed so well.

Shaniece shared her struggles as an actress auditioning for roles. "If you walk in and don't look the way producers want you to look, you can't play a role that you know in your heart and mind you can portray because you have to fit what *they* think a Latina is."

Claudio chimed in. "The Latinos on TV, you're not necessarily thinking of the Latinos that may be represented in this room. Unfortunately, you're thinking of Sofia Vergara and those other types. When you think of a Latin lover, you're not necessarily thinking of me." We all laughed but sadly knew it was true.

I stood there watching these minds ablaze with Black consciousness in our small Grio office and felt a moment of pure satisfaction.

These were my people too. Terminology aside, as Black people with connections to Latin America, we all felt we had a shared experience of being both insiders and outsiders at the same time. After the panel, I felt a spark. I would commit to finding a way to tell stories of Black people from across the African diaspora, Afro-Latinos included. We had a lot more in common than people realized. But soon I would be reminded that for some people, it wouldn't be enough.

15

Black Like Negra

Why is a Dominican running theGrio?

I stared at my phone screen: besides the questioner mistaking the Puerto Rican flag in my Twitter bio for a Dominican one, I was baffled by the tweet on my page. Another poster—who looked like she could have been a cousin of mine—cosigned the comment.

"Whew the ignorance," I replied defensively in a tweet. "Ever heard of Afro-Latinos? I'm also African American a.k.a. BLACK," I tweeted back before eventually muting the thread, vowing to follow my rule of not arguing on the internet.

Still bristling hours later, I realized the back-and-forth had in fact touched a nerve.

Not once in my life had anyone ever questioned my Blackness or belonging in Black spaces—at least not to my face.

Perhaps the critics were not upset about my Blackness, but what they perceived as my ethnic outsider status. It reminded me of our college debates about generational African Americans being outnumbered by other Black groups in the Ivy League. In a strange way it gave me empathy. Clearly, there was concern about taking up space, and the assumption that a space like theGrio was for African Americans exclusively, despite the very name of our site having Afro-diasporic origins. The irony was these same critics would likely be judgmental of an Afro-Dominican or Puerto Rican who didn't want to claim their Blackness.

As I nursed my wounds, my thoughts wandered to something I'd seen the other day while walking through Harlem.

It was a spectacular glass building on 135th Street and Malcolm X Boulevard. I'd seen the sign—SCHOMBURG CENTER FOR RESEARCH IN BLACK CULTURE—many times before, but never had realized that the namesake of the institution was a Black Puerto Rican man who played a major role in elevating Black history in America.

Arturo Alfonso Schomburg was born to a Black mother from St. Thomas and a white German father in Puerto Rico. He attended a school where a teacher told him Black people had no historical accomplishments worth noting. In 1891, while still a teen, Schomburg moved to New York City, eventually becoming an archivist, writer, and documentarian of African history around the world. He ran with the likes of Langston Hughes and joined the Masons. His first wife, Elizabeth Hatcher, was an African American woman from Virginia. Jamaican journalist and writer J. A. Rogers dubbed Schomburg the "Sherlock Holmes of Negro History," according to scholar Robin Kelley.

"The American Negro must remake his past in order to make his future. History must restore what slavery took away," Schomburg wrote in his famous essay "The Negro Digs Up His Past." "The Negro has been throughout the centuries of controversy an active collaborator, and often a pioneer, in the struggle for his own freedom and advancement."

Schomburg made it his life's mission to document the genius of Black people in America and globally, conjuring points of pride that did not require us to imitate or become anything other than who we are.

The fact that we had an African diaspora was because we had been tragically scattered across the world, creating breaks and fractures in our connections, and at times our understanding of shared history. It reminded me of another critique I'd seen recently going viral online.

"You're NOT Afro-Latino if you have an African American parent and a Latino parent—just FYI," a snappy Instagram creator explained, drawing the lines clearly.

The claim was an effort to draw clear lines and boundaries—perhaps an attempt to center the Afro-Latin Americans in different countries who had different lived experiences from Afro-Latinos in the United States. Protecting the culture from imposters was important too, pretenders like Jessica Krug, an educator at George Washington University, who was called out by Afro-Latinas for cosplaying as an Afro–Puerto Rican woman for years, by dyeing her hair dark and wearing big hoop earrings—even though she was actually a white Jewish woman.

As Afro-Latino recognition by the mainstream continued to grow, there also remained the issue of colorism, where only the lightest-colored Afro-Latinas, with barely a trace of African ancestry, are frequently promoted as the face of the community, relegating darker-skinned Afro-Latinas to the margins yet again. I'd recently interviewed a renowned Puerto Rican scholar in Afro-Latino studies, Miriam Jiménez Román, who cautioned against using "Afro-Latino" too liberally when it came to tracking populations. "To say that we are all Afro-descendiente is to basically say nothing. Everybody on the freaking planet is Afro-descendiente. We all come from Eve. You're not saying anything new." I chuckled at her realness and took notes diligently. "You're not saying anything that's going to make any fundamental political difference in the way people are situated in their socioeconomic lived experience. It's partly being conciliatory. You know, 'We are all one,' but we are not all one. The real issue today is an anti-racist struggle." Her honesty was refreshing. The drawing of boundaries around Afro-Latinidad was understandable.

But I still wrestled with what seemed like a fluidity of ethnic borders. Not only had African Americans and West Indians migrated to places in Latin America, contributing to the Afro-Latino populations who lived there, but also there were Afro-Latinos who had themselves been absorbed into African American community and culture, and were simultaneously claimed as Black American. People like Baltimore's Carmelo Anthony, New York City's Noreaga and the Bronx's Sunny Hostin, all had an African American parent but also were recognized as Latino. I cheered as track star Jasmine Camacho-Quinn was celebrated across the island of Puerto Rico, after the South Carolina native represented the Puerto Rican team and won the island's first gold medal in the women's 100 meter hurdle at the 2020 Tokyo Olympics. The daughter of a mestiza Puerto Rican mother and African American father, Camacho-Quinn was hailed as an Afro-Latina history maker, despite one vocal hater who in typical "prove your Latinidad" fashion, questioned if she even spoke Spanish, sparking strong public defense of Camacho-Quinn.

Raymond Santana of the Central Park Five, had a Spanish surname, and his Spanish-speaking grandmother's inability to understand English was a disadvantage in the aftermath of his arrest. According to scholars Elizabeth Hordge-Freeman and Angelica Loblack, years later when Santana was exonerated and giving a talk at a Hispanic Heritage event, he credited his interactions with other Black friends and influences like Malcolm X with his social justice work. As an Afro-Latino growing up in the United States, Santana has a story interwoven with contemporary Black history. We were a transnational people, and even in modern times, had history to reclaim, relearn, and dig up, as Schomburg suggested.

I read more of Schomburg's writings and story in Vanessa K. Valdés's book *Diasporic Blackness: The Life and Times of Arturo Alfonso Schomburg* and felt an affinity toward him. This man was Puerto Rican by nationality, Black racially, mixed ethnically, with a non-Spanish surname, and embedded in the African American community. Schomburg even contended with criticism that he'd been too focused on Blackness at the expense of his Latinidad, and yet he saw the value of showing Black people their contributions in a world that acted as if they had none. He surely knew what it meant to live between multiple worlds.

As a woman with a Latina mom married to my Black American father, I've also considered the implications around gender dynamics between the two groups. What did it suggest that my father—who taught me to be proudly Black—married my mother, who, although she had Black ancestors, was not African American? Daddy always explained that he just unexpectedly fell in love with Mamí for who she was—he had dated all kinds of women before her—and I believed him. And yet I was disturbed that there were some non-Black Latina women who felt a sense of superiority to Black women, particularly African American women. And that there were Black men, of all ethnicities, who exoticized certain Latina women in the same spirit, pitting them against Black women in the process.

As I interrogated these numerous intersections of identity, I decided to get to work. After attending a workshop facilitated by the OpEd Project, I set out to write about this journey for another publication that would be able to reach additional audiences outside the one I had at theGrio. My program mentor, journalist Jamil Crews supportively put me in touch with Jenée Desmond-Harris, an affable and talented editor then at the *New York Times*, who eased any intimidation I had about the project and began to research for my op-ed.

I wrote about Schomburg and many other Afro-Latinos who inspired me, from actress Gina Torres to Janel Martinez of *Ain't I Latina?* When I opened the Sunday paper and saw my op-ed, I sat in my Harlem sublet in awe of the power of manifestation.

Within just a few years, I had created and fallen in love with not only my job but also my new life in New York City. Even with theGrio's shaky rebirth and my having had to pinch pennies to make ends meet each month, in the words of the great Toni Morrison, this was what it felt like to "surrender to the wind."

———

As much as I wasn't initially attracted to celebrity coverage, I'd now started to build a serious roster of incredible interviewees, including everyone from Viola Davis to Denzel Washington, Spike Lee, the late Chadwick Boseman, and Will Packer. Each time I took a picture, Daddy would get it enlarged as an eight-by-ten or poster and display it in the basement, making a living museum of my budding journalism career.

However, even in these exciting times of my new career, my father and I had our usual tensions. During one visit home back in Syracuse after we'd eaten at Chili's, Mamí told me Daddy thought it was rude I'd sent a salad back to the kitchen and asked for a change in my entrée. He also went off on me after I made a joke about him wearing sunglasses indoors in the house.

"If you got a problem being respectful, you can leave this house, you hear me?!" he barked while I stood still, caught off guard by the perceived offense, not knowing where I'd go if he was serious.

Once, on a father-daughter vacation, I'd saved up some cash, proud that I could finally afford to fly us on a long-dreamed-of trip to an amusement park in Florida. But just one day into the trip after reprimanding me for being on the phone texting too much, I carelessly replied, "Not right now Dad, please," leading Daddy to seethe quietly for five minutes then cancel the entire vacation on the spot. I begged for forgiveness, swallowing my pride, promising to not talk back again so we could enjoy the rest of the vacation. But Daddy's mind was made up. He refused to speak to me the entire flight back to Syracuse, his silence tragically familiar, before I took another plane back to New York City, promising myself, this time, I would never speak to him again.

At this point in my life, I surrendered to the reality that the longer I stayed away from home and even sometimes my own family, the more I would come back and see that many of my bad habits and mistakes were trauma-informed. I wanted to make my family happy, but I could not do so at the expense of my dignity or peace.

In the realization was, in many ways, the cost—and the curse—of growth. You will see what you did for survival and for love. And your new life will present the choice to live differently, to thrive and love

yourself. I would also conclude that I would need to eventually forgive him, even if he didn't ask for it. There were things I wanted
from him that he could never give me, because he had never experienced them himself. My life had still been blessed in spite of it all.

Any disappointment on the home front only further highlighted
the joys of the life I had made for myself down in New York City. I
was becoming who I needed to be in the world—and it was worth
fighting for.

———

As part of the season finale of the hit show *Queen Sugar*, I was invited to Oprah Winfrey's OWN studios in Los Angeles to enjoy a
postshow taping. James Ward III, OWN's publicist at the time, had
always heard me say it was my dream to meet her. And just like that,
he kept me in mind during this trip. There were no promises made
to meet my longtime idol, but just being in the audience during a
postshow interview meant I got to see Oprah and the show's cast.

When Oprah came out onstage, the entire room erupted in
squeals. She floated across the room, her ponytail swinging back
and forth, with her signature glasses on her face and a big smile. It
made sense that people loved her.

After the taping, I and my fellow colleagues from the Black
press, Keyaira Kelly from *HelloBeautiful*, Brande Victorian from
MadameNoire, and Panama Jackson from *Very Smart Brothas*, were
informed that we'd been invited to the exclusive cast after-party at
SoHo House. Here in Oprah land, the Black press were treated like
royalty—not last in line on the red carpet—and I felt like I'd entered an alternate realm.

Keyaira, Brande, Panama, and I all stuck together, milling about
the garden-themed room as waiters served hors d'oeuvres. Then
Oprah walked in.

We all took a deep breath and tried not to get too excited, but the
four of us each gave a look that said, *Let's go for it.*

Oprah went straight to the bar, and we casually hovered, trying not to scare her off. Panama was brave and began to speak while the rest of us looked on.

"And what exactly are YOU drinking?" he said casually.

"I love tequila!" she replied with a smile, and then went on talking about her obsession with Casa Dragones. "Bartender, let's get some shots, please!" she said, ordering a round for the group.

I couldn't believe it: we were about to do shots with Oprah Winfrey. I was sure no one would believe the story. I took a glass from her, and we all toasted before tipping our heads back and letting the tequila warm our bellies.

Once the toast was done, Oprah stayed to chat with us, and we each told stories of how something she'd said or done had changed our lives.

When it was my turn, I laid it all out. "I started off in a job at a hedge fund, and I knew deep down I wasn't happy. When I saw you speak at the Harvard commencement the year I returned for my reunion, Ms. Winfrey, your speech gave me the courage to really go after my big dream. I left my job and became a journalist."

"You had to answer the calling, huh?" she said, warmly looking into my eyes.

"Yes, I had to. And my whole life has changed ever since."

Oprah said the calling would keep speaking to us throughout our lives; it was our choice whether we heeded it. We each took turns snapping pics for each other with her. As she walked away, Keyaira and I squealed quietly together, grabbing each other's arms and quietly mouthing: "WE MET OPRAH!"

I looked around the room at Ava DuVernay casually mingling with *Queen Sugar* stars Kofi Siriboe, Bianca Lawson, and Rutina Wesley. I was *in* the room—not trying to *get in* anymore. Oprah was the biggest idol I'd ever dreamed of meeting, and I had just met her. It was time to dream an even bigger dream for myself.

Oprah was right. My entire life really had changed by listening to that small voice inside me, rather than continuing to try to appear successful. Everything I wanted and was destined to do had been there all along, even when I was in the so-called wrong place or job.

"Do not despise these small beginnings, for the Lord rejoices to see the work begin," reads Zechariah 4:10, a verse I would highlight in my digital Bible after the trip to LA. This life chapter, the act of becoming a Grio, had been portrayed as so small in the beginning. But now, after much struggle within and outside myself, I was in the "rejoicing with the Lord" phase, ready to finally see real work begin.

16

Beyond Invincible

I was in Los Angeles just returning from a visit to the set of the hit HBO show *Insecure*, at invitation of Prentice Penny, the ingenious showrunner whom I'd kept in touch with after interviewing him for theGrio a couple years before. I'd hustle from there to see Byron's production lots in Century City, where our parent company filmed court shows. The visits had come on the tail end of a whirlwind week of reporting on HBCU SpringComing weekend back in New York City, and suddenly, my lungs exploded with pain that indicated I was in the midst of a lupus flare.

Even with the support of others, I still spent the first two years of my diagnosis in denial and passive resistance, "forgetting" to take my medicine daily, continuing to work at the same pace and intensity that I had when I first moved to New York City and was trying to get hired in media, still hiding my diagnosis out of fear of being judged.

But every time I thought I'd gotten away with beating this lupus thing, which wasn't "real" anyway to me, I'd land flat on my butt to face the consequences of what not accepting my diagnosis meant.

The year before, covering Donald Trump's inauguration, running through the streets of DC conducting interviews, and at one point dodging pepper spray and rocks while protests erupted, I landed in the ER, with fluid in my lungs and an active flare making it hard to breathe and move.

The lupus loved my lungs, as if it knew that the organs were the core of my passion, where I pulled oxygen to speak, interview,

tell stories, and command the room. This ailment had chosen to settle into my body in a place I couldn't ignore.

*You will not overwork your body, and if you do, your body won't
work for you.*

And just like that, I raced from the glamour of Hollywood life
over to Cedars-Sinai Medical Center ER in a cab, to try to get my
flare under control.

As I looked at the unfamiliar hospital room, I panicked as I felt
the ceiling caving in, my anxiety flaring at the realization I was
thousands of miles from home.

Sad as it sounded, I felt safest in hospitals. It was the one time
I was cared for and physically attended to, as in the old days when
Mamí would rub my chest with Vicks and wait on me hand and foot.
I was safe from myself in the hospital, forced to cancel commitments
and call into work—things I wouldn't do if I were free to choose.

Sitting in the hospital bed in the sterile gray room thinking about
how my entire trip had just blown up before my eyes, I heard my
cell phone ring and looked down.

It was Dorothy Tucker, then the president of the National Association of Black Journalists. Hardwired to pick up my phone no matter
what, I pulled my IV cord a bit to sit up and sound professional and
energetic as I answered.

"Hello, Dorothy, how are you? How can I help you?"

"Well, Natasha, I'm calling to inform you that you've been named
Emerging Journalist of the Year!" she said pleasantly.

I was stunned with joy. I couldn't believe they'd picked me. More
importantly, I was overwhelmed with gratitude that a journalist at a
Black-owned outlet like theGrio was finally getting the recognition.
I thanked President Tucker profusely.

"What's more is that this will be the first year the award is named
after Michael Feeney," she followed up warmly, with a tinge of sadness in her voice.

Michael Feeney was a journalist who was more than a journalist
to the NABJ community. He had a reputation for being a friend to

all and served as president of the New York chapter of NABJ. Tragically, just as Feeney was preparing to start his dream job at CNN, he fell ill with symptoms related to a chronic illness. While in the hospital he got a sepsis infection, and at just thirty-two years old, he passed away, shocking the journalism world.

I'd had the good fortune of meeting Feeney once at an NYABJ event, and of course he'd offered to give me some advice about navigating theGrio, where he'd previously freelanced, but tragically he died before we could connect.

Yet again I felt God's hand all over this phone call. I heard the message loud and clear: If I did not accept my new normal, and manage lupus, I would not be able to enjoy the fruits of anything I was working for.

That phone call was a turning point for me, and it began a process of acceptance, in which I tried taking doctor's orders seriously. After all the shame and stigma of being "sick," and much internal deliberation, I decided to publish a piece about my diagnosis in XONecole, a Black women's online lifestyle magazine, hoping to destigmatize sickness, but most importantly, to set myself free.

If I wanted a public career, I didn't want to spend my life hiding moments when I was down. Celebs like Toni Braxton and Selena Gomez all had their own thriving careers despite having lupus, and there was no need to internalize the idea that this condition would prevent me from having my own as well.

But there was still something troubling about my thinking. So much of my obsession with getting healthy was in relation to getting back to work—to so-called productivity.

My entire life, I'd found value in what I could achieve and do, whether at school or in my career. I'd now been handed the ultimate antagonist, an unpredictable ailment that carried both the blessing and the curse of not being visible. To redefine my worth as a person when I didn't feel useful or productive would require an entire reorientation.

After being discharged from the hospital, I vowed to take my health seriously and started to seek out help from some of the best lupus doctors in the country.

But later that year, as a result of my search to better understand the lupus, I got a new diagnosis—avascular necrosis in my hip. My hip joint was seeing erosion due to blood loss—likely the result of taking so many steroids to treat lupus over the past few years. Doctors told me that I'd need to be on crutches for weeks, bursting my health secret wide open like a huge bubble.

Surely, working in media I could no longer hide; and at every turn I would be asked what was wrong with me. I had now been at theGrio over four years at this point, and the original crew of coworkers-turned-family who'd nurtured my career, like Todd and Gerren, had all moved on. I felt literally and figuratively alone during one of the most somber seasons of my life.

With my awkward crutches and the impossibly un-disability-friendly landscape of NYC of stairs, crowds, and broken sidewalks, at first I trudged everywhere, including into the office, hoping people would see me as able to work. It was illogical and borderline crazy, and I felt (or imagined) quiet judgment from some of the people around me. When you're sick, it can feel as if the world wants you to go away until you "get better" enough to be seen. However misguided it was, I insisted on not being discarded in my state.

Eventually, I headed to Mamí and Daddy's to work remotely from Syracuse and explore treatment options. I'd watch from the sidelines as work initiatives I was told I'd be included on happened without me. I admittedly struggled to keep up and produce. I was so discouraged by the loneliness of this season of my life that I entertained actually throwing in the towel, turning my short-term leave in Syracuse into a permanent stay.

Years later, when the great actor Chadwick Boseman died of colon cancer in the wake of his blockbuster success with *Black Panther*, I more than understood why he chose not to disclose his illness to the world. Even when people mean well, they see you differently when you are sick or appear unable to perform. And sometimes they simply don't mean well, and your disability is yet another reason to count you out. Whatever the reason, they take away your choice. And what's so devastating about being chronically ill is that, forced into a fate you didn't select for yourself, you already feel robbed of choice.

Chronic illness is like a playground bully who laughs in your face, beating you down and promising to come back and see you at lunch for more. Which lunch and what day, you don't know. But you know they are coming back and live with the dread of it interrupting your joy.

Each day during this season, I delayed even thinking about the hip surgery I was advised to get, to avoid missing a beat in my career.

I didn't want time off. I wanted to do what I loved.

Despite years of being told that if I worked twice as hard and was excellent I would succeed, I was now at the mercy of a body that I couldn't control.

Close friends stepped up for me with hospital visits and encouragement; one friend texted every morning to ensure I took my medication. But as with all things, concern fades with time, and the check-ins stop. You don't want to be a burden on others and simultaneously feel that if you have to ask for help, you may as well just handle it yourself.

Acceptance came in the form of a Grio assignment: an interview with the social justice activist the Reverend Dr. William Barber II in the wake of his winning a MacArthur "genius grant." He shared with me his journey living with ankylosing spondylitis, a rare form of arthritis that practically locked his spine in his early twenties, putting him in a wheelchair. Dr. Barber fought depression by leaning on a community of prayer warriors and reading the autobiographies of other changemakers, finding similar themes.

"A whole lot of people who made a difference in history had some ailment," Dr. Barber told me during our phone call. "Moses stuttered. Elijah in the Bible often faced depression . . . Paul had his own thorn in the flesh. Martin Luther King was stabbed and had breathing issues and sometimes had challenges with his own emotions. You look at all of them throughout history and come to see that brokenness is not necessarily final; disability can actually give you abilities."

His words nearly brought me to tears as I took notes at my desk in the Sixth Avenue office that day.

I thought about the women in my life who had been lifelong workers outside the home, who ended their working years with physical ailments to fight: Mamí working herself to exhaustion teaching children for almost three decades; Abuela putting in her years at the factory, then fighting breast cancer twice while she helped raise my titi's kids; and Grandma, serving others in a nursing home kitchen most of her adult life, then dying of Alzheimer's and dementia.

A cycle of work, suffering, and struggle had been normalized for me; it was just what women like us went through. But I didn't want that version of womanhood anymore.

I wanted not to feel guilty about prioritizing healing.

One year after my avascular necrosis diagnosis, during the height of the pandemic, I sat back in a hospital bed and extended my arm once more for an IV.

This time I was getting the surgery I needed for my hip—the one I'd delayed out of fear that I'd be replaced or pushed aside in my work. Now I finally understood that much as the world had stopped to adjust to the reality of COVID-19, I had the power to stop too.

I would honor the body that had carried me this far. Not because I'd earned it—but simply because I deserved it. And this would be a story—a truth—I could never tire of telling.

17

DiaspoRican

After years of growing pains and organizational changes at theGrio, Byron promoted me to vice president. I was no longer the opinionated journalist wishing our small newsroom could be more relevant in the media landscape—I now had the privilege of leading and the joy of recruiting many of my former Grio coworkers to come back for this new era of the brand. I celebrated as journalism stars like April Ryan came to join our team, and I worked on the initial launch of theGrio's television channel in awe of our growth—long past the days of the one-room coworking space. The job was humbling. Despite the perks, like my own office overlooking Sixth Avenue in a city I once couldn't afford to pay rent in, being a news boss took more than dreaming big. I realized that many of the standards I'd held for my former bosses throughout my life, not just in news, had been impossibly high.

My media executive era taught me there were frequently competing agendas, misunderstandings, and other internal and external forces that made the job of newsroom leader about more than the idealized search for truth. I was now learning the *business* of media, with a ten-thousand-foot view that made me, at times, dislike heights. I longed to be a storyteller full-time again but was grateful for the ways this season of my life was forcing me to grow up, learn from mistakes, and get the job done.

If there ever were a time for principled leadership, it was now, in this era of American political unrest, pandemic, and Black Lives Matter, when it seemed all of our institutions, principles, and commitments to democracy were being tested. Journalists were on the front lines of democracy, doing "knowledge work," trying to inform audiences who were constantly bombarded with misinformation. It turns out I had found the right career path after all.

As I sat at my desk, working on our content plan for the upcoming Black History Month, I got a call from home. It was Daddy. It was the middle of the day.

"Hey, Boonky, you got a second to talk?" He was trying to sound upbeat. Something was wrong.

"Hey, Daddy . . . what's going on?" I said, stepping into a conference room and closing the door.

"Well, Natasha, I just wanted to let you know, the doctor said I have cancer again."

Everything stopped, from the cars and taxis on the street below, buzzing and beeping, to the noises of the printers and computer keyboards clacking away. I could only hear my heart pumping, breaking, twisting into knots.

"It's Hodgkin's lymphoma this time. Stage four. It's gonna be okay, I start chemo next week and your moms is taking care of everything, but just wanted to let you know."

As my eyes welled, I swallowed down the fear so he would not hear it in my voice.

"Of course, Daddy, everything's gonna be fine. You'll beat this like you beat it last time."

"Yup! My first day of my chemo, I'ma be clean. I have my pants, my shirt, my hat. Anything like that, that got potential to hurt yo health, you gotta go wit it, positive."

"You're right, Daddy, that's true."

"All right then, well, I'ma let you go. I'll talk to you soon, just wanted to let you know."

"Bye, Daddy, I love you."

"Love you too."

We hung up and I texted Todd:

CAN YOU MEET ME IN THE HALLWAY?

As soon as he stepped outside, and before I could utter a word, my fears spilled into sobs. No matter how Daddy and I had butted heads over the years, our similarities too strong to not produce friction, I could not imagine a world without him.

"Don't worry about the rest of the day at all, just go home," Todd told me empathetically, the father he'd loved having died from cancer years before. "We'll take care of things, just go home."

I rode the B train back up to Harlem in a daze, seeing nothing with my eyes, hearing nothing with my ears, standing and exiting the train on instinct at my stop on 135th Street.

As always, there were long to-do lists in every realm to distract me. The Grammys were coming up in LA, and I needed a dress. I'd need to contact the subjects for my *New York Times* piece to get permission for their photos. And then I had a story on two young Black boys in juvenile detention back in Syracuse that would soon come out in the local paper, a special journalism project I did to stay connected to my hometown roots. Although I'd long been acting as VP since the previous fall, my official promotion announcement would hit the PR wire that week.

I had chosen a career that kept me too busy to wallow in private agonies. If I immersed myself in the gravitas and brokenness of the world, I knew I'd never have a right to feel sorry for myself. There was always someone who had it worse, and always a deadline to meet. Unlike the last time Daddy got cancer, I insisted I would not fall apart. I would take this day off but keep my head in the game. I had perfected hiding myself in my work, and on this day, I was grateful I had plenty of work to do.

————

In the summer of 2019, there was a massive uprising on the island of Puerto Rico, where its people flexed their power by the hundreds of thousands and demanded the resignation of Governor Ricardo

Rosselló. Leaked text messages revealed members of his administration mocking Hurricane Maria victims, and making sexist and homophobic comments. After years of political mismanagement, the texts were the straw that broke the camel's back. People took to the streets. I'd traveled down to San Juan in the weeks after to do a series for the Pulitzer Center about Afro-Latinos and their experiences during this revolutionary time.

The trip opened my eyes to how women in particular were leading the way, with activists like Gloriann Sacha Antonetty Lebrón and Maricruz Rivera advocating for racial and environmental justice, in the aftermath of Hurricane Maria. I wished I'd known these Afro–Puerto Rican women my whole life; spiritual power and moral authority emanated from every word they spoke. Sacha shared with me details about the growing movement of Afro–Puerto Rican women embracing their natural hair textures in the wake of Hurricane Maria, when hair-straightening tools like curlers and blow-dryers couldn't be used after most of the island lost power.

While looking for interviewees, I met a small business owner named Alfredo who ran an empanada shop in Old San Juan. He told me how he was on the front lines of seeing people's economic struggles, the three-dollar empanada sometimes being too much for them to afford. But he also shared that he, too, was witnessing a sort of racial awakening on the island, reflecting on his own evolution of identity: after calling himself "Hispanic" all his life and being listed as "white" on his birth certificate (despite being three shades darker than me), a DNA test revealed he had 39 percent African ancestry. Soon, Alfredo began to acknowledge his own ties to Blackness.

I also met with Marcos Rivera, an attorney who was referred to me by a local activist. He was akin to a Puerto Rican Ben Crump; people would call Marcos when they had concerns they'd been mistreated and were seeking justice. He said he opened his private law office, co-run with his attorney daughter, specifically to help Black Puerto Ricans like himself, who navigated a society that often denied the existence of racism and gaslighted its victims in the process.

"Mr. Rivera, can I ask—why is it that you all don't have something like an NAACP here? Or racial justice organizations with sustained history, the way we do in the United States?"

Marcos explained that he had been involved with groups, but they lacked sustained support. To Marcos, many of the people of Puerto Rico weren't angry enough; it was a by-product of colonization. To him, while some citizens resisted, others were resigned to their fate.

"Negros have not learned to unite," he said. "People don't know the importance we have as a Black culture because we're told we're inferior to whites. Schools in Puerto Rico don't teach anything about the importance of blacks in world history. Until we learn to have that awareness, to know what we are and what we are worth, we cannot defend ourselves."

I left Puerto Rico with his words heavy on my mind. On February 9, 2020, my second piece in the *New York Times* was published—this time a reported story on how Sacha and other activists were encouraging more Afro–Puerto Ricans to pick "Black" on the census, despite decades of surveys portraying Puerto Ricans as a predominantly white population. By being counted, these activists dreamed of a world where data could spark policy change and community support. I opened the newspaper in awe at the story's featured photo of girls in colorful skirts dancing at Maricruz's community center. We had gotten bomba on the front page of the *Times*.

The high from that story lasted awhile, until, like so often in the news, joy was replaced with tragedy.

George Floyd was killed on May 25, 2020, by Minneapolis police officer Derek Chauvin, in a murder that would be seen around the world thanks to a young citizen journalist who recorded the incident on her phone.

The death sparked global protests. The sudden interest in police killings of Black people and racial justice meant an insane amount of traffic to theGrio. It seemed as if the world was just catching up to what we Black media had always known was important.

Covering killings of Black people in the 2010s had been so common that I honestly hadn't initially thought much of the power of George Floyd's death to spark change when I heard the alert. My spirit had grown wearier, year after year, as the death toll piled up with new hashtags: Rekia Boyd, Eric Garner, Philando Castile, Tamir Rice . . . the list went on.

For Black journalists, there was nothing new about these stories. We knew the predictable media cycle: death, social media outrage, protest, blaming of the victim and unearthing or spinning of damaging information, trial, acquittal, collective disillusionment, rinse and repeat. But the Floyd killing was caught so fully and clearly on camera, it seemed as if enough of the world collectively opened its eyes and all together said: No more.

The streets flooded with protestors by the millions across the United States. Soon countries like France, Germany, Australia, Hungary, and Brazil joined in, and George Floyd was not just another Black person in America who died unnecessarily. Even Puerto Ricans joined in protesting, marching in the streets and waving Black Lives Matter signs. It made me proud that many people were not turning in the other direction and distancing themselves. Now it seemed the two worlds I'd been trying to negotiate between my entire life were closer than ever.

I called Mikey Cordero, a New York–born Puerto Rican, and the videographer referred to me by Puerto Rican activist and scholar Rosa Clemente. Mikey and I had worked together on the Pulitzer series and had a trove of unpublished interviews from the trip still.

"Hey, Mikey, it's time we do something with all that footage we shot in Puerto Rico. Now just feels right with the world talking about Black Lives Matter, race, and identity. We can make it a full documentary and help people understand Afro-Latino identity and how it's part of the larger movement for racial justice. Wanna make it happen?"

"Let's do it," he replied.

Mikey and his producer Frances Medina reconnected, pulling

the interviews we'd shot in Puerto Rico the summer before and shooting new material to reflect the Black Lives Matter shows of solidarity that had been happening on the island. A small grant from the Pulitzer Center helped it across the finish line.

I called the film *Afro-Latinx Revolution: Puerto Rico*, optimistically hoping that someday I'd get to return and shoot more stories of Black people in other Latin American countries. Initially I had written "Afro-Latino," but then I changed it to "Afro-Latinx," mindful that many of the stories I'd heard in PR were also about LGBTQ+ people fighting for inclusion and facing physical violence.

From my understanding, the *x* was gender-neutral and defied the strict *a* or *o* ending that signaled masculine or feminine. If I had a choice, I wanted to be more inclusive and not less, and although I sensed some people might not like that approach, I was willing to take the risk.

Despite my good intent, a culture war around the word *Latinx* would soon erupt, as many conservatives, right-leaning cultural critics, and plenty of randomly surveyed tíos and tías deemed the word out of touch with everyday people. It was allegedly just vocab of the elites—academics who wanted to impose their will on people.

Mamí had simply not heard the word before.

"Well, we've always just been Puerto Ricans anyways," she responded with a shrug when I explained all the terminology sparking debate.

Latino thought leaders took different stances. Afro-indigenous writer and professor Dr. Alan Pelaez Lopez called the word *Latinx* a necessary "linguistic intervention," but they cautioned that it was not necessarily a word that all people were entitled to use. Dr. Pelaez Lopez argued that the word should be used to engage in critical reflection around the brutality that caused LGBTQ+ people to have to use it in the first place.

Trans women like Chanell Perez Ortiz, who was shot to death, and Layla Pelaez Sánchez and Serena Angelique Velázquez Ramos, who were found killed in a burnt car, were examples of LGBTQ+

people brutally killed for daring to exist. Any conversation about revolution *had* to include them.

Title aside, I hoped the documentary would start new conversations across cultural media silos with its publication on theGrio. Wanting to get this story right kept me up at night, and I hired Afro-Latina scholars and teachers like Zaire Dinzey-Flores and Dash Harris as consultants to read it and assess it for any flaws or blind spots.

It was also important that the doc be accessible to as many people as possible, so I asked the production team at Entertainment Studios to caption the work in both English and Spanish.

With Byron's support, I got Entertainment Studios to agree to publish it on Amazon Prime Video once finished.

I thought about the point of all this. For periods of my life, Puerto Rico had seemed so far away, completely disconnected from my reality in the continental United States and from my experience as an American. And yet, with every news story, from hurricanes to bankruptcy to political unrest, there was a tug on my soul.

It was a phenomenon best described by Mikey Cordero as being a "diasporican." We, the descendants of the island, had ancestors who had come to the mainland looking for opportunity. And yet as we watched the island's struggles, we were reminded we had a responsibility to care beyond waving a Puerto Rican flag at parties or bumping reggaeton.

Through this reporting project I'd learned that the island of Puerto Rico represented an inconvenient truth: as much as we hailed ourselves "land of the free," the America I had praised during oratorical competitions as a teen was still a country that colonized another one, and that country was still living with the effects of it daily.

Many of the younger generations of DiaspoRicans were repatriating and going back, hoping to reconnect with the land and culture in ethical ways. It reminded me of how so many Black folks back in Syracuse returned down South after years of living in the northern cold, to feel the warmth of not only the sun but the soil our Black ancestors tilled.

My ancestors from South Carolina and Florida had died, some of them having never tasted freedom, but strived for better so that I could inherit and savor the promises of this land.

And yet here I was, living a dream come true. In fact, I had lived some version of the American Dream each step of the way to get here.

From boardrooms to classrooms to TV stations, I put on someone's version of the American Dream to see how it fit on my skin. Whether it made me whole or not. If it settled the guilt about making it through and out of systems that not everyone had. Now for truly the first time in my adult life, I was speaking in a voice that actually sounded like mine.

As a Black American, I'd been told that to make it in this country, it would sometimes mean going to places where I would have to leave myself behind. And yet, it was in staying true to myself, and my passion for these stories that America—not just Black people—needed to know, that I found myself.

Yes, both of my peoples had been so-called boat stops away, stripped of the languages, customs, and faiths of our origins. Yet in each place we'd found a way to survive in spite of our suffering. Our futures would rest on the self-love, justice, and facing of history that Marcos had invoked. The kind MLK and Malcolm were both killed for having. The kind I'd reported on in communities across America from theGrio.

Facing history would not just save "us," but it had the power to save all. To transcend ethnic, racial, and political divides. Too many Americans believed we needed to avoid the past and move "past" it, when in fact, we could never move forward if we deprived ourselves of the honest answers to the question: How did we get here? How could we restore that which we couldn't admit had been damaged—and was still hurting?

When we bore witness to the urgent truth in our souls, we could speak ourselves, the nation—even the world—into liberation.

Maybe even into healing.

———

The Syracuse cold is bitter today. I tug my scarf around my neck tighter, wishing I had put on the layers that Mamí once dressed me in, and a layer of Vaseline on my cheeks for good measure. I knew better than to come outside in December without extra warmth. Especially at Oakwood Cemetery.

It is just a week before Abuela's eighty-fifth birthday. We are here to lay her body to rest.

Mamí and my prima Maxnina were by her side when her spirit left. They said that at approximately three in the morning on December 21, 2021, her breathing slowed and her hand turned cold in the bed of her tiny West Side apartment. Then suddenly a burst of cool air shot through the room, as her soul took flight.

Pancreatic cancer is swift and merciless. I'd tried to bend time to my will two weeks before, taking her on a drive, hoping to make her smile. But she could barely speak or recognize me, weakly nodding in my direction. Already without the language to express the depth of my emotions for her, I told her *"te quiero"* and we started preparing for the end.

And so when it came, I dropped everything, canceling work and appearances for the television analyst gig I'd finally gotten, racing back to upstate New York to be by Mamí's side.

Mamí was surprisingly calm, stoic. I'd braced myself to see her cry, but instead she did as I should've predicted she'd do—busied herself with logistics, ensuring that every chair and flower arrangement was perfectly in place, and everyone else taken care of. Titi Nina had shown up to the wake with the girls, wearing matching custom T-shirts with pictures of Abuela on them, her favorite animal, the butterfly, emblazoned everywhere.

I listened as a Catholic priest who had never met Abuela did his best to inspire us to stay hopeful and grateful for the good years she'd lived on this earth. He got us to share happy memories of her out loud, causing us to chuckle as we thought of how feisty and joyous she was, never bitter about the cruel hand life had often dealt her.

I feared seeing my grandmother's body in the casket, our faces so similar. It would be as if I were looking at myself in part. And yet I needed to face the finality of this moment, that her story had ended here, so that I could continue mine with closure.

I took in Abuela's image from far away at first and then approached, the fear leaving me as the reality sank in: I was looking at nothing but an old home, no longer occupied.

Now, at the cemetery, as we lower the casket into the ground, the wails of my titi and cousins piercing the cold, and the wind whipping our faces, I remember these final moments with the matriarch whose faith brought us north, far from the warmth of her island.

I grip my young son close to my chest, his coos occupying my mind as I transform from little girl back into parent, calculating how long we can be outside before he catches cold, and how long I'll need with the casket before I break down with regret.

When the cold becomes too much, I start to head back to the car, handing him to his father, who cradles him tenderly, then watching as Titi Nina approaches Mamí and Daddy.

"Thanks fa' coming," she tells Daddy, her signature Bronx accent not a single iota changed from the day she moved upstate twenty years before.

I'm watching them hug when my eye catches another sight I haven't expected.

There, just thirty feet away from Abuela's final resting place, sit two headstones with the engraving:

ALFORD

There they are, my grandpa and my grandma, all in the same section.

Both sides of my family sought the North through divergent pathways, yet fate brought us together through to the very end.

This was my American family.

I don't know how I will pull it together to get back to life and work in the big city in just a couple days, to appear on TV, to be insightful and inspiring, ready for the coveted seat at the table I'd yearned to have for so many years and now do. I've ended up at this table not by taking a straight path. Standing, looking out at the sprawling green hills of Oakwood, kissed with snow, I wonder if I can navigate the next leg of this journey now that I'm really on my own. As I watch my parents duck into their car together, I remember a message Mamí relayed to me from Daddy in an email all those years ago, when I was a college kid trying to finish my thesis and prove to myself that I could find a story worth telling.

"Your daddy said keep to your dreams. We love you. Okay, negra chula?"

Keep to your dreams.
Keep to your dreams.
Keep to your dreams.

It feels like, finally, I can hear them all loud and clear.

Acknowledgments

This book exists because of the many people who believed in and championed it into being. To my literary agent, Johanna Castillo, thank you for having faith in me, even though I was a week away from giving birth when we met, and you could've easily surmised I had my hands full! You embody the spirit of women supporting women, and I am grateful for all you have taught me. To Maya Payne Smart and Lisa DiMona, you were the missing puzzle pieces in my quest to become an author. Thank you for affirming this book's potential. Nancy Redd, you pushed me from day one to follow through on this book dream. Thank you for loving and supporting me through this process. Gail Winston, this book, in this form, wouldn't exist without your faith—thank you. Thank you to my entire HarperCollins family, including Liz Velez, Leslie Cohen, Samantha Lubash, and my editor, Adenike Olanrewaju. Adenike, thank you for your wisdom in seeing this book's potential, inspiring me as I brought it to life, and leading us across the finish line—we did it! Brea Baker, thank you for bringing your magic, talent, and heart to year one of line-editing this book, giving me the foundation for the pages we have today. Krishan Trotman, you have my eternal gratitude as a mentor, literary adviser, and so much more. Thank you for all the ways you have supported me, seen and unseen. To Ms. Marie Brown, the literary legend, thank you for cheering, coaching, and guiding me at the most crucial writing milestones (always with a few lifesaving line edits). I wanted to make you proud, and the vision of you holding this book motivated me. To the authors I admire: I extend my deepest gratitude to Kiese Laymon, Elizabeth Acevedo, Michael Arceneaux, Darnell Moore, D. Watkins, Claire

Potter, Joi Marie McKenzie, Michael Harriott, Marc Lamont Hill, Panama Jackson, Ashton Lattimore, Jenisha Watts, and every writer who affirmed that I could and should tell my story, even as a young person, even as a new author. I kept your generous advice close to my heart in this process.

To Professor Reena Goldthree of Princeton University, thank you. Taking your Afro-Diasporic Dialogues course as I finished this book (in a building named in honor of the great Toni Morrison of all places!) was a priceless gift. To the professors and *profesores* who offered inspiration and lent an ear in my quest to tell the stories in *American Negra* as accurately as possible: Dr. Lorgia García-Peña, Dr. Alan Pelaez-Lopez, Dr. Zaire Dinzey-Flores, Dr. Jennifer L. Jennings, Dr. Christina Greer, and Dr. Carlos Vargas-Ramos, thank you sincerely. To Dr. Henry Louis Gates Jr., Lourdes del Pino, and Nicka Sewell-Smith, thank you for your transformative support with the genealogy research for this book. To Dash Harris, for your insightful research, dedication, and the innovative Black Latin American history workshops you held with Javier Wallace through Afro-Latinx Travel that inspired me as I wrote over the years—thank you always. To Edgardo Miranda-Rodriguez, thank you for La Borinqueña and for encouraging me to follow through on coming back to Puerto Rico. To the organizations, institutions, and experts that have supported my research or work on this book directly or indirectly: Robert Searing of the Onondaga Historical Association, the Center for Puerto Rican Studies at Hunter College, the Schomburg Center for Research in Black Culture, Dr. Marta Moreno Vega of the Caribbean Cultural Center African Diaspora Institute (CCCADI), the Pulitzer Center on Crisis Reporting, Princeton University SPIA (School of International and Public Affairs), Michele Filgate of the Sackett Street Writers' Workshop, Marie Carter of Gotham Writers, Harvard University, and Northwestern University's Medill School of Journalism, I am eternally grateful. To Ava Reese, thank you for your superb archival research. To GOLDEN (Amara, Ashton, Shera, Chenelle, Emi, and Sam), Tiffanye, Uju, and Alessandra, thank you for supporting this book with interviews, edits, and reading, and for our enduring friendships. To my Grio family, past and present—thank you for bringing this book into being by being such a major part of my story. TheGrio is not one person's story but many stories and examples of embodying our ancestors' wildest dreams. I'm grateful for each of you, no matter how or when we met along the way. Special thanks to my chosen brother, Gerren Keith Gaynor—your kind spirit has fortified me in writing this book and beyond. Thank you, Duanecia Clark, for pouring into me and *American Negra*'s branding creatively. Thank you, Jasmine Hardy, for your support. To Byron Allen, thank you for reading and blessing the stories shared within. Your investment has helped me experience my American Dream. To my agent Traci Wilkes Smith, and the mentors who've guided me in this process and throughout the years, thank you. To the dozens and dozens of people I interviewed for this book, thank you for letting me share your sacred stories on these pages, whether I used your real names or not. To every person mentioned in this book, I thank you. To the teachers who taught me how to write and told me to use my voice, thank you. To the numerous friends who encouraged me throughout this process with texts, coffee shop writing sessions, and motivation, thank you. To the Black Diasporic and Afro-Latin@/x communities and scholars who have taught me so much and collaborated throughout the years, this book wouldn't exist without you—thank you. To the ancestors, from anonymous monument builders to the Young Lords to SNCC, I acknowledge your place in history and impact on the present. To my family, the Alfords, Cuylers, Pagans, Ortizes, and more, thank you for helping me reconnect with our roots for this project. To my parents, I owe you everything. Your love and support made this book possible. Thank you for the interviews, phone calls, digging up old photos, fact-checking, and giving your blessing to share these stories with the world. To Meme, Lailah, the babies, and all children around the globe—wherever you are when this book meets your hands, know that you are perfectly made and powerful at any age.

To Vlad, my love, thank you for being by my side every step of the way. For all the mornings and nights, assurance, laughter, cups of tea with honey, and sacrifices that people will never know, thank you. We have a book right now.

To Julian, my son, you are the light of my world. Thank you for inspiring me to finish this book and bringing me joy daily. Bloom freely wherever your journey takes you.

To the Most High, thank you for the blessing of life and the grace to start anew each day. And finally, to the readers, wherever your roots may lie, thank you for opening your hearts and minds to this story. May the beauty of your own be as clear as ever. May our ultimate tie as human beings inspire us to create a more just and peaceful world.

Selected Bibliography

Alexander, Leslie M. 2022. *Fear of a Black Republic*. University of Illinois Press.

Algarín, Miguel, and Bob Holman. 1994. *Aloud: Voices from the Nuyorican Poets Cafe*. Macmillan.

Alvarez, Julia. 2008. *Once Upon a Quinceañera: Coming of Age in the USA*. Plume.

"Bad Press, Good Press and the Reception of Puerto Ricans in New York City, 1946–1948." 2017. Center for Puerto Rican Studies. https://centropr-archive.hunter.cuny.edu/digital-humanities/puerto-rican-labor/bad-press-good-press-and-reception-puerto-ricans-new-york-city-1946-p2.

Brotemarkle, Benjamin D. 2004. *Titusville and Mims*. Arcadia Publishing.

Busey, Christopher L., and Bárbara C. Cruz. 2015. "A Shared Heritage: Afro-Latin@S and Black History." *The Social Studies* 106 (6): 293–300. https://doi.org/10.1080/00377996.2015.1085824.

Byrd, Ayana, and Lori Tharps. 2014. *Hair Story*. St. Martin's Griffin.

Denis, Nelson A. 2016. *War Against All Puerto Ricans: Revolution and Terror in America's Colony*. Bold Type Books.

Dubois, Laurent, and John D Garrigus. 2017. *Slave Revolution in the Caribbean, 1789–1804: A Brief History with Documents*. Bedford/St. Martin's, Macmillan Learning.

García-Peña, Lorgia. 2016. *The Borders of Dominicanidad Race, Nation, and Archives of Contradiction*. Duke University Press.

Goldthree, Reena N. 2018. "Afro-Cuban Intellectuals and the New Negro Renaissance: Bernardo Ruiz Suárez's the Color Question in the Two Americas." In *New Perspectives on the Black Intellectual Tradition*, ed. Keisha N. Blain, Christopher Cameron, and Ashley D. Farmer, 41–57. Northwestern University Press.

Gray, Lois S. January 1975. "The Jobs Puerto Ricans Hold in New York City." *Monthly Labor Review*.

Greer, Christina M. 2013. *Black Ethnics: Race, Immigration, and the Pursuit of the American Dream*. Oxford University Press.

Grillo, Evelio. 2000. *Black Cuban, Black American*. Arte Publico Press.

Harvard Black Students Association, The. 2002. *The Black Guide to Life at Harvard*. Edited by Kiratiana Freelon and Marques J. Redd.

Hernández, Tanya Katerí. 2022. *Racial Innocence*. Beacon Press.

Hrach, Thomas J. 2016. *The Riot Report and the News: How the Kerner Commission Changed Media Coverage of Black America*. University of Massachusetts Press.

"Ladinos and Bozales | First Blacks in the Americas." Accessed October 26, 2023. http://firstblacks.org/en/summaries/arrival-02-ladinos-and-bozales/.

Laviera, Tato. 2003. *AmeRícan*. Arte Público Press.

Lupus Foundation of America. n.d. "Health Disparities in Lupus." Accessed October 29, 2023. https://www.lupus.org/health-disparities.

Martinez, Janel. September 17, 2018. "'Negra Soy': Why I've Moved Away from the Term Afro-Latina." Remezcla. https://remezcla.com/features/culture/negra-vs-afro-latina/.

McCall, Nathan. 2016. *Makes Me Wanna Holler: A Young Black Man in America*. Random House.

Mulcahy, Matt. February 23, 2021. "The Map: Segregated Syracuse—See First Documented Association of Race and Redlining." WSTM. https://cnycentral.com/news/the-map-segregated-syracuse/the-map-segregated-syracuse-see-first-documented-association-of-race-and-redlining.

Pelaez Lopez, Alan. September 2018. "The X in Latinx Is a Wound, Not a Trend." *Color Bloq*, The X Collection. https://www.colorbloq.org/article/the-x-in-latinx-is-a-wound-not-a-trend.

Presidential Committee on Harvard & the Legacy of Slavery. 2022. "Harvard & the Legacy of Slavery." Radcliffe Institute for Advanced Study at Harvard University. https://legacyofslavery.harvard.edu/.

Rampell, Catherine. December 21, 2011. "Out of Harvard, and into Finance." Economix Blog. https://archive.nytimes.com/economix.blogs.nytimes.com/2011/12/21/out-of-harvard-and-into-finance/.

Rivera-Rideau, Petra R., Jennifer A. Jones, Tianna S. Paschel, and Springerlink (Online Service. 2016. *Afro-Latin@S in Movement: Critical Approaches to Blackness and Transnationalism in the Americas*. Palgrave Macmillan US.

Román, Miriam Jiménez, and Juan Flores. 2010. *The Afro-Latin@ Reader.* Duke University Press.

Schomburg, Arturo. March 1, 1925. "The Negro Digs Up His Past." *Survey Graphic.* Schomburg Center for Research in Black Culture, Manuscripts, Archives and Rare Books Division, New York Public Library. https:// digitalcollections.nypl.org/items/61304dd0-ea1f-0138-4343-0242ac 110004.

Semuels, Alana. November 20, 2015. "How to Decimate a City." *The Atlantic.* https://www.theatlantic.com/business/archive/2015/11/syracuse-slums /416892/.

Shereen, Marisol Meeraji. January 22, 2014. "English Only? For Mainland Puerto Ricans, the Answer Is Often 'Yes.'" *Code Switch.* https://www .npr.org/sections/codeswitch/2014/01/22/262791008/english-only-for -mainland-puerto-ricans-the-answer-is-often-yes.

Song-Ha Lee, Sonia. 2014. *Building a Latino Civil Rights Movement: Puerto Ricans, African Americans, and the Pursuit of Racial Justice in New York City.* University of North Carolina Press.

Steele, Claude. 2010. *Whistling Vivaldi and Other Clues to How Stereotypes Affect Us and What We Can Do.* Norton.

Tabron, Lolita A., and Terah T. Venzant Chambers. 2019. "What Is Being Black and High Achieving Going to Cost Me in Your School? Students Speak Out About Their Educational Experiences Through a Racial Opportunity Cost Lens." *High School Journal* 102 (2): 118–38. https://doi.org /10.1353/hsj.2019.0002.

Tatum, Beverly Daniel. 2017. *"Why Are All the Black Kids Sitting Together in the Cafeteria?": And Other Conversations About Race.* Basic Books.

Thomas, Piri. 1991. *Down These Mean Streets.* New York: Vintage Books.

Valdés, Vanessa K. 2017. *Diasporic Blackness.* State University of New York Press.

Wai, Jonathan, and Frank C. Worrell. 2020. "How Talented Low-Income Kids Are Left Behind." *Phi Delta Kappan* 102 (4): 26. https://doi.org /10.1177/0031721720978058.

NATASHA S. ALFORD was born in Syracuse, New York. As the only child of a public school teacher and a U.S. Army veteran, she honed a love for oratory and writing while attending the Syracuse City School District. She is a 2008 graduate of Harvard University and a 2010 alumna of Teach for America's D.C. Corps. Natasha is also a graduate of Northwestern University's Medill School of Journalism, where she earned a master of science in broadcast journalism in 2014.

Natasha has built a career as an award-winning journalist, host, and TV commentator, highlighting overlooked stories, histories, and perspectives.

In 2018 she was named the National Association of Black Journalists' Emerging Journalist of the Year. In 2020 Natasha was awarded a Black Voices for Black Justice grant for her work and announced the formation of a new scholarship to support aspiring journalists of color. She is a graduate of the Poynter Women's Leadership Academy and a Maynard 200 Fellow.

Natasha served as the deputy editor of theGrio for four years before becoming vice president of digital content for theGrio, overseeing the launch of numerous video initiatives and the brand's first podcast. She also executive produced the documentary *Afro-Latinx Revolution: Puerto Rico* (2020) and her first feature-length film, *Surviving Solitary*. She is currently an anchor for theGrio's cable TV network.

Natasha has served as a CNN political analyst since 2021, offering insights on the news and stories shaping our nation. Her work has also been published in the *New York Times*, the *Guardian*, the *Oprah Daily*, *Time*, and *Vogue*.

Natasha is currently completing a master of public policy at Princeton University, specializing in domestic policy with a certificate in urban policy. She resides with her family in New Jersey and devotes her free time to mentoring aspiring journalists and youth through organizations like The OpEd Project.